110-E

AF529222

Information Technology For All

Information Technology For All

(Volume – Two)

Editor-in-Chief
Arvind Kumar

INSTITUTE FOR SUSTAINABLE DEVELOPMENT
LUCKNOW
&
ANMOL PUBLICATIONS PVT. LTD.
NEW DELHI - 110 002 (INDIA)

ANMOL PUBLICATIONS PVT. LTD.
4374/4B, Ansari Road, Daryaganj
New Delhi - 110 002
Ph.: 23261597, 23278000
Visit us: www.anmolpublications.com

Editorial Board
Mr. Arvind Kumar, *Editor-in-Chief*
Smt. Neelam Singh, *Member Secretary*
Dr. Arun Kumar, *Director Bihar Branch*
Mr. Kashi Yadav, *Member of the Board*
Dr. C.P. Yadav, *Member of the Board*

Information Technology for All
© Institute for Sustainable Development, Lucknow

First Edition, 2004

ISBN 81-261-2016-9 (Set)

[Responsibility for the facts stated, opinions expressed, conclusions reached and plagiarism, if any, in these volumes is entirely that of the ISD, Lucknow. The Publisher bears no responsibility for them, whatsoever.]

PRINTED IN INDIA

Published by J.L. Kumar for Anmol Publications Pvt. Ltd., New Delhi and Printed at Mehra Offset Press, Delhi.

CONTENTS

PREFACE

All modern complex organizations deal with men, material, machinery and, of course, money. This was postulated long ago by Forrester who added information to the list. Information is as vital a component to an organization as the other four, and is as crucial to its continued viability as the others put together. The analogy is to the genetic code carried by our chromosomes in a highly formal manner, — the sheer regularity and carrying forward is essential for the organism to survive. Any departure can only lead to a cancerous decay process.

The long talked about growth of computers and the "information explosion" are today's realities in our social and economic institutions. The purpose of this work is to provide the fundamental knowledge to enable one to participate in the development and use of information systems in modern organizations.

The Internet is *not* owned or funded by any one institution, organization, or government. It does not have a CEO and is not a commercial service. The Internet is, however, directed by the Internet Society (ISOC), composed of volunteers. The ISOC appoints a sub-council, the Internet Architecture Board (IAB), which works out issues of standards, network resources, network addresses, and so on. Another volunteer group, the Internet Engineering Task Force (IETF), handles day-to-day issues of Internet operation. Practically speaking, the Internet is composed of people, hardware, and software. With the proper equipment on both ends, you can sit at your computer and communicate with someone any place in the world. You can also use the Internet to access vast amounts of information, including text, graphics, sound, and video. From your computer, you can send e-mail, "chat" with others on another continent, work with others on an electronic whiteboard, and, with the appropriate equipment, video-conference. The Internet grew out of a series of developments in the academic, governmental, and information technology communities. In 1969, ARP Anet, an experimental 4-computer network, was established by the Advanced Research Projects Agency (ARPA) of the U.S. Department of Defense so that research scientists could communicate.

'Informational Technology for All', as is obvious from the name of the title, this work contains very judiciously selected succinct information on Information technology, meant for one and all. The beginners as well as experts will find the contents of utmost use. The entire information is covered under twenty two chapters, followed by appendices and bibliography.

To make the information reliable, we have borrowed the matter from various authoritative sources. Expert opinions are also consulted. We owe a deep sense of gratitude to all those whose works are cited and substantially reproduced.

Finally, we will be failing in our duty if we do not acknowledge the kind of assistance we receive from our colleagues at the Institute in completion of this work. We are equally indebted to Shri J.L. Kumar, Managing Director, and Mr. Kripal D. Joshi, Editor, Anmol Publications Pvt. Ltd., New Delhi for publishing this manuscript in a very limited time.

Arvind Kumar

12

GROWTH OF LIBRARY AND INFORMATION SCIENCE IN INDIA: SOME THOUGHTS

1. Introduction

When a philosopher was asked what was the permanent thing on this earth, he answered aptly but philosophically that "change is the only permanent thing on earth". Now when we are in the last decade of 20th century and soon shall be entering the 21st, it is crucial for the educationists and educational planners to assess the growth in terms of changes brought about by such forces as technological, economic, social, etc during this century in our country. In a changing society social agencies and institutions will reflect in them the corresponding changes in their nature and functions.

It has been true in the case of library and the profession of librarianship as such. The library as a social agency had to go through successive stages of development in its nature and functions though it retained its basic social purpose of facilitating human communication through documents. Thus it leads to the new era of librarianship which has come on the frontline as a result of the impact of new information technology. The development and application of new technology brought a significant social change; a shift in the profile of the working population towards information related jobs. According to an estimate about 60% of the workforce in the USA and the UK is engaged in the information sector.

Aim

The growth of the profession of library and information science has its direct bearing on and influenced by the growth of library and information science education, as it is the education and training that provides direction to the profession. With this in mind the aim has been to discuss the growth of library and information science education in India, look at the trends and issues, perspectives, performance, and strategies for change in the new social, economic, and technological environs.

2. LIS Education: Indian Scenario

1. Background At a Glance

While discussing the present scene of LIS education in India, it is almost essential to outline briefly the background. It is now a part of the library history that the foundation of LIS education was laid about 80 years ago in Baroda in 1911. Some more training courses were, set up after this at the Punjab University, Lahore, Madras, Andhra University, Imperial Library Calcutta, etc. The first one year post-graduate Diploma Course in Library Science was started 55 years ago by none other than S R Ranganathan at the University of Madras in 1937. It may be mentioned here that this Course served as a model for developing library science training programmes in the country during the next three decades or so. This also shaped the growth of the profession of library and information science as Ranganathan not only served at Madras but at Varanasi and Delhi also. The impact of his ideas was all around.

The second such Diploma Course was set up at the Banaras Hindu University in 1942, 50 years ago; the third at Bombay University in 1943; Calcutta University in 1946; and University of Delhi in 1947, taking the number of five Diploma Courses at the University level at the time of Independence of India.

2. Present Scene: Overview

The growth and development of LIS schools became quite steady in the post independence period as it synchronised with the growth and development of the institution of higher education, libraries, documentation centres, information centres, etc. As a result of these and other developments LIS today is a well recognized discipline of study and research at the post-graduate level in about 70 universities in the country. All these 70 university level LIS schools, and some colleges also, conduct one-year post graduate course leading to the award of B. Lib Sc. Degree. Between 45 and 50 schools offer courses at the Master's degree level; while about 35 universities enrol students for Ph D degree; whereas about 5 university schools now offer M Phil course (These are University of Delhi; Anand (Gujrat); Gulbarga; S V University, Tirupati; S K University (Anantpur).

In documentation/information science specialised training courses are offered by the DRTC, Bangalore and INSDOC, New Delhi leading to the Associateship in Documentation and Information Science.

Besides, a few women's polytechnics, library associations, etc also offer undergraduate level training known as Diploma in Library Science.

In addition to the above, some Open universities like the IGNOU, New Delhi; APOU, Hyderabad; Kota Open University; Annamalai; Madras also offer courses at various levels through distance education.

3. Library & Information Development Programme: Infrastructure

After the four decades of planned development since the First Five Year Plan in the country the picture of library and information sector emerges as given below:

1. *National Libraries:* India has now (a) National Library at Calcutta, (b) National Science Library at New Delhi, (c) National Medical Library at New Delhi, (d) Indian Agriculture Research Institute Library at New Delhi which is the national agricultural library, (e) National Library for the handicapped has been set up at Dehradun.

2. *Public Libraries:* The country has been setting up an infrastructure of public libraries and public library services in several states of Tamil Nadu, Andhra Pradesh, Maharashtra, Karnataka, West Bengal Manipur, Haryana, and Kerala. Some more states of MP, UP, etc are on the way.

3. *Academic Libraries:* In about 6,000 colleges and 190 universities and other institutions of higher learning, libraries have been set up to cater to the academic information needs of the students, researchers, teachers, scientists, and others. The academic libraries are now being modernised by acquiring new tools of new technology.

4. *Special Libraries:* Various scientific and technical institutions, R & D centres, scientific laboratories, etc have also set up good to better libraries to meet the specialised information needs of the scientists, engineers, and technologists.

5. *Government Departments Libraries:* The Central Government ministries and departments, the state governments, the union territories governments have also established libraries, to fulfil their own requirements.

6. *Documentation/Information Centres and Services:* At the national level various documentation/information services are being Provided by the centres set up for this purpose, viz., INSDOC, New Delhi; NASSDOC, New Delhi;, DESIDOC, New Delhi; SENDOC, Hyderabad; DRTC, Bangalore.

7. *Library Associations:* Many library associations are currently working at the national level such as Indian Library Association, IASLIC, SIS, AGLIS, IATLIS, INDAAL. Besides, almost every state has its own state library association such as Punjab Library Association, Maharashtra Library Association, Gujrat Library Association, etc. Similarly, there are some local level library associations and/or study circle, such as UP Library Associations (Lucknow chapter), or IASLIC Study

Circles spread all over India.

8. Library Literature; The output of library and information science literature in various forms such as book, periodical article, seminar/conference paper, Ph D thesis, etc. has been steadily growing at an impressive rate during all these years.

9. Bibliographic Control: The Indian National Bibliography since 1958, Indian Books in Print upto 1991, Indian Periodicals in print, various union catalogues as National Union Catalogue of Scientific Serials in India (NUCSSI) of INSDOC, Union Catalogue of Social Science Periodicals in India of NASSDOC, some other union catalogues prepared at the regional or local levels, and many more bibliographic control tools in the form of bibliographies, indexing/abstracting services, documentation lists, etc are being produced in the country to help exercise bibliographic control of Indian publications at least in English language.

10. Information Systems: The Government of India, Department of Scientific and Industrial Research has already started the implementation of its plan for National Information System in Science & Technology (NISSAT), and eight Sectoral centres have been established to provide bibliographic information, and current awareness services, among others.: These centres are Leather Technology (NICLAI) at the CLRI, Madras; (ii) Food Science and Technology (NICFOS) at CFTRI, Mysore; (iii) Machine Tools (NICMAP) at the Central Machine Tools Institute, Bangalore; (iv) Drugs and Pharmaceutical (NICDAP) at the CDRI, Lucknow; (v) Chemistry & Chemical Technology (NICHEM) at the National Chemical Laboratory Pune; (vi) National Centre on Bibliometrics at the INSDOC, New Delhi; (vii) Computer Disk (NICDROM) at the National Aeronautical Lab, Bangalore; (viii) Besides, NISSAT has also set up three information analysis centres: (i) Crystallography (NICRYS) at the University of Madras; (ii) Advanced Ceramics (NICAC) at the Central Glass and Ceramic Research Institute, Calcutta; and (iii) Resource Centre on Software for bibliographic Applications at the Andhra University.

The ICSSR is making a proposal to set up a National Information System in the Social Sciences (NISS). BARC Bombay and ICAR, New Delhi have been working as national input centres for the international database INIS and AGRIS respectively. With several global information systems such as UNISIST, ASTINFO, APINESS, India has developed collaboration and cooperation to have quick access. More specialised information systems such as Biotechnology Information System (BTIS), Environmental Information System (ENVIS), Patent Information System, etc have also been set up.

11. *Library & Information Network:* In addition to the general net work like NICNET, INDONET, etc the UGC has brought out a report entitled *Development of Information and Library Network* (INFLIBNET) in Dec 1988 to forster cooperation and coordination amongst library and information systems and services in the land. In March 1991 a local area network for some important libraries in Delhi, DELNET, has been initiated which would help in resource sharing at local level. A similar network CALIBNET, is being finalised for libraries of 38 participating institutions mainly in the field of science and technology. In addition, CSIR, ICAR and DRDO are building their own networks as SIRNET of the CSIR, DESINET of DRDO, and so on. Then there are VIDYANET and ERNET which provide for the transfer and sharing of information and computing resources within India and for online access to remote databases and computing resources worldwide via communication gateways.

12. *Development in Information Technology:* In addition to what we have just discussed in the preceding two paragraphs , it may be pointed out that the UGC has set up a National Science Information Centre at the Indian Institute of Science, Bangalore which has been obtaining databases such as Chemical Abstracts, BIOSIS, and COMPENDEX on magnetic media and provides SDI services to scientists in the country. Information resource centres are being set up linking local libraries in universities and other institutions of higher learning in Bombay and Calcutta. There are also information systems and local networks in specialized fields such as hydro-power, oceanography, steel, petroleum, coal, agriculture, marine resources, health sciences, etc. Even experimental use of CD-ROM databases have been successful. Electronic publishing and office automation are becoming popular day in and day out. It can therefore be said that the library and information centres could be among the significant beneficiaries of the IT developments in the country provided the library and information profession prepares itself.

13. *Other Developments:* The Planning Commission of the Government of India has been appointing Working Groups from lime to study the situation of libraries in the country. First such Working Group was appointed in 1964. Its report was the first publication of its kind in India, containing detailed information on the resources and service of public libraries in the country again, the Planning Commission appointed a Working group on the Modernisation of Library Services and Information for the Seventh Five Year Plan (1985-90) which submitted its report in 1984. Recently, the Planning Commission has appointed another Working Group to make recommendations for the Eighth Five Year Plan (1992-97) in view of the impact of the new IT.

Another important development has been the Report of the Committee appointed by the Department of Culture, Government of India, on the 'National Policy on Library & Information Systems' submitted in 1986 which has now been approved.

14. Salary Scales and Academic Status: The UGC has granted salary scales at par with the university teachers to librarians and other senior staff working in college and university libraries; while for other libraries the scales have been revised as per the recommendations of the Fourth Pay Commission. However, there still remain some anamolies, which could be removed with the passage of time. The release of teachers' grades to the librarians in colleges and universities has also ensured the academic status. This has changed the thinking of the library personnel as well as that of the teachers and others.

4. Library & Information Development and LIS Education

These developments highlight the existing scenario of library and information services in the country. All these libraries, documentation and information centres are manned by professionally qualified manpower who provide such services as SDI, GAS referral services, repackaging of information, and the like. Some of the libraries, particularly in the science and technology sector, specialized information and data centres, have either already started providing computerised information/ documentation services or are in the process of introducing them. These centres call for specialised skills, ingenuity, imagination, and expertise on the part of library personnel, but as ill luck would have it most of them are trained in only conventional methods and technique of providing services and are not exposed to the new knowledge and skills required for designing, organising and operating the newly emerging information systems. This product with conventional LIS education lack the information science-content—Information—science which is multi-disciplinary field includes elements in the processes of communication, problem solving, decision-making, learning, computer science, etc. Such a composition of information science calls for appropriate knowledge and skills and capabilities in the practitioners as well as the faculty.

5. LIS Education: Course Contents

In the light of the above, it is imperative to acquire appropriate knowledge and skills required not only to handle the hardware and software but also to operate them for various types of jobs and services such as circulation control, document acquisition, serials control, cataloguing, management, SDI, CAS, etc. This brings into play the new elements of course contents or even the restructuring the conventional course contents so as to incorporate the information science concepts to make it applicable to the present and future developments in library and information services.

As of today, it may be pointed out that though the library and information service scenario has been undergoing a metamorphosis yet a large majority of the libraries in our country are without any computer facilities, and they are likely to take some more time before a computer is installed there. The programme of LIS education, therefore have to be developed, designed and restructured in such a way that they fulfil the changing requirements of the libraries/documentation and information centre at two levels:

(i) to impart training in knowledge, skills and techniques required to handle the immediate jobs, operations, services as obtained in a majority of libraries; and

(ii) to impart training in knowledge and skills required to develop programmes, procedures, and services on modern lines with the assistance of computer technology, telecommunication technology, reprography technology, etc.

The need of the hour is not to dispense with the old conventional educational programmes altogether, but to continue these with the elements and concepts of the new IT. At the first degree level a paper about 'Introduction to Information Technology' may be added to the core of the conventional programme while at the Master's level in addition-to-the-papers-on-Information Systems and Information Technology, etc a full paper on 'Computer Application to library and Information Activities' may be added. Such a blending of the traditional and new courses would meet the requirements of public libraries, school, college and also that of the scientific and technological libraries. This has been supported and recommended by the UGC panel on Library &. Information Science.

It is experienced that the new programmes with the concepts from the new IT incorporated are being taught for the last 5 years or so, and with an annual average turnover of about 400 to 450, by now 2,000-2,200 M.L.I.Sc. students must have been in the market serving various libraries across the country, where they are face to face with the computers, and other machines of hi-tech. The new knowledge and skills they have acquired during their training period must have given them more confidence to provide computerised services more quickly and effectively. This therefore, calls for restructuring of course contents at B. Lib. Sc. and M. Lib. Sc. levels, as the information science and technology content in the existing curriculum is quite inadequate. The reformulated course contents would benefit both the library &

information profession and the society it serves, as the professionals would make effective use of and manage the emerging IT in the area of information resource management.

6. Faculty

Although in most of the university level LIS schools full-time faculty has been working, yet there are some schools where either the Head is the University Librarian or/and the teachers are also borrowed from the university library. The growth of faculty has been slow and the number is very small when compared to other disciplines. The position of the LIS faculty is given in Table 1.

As far as their qualifications, status, salary, promotion, study leave, vacation, and other facilities are concerned they are at par with other teachers in the university. But the faculty strength is much wanting in that the most of the LIS schools do not have a post of Professor; nor do they have other cadres of teachers according to the recommendations, of the UGC.

Though it has been difficult to recruit suitable teachers with higher qualifications, the situation has now undergone a change since the eighties, and as of now the number of Ph D teachers in our schools has gone to about 60. However, it will be still difficult for some more time to recruit faculty with background of computer and computer applications to library and information activities.

TABLE 1

LIS Faculty

Cadre	*Position in* 1987	1989	1991
Professor	21	25	30
Readers	77	80	80
Lecturer	86	100	140
Total	184	205	250

7. Research Activity

The quality of LIS education can be linked with the interest of the faculty in the subject to keep themselves uptodate, and also their interest in carrying out research activity. Interest in research would always goad them to do intensive as well extensive reading on the core subject(s). Any relaxation in the preparation of the courses would certainly deteriorate the product of these schools. There were times when many believed that the poor quality of LIS education is the result of the dearth of competent, if not also inspired, teachers to man our library schools. This situation is changing fast as some of them, if not all, have started taking interest in research activities in recent years. The teachers themselves are also doing their Ph. D degrees-mostly in library and information science. According to the information of this author, as of now, about 65 teachers hold Ph. D degrees.

Besides the teachers, the LIS professional in general have also started taking keen interest in research activity. Although the first Ph. D degree in LIS was awarded by the University of Delhi way back in 1957 to a working librarian, yet the development of research activity in LIS schools has been rather slow till recent times for various reasons. For instance, (i) Ph D degree was not required for various job opportunities, (ii) lack of research degree among the LIS faculty who were to be the supervisor, (iii) non-availability of the essential data from the libraries, (iv) lack of proper and adequate and proper library facilities, (v) non-availability of financial support in the form of fellowships, scholarships, research grants, etc. But the situations has changed since, and the professionals all over the land have been coming forward to do research. According to an estimate about 80 candidates are registered for this degree in the 30-odd LIS schools; while about 55 professionals of all cadres have received their Ph D degree from these institutes during 1985-89. Some of the LIS professionals have also done Ph D in other subjects for which records were not easily available.

But inspite of all this development in research by the faculty, the working librarians, and the fresh students, no LIS school in the country has so far attained the status of 'Centre of Advanced Study under the UGC scheme. May be , that research has not percolated deep into the faculty activities. This becomes more pronounced from the fact that the number of research projects completed by them has not been more than six or seven which is by no standards praiseworthy. However, in order to promote research activity and create research environment, it is suggested that a 'Centre of Advanced Study in LIS' should be set up taking into view the infrastructure in terms of resources and facilities.

8. Publication Activity

The LIS faculty and likewise the other professionals, have, in recent times, developed interest in writing and publishing their papers on various problems of librarianship in the professional journals in India and abroad. There was only one professional journal being published in India when Ranganathan appeared on the horizon of Indian Librarianship; and even at the time of Independence the number of active journals could not go beyond two. However, more new journals started appearing during the 1950s, 1960s, 1970s and more in the 1980s. And in 1990 two more journals have been instituted: (1) *Granthana,* by Raja Ram Mohun Roy Library

Foundation, Calcutta, and (2) *Journal of Information Science, form* Chandigarh. Besides, the two old journals are being revived; these are: *Timeless Fellowship,* and *National Librarian.* As a result of this, there are about 25 LIS journals currently being published in English Language only. This speaks of the maturity and growth of the subject, and the interest evinced by the professionals in publishing their research and technical papers.

On the basis of the two bibliographies complied by this author for the 1980s (one covering the period 1981-85 and the other 1986-89), the average annual output of Indian authors in LIS is about 450 articles and about 30 books. However, for the last four years of the eighties (i.e., 1986-89) a total of 2,789 items are recorded which includes 336 items published by foreign authors giving the net total of publications by Indian authors at 2,450 items. This gives us an impressive annual average of about 612 items by Indian professionals.

If we look at the contribution made by the LIS faculty only then it comes to about 800 items for these four years. Out of this the share of Professors is about 290 items; that of the readers is about 340; and about 250 of the Lecturers. The yearly average of about 25/30 Professors is 72 items; that of 80 Readers is just 85 items; and only 62 items of about 140 Lecturers. This data paints a miserable picture, but on looking at the total contribution for 1986-89, the growth is clearly visible because for the first half of the eighties (1981-85) the annual average contribution of the faculty was just about 100 items. Thus for the 1980s (1981-89) the annual average publications of the faculty stands at about 150 items.

If we look at the working librarians contributions for the period 1986-89, it works out about 400 items per annum which is not bad. Their publications for the years 1981-85 stand at the annual rate of 210 items; and collectively for the eighties at about 310 items per year, which is better than that of the faculty. But then the numerical strength of the faculty is not comparable with the librarians in the country.

9. Students Intake

It has been experienced during the last two decades that the students who come to seek admission in the first professional degree in the LIS schools now have higher academic qualifications than what their counterparts had 20 years ago. Although the eligibility qualification is BA/BSc/BCom, yet most of them who are admitted hold Master's degree with good academic record. It has also been found that their general awareness level is fairly good, and they also show interest in learning new skills and knowledge about the tools of new technology. But inspite of this, if we give a hard work at their calibre the picture turns a bit dismal, probably for the following reasons:

1. It is generally experienced, and this view is corroborated by others also, that not all students join the LIS courses with a carrer planning. For many of them it is the last resort; they come to it when they fail to get admission in other courses. Even though they are admitted in the first degree course, they go on appearing in various competitive examinations, and pay very less attention towards the studies in librarianship.
2. As a result of the overall deterioration in the educational standards in our country, what we get in LIS schools is the run-of-the-mill stuff. This deterioration may be traced, inter alia, to two reasons: (a) unhindered expansion of educational institutions at higher level, and (b) menace of unfair means in the examination system.
3. The girl students, in some schools enter only to enhance their marital opportunities, and are scarcely concerned about the profession as such.

10. Avenues of Employment

According to the report of the survey on the library and information manpower need in India conducted jointly by the ISALIC and Burdwan University, about 2,700 qualified personnel join the workforce each year from the existing 75 graduate library schools. They are not so sure as to where they will get employment. In most of the cases, they join the college and university libraries; some in the special libraries, and few in public libraries. But the situation in the country even after unhindered spurt of education about 190 universities, and about 6,000 colleges-is such that they can't provide suitable employment to all those who pass out of these schools. Besides, there is an unspecified number of persons qualifying from the open universities, correspondence courses, professional bodies, polytechnics, colleges, etc. again (with due apology to my women colleagues), the girl students having limited mobility further restrict the job opportunities.

With the enactment of library legislation in eight states more employment avenues are generated there. But the remaining states have yet to pass the library laws; and if they also enact it one by one more employment avenues will be provided to the qualified persons.

It is estimated that in the roughly 300 special library units in the country, about 10,000 professional staff might be recruited in the next 5 years.

There are employment opportunities for the trained librarians in sectors other than libraries, such as publishing industry. The publisher employ graduate librarians for preparing indexes for books they publish, because many authors do not want to do the job of index preparation; and even if they prepare these are ill-prepared in many cases.

The librarians can also bring out systematically the publishers catalogues and other book lists.

Well qualified librarians can also work as better copy editors if they have proficiency in English.

Further, a librarian working with a publisher can always prepare the cataloguing in Publication CIP data which is to be included at the verso of the title page (as we have in the books from the UK and the US) for multiple use.

There are avenues of self-employment for the trained librarians. The most useful, urgently required, and lucrative also are the areas of compiling bibliographical control tools such as indexing and abstracting services, bibliographies in subject fields not covered so far. They can also prepare directories, state-of-the-art reports, and the like.

Librarians can also employ themselves in other areas such as stationery, furniture and equipment suppliers to the libraries. Since they are more familiar with the library needs they can always supply quality items to them.

In view of the computer applications to libraries and information centres the job opportunities of trained librarians with computer qualifications and skills will be immense in the future.

11. Need for Accreditation

At present when we look at the LIS schools in the country the following aspects are reflected.

(i) Increase in the number of institutions imparting LIS education at different levels ; (ii) Increase in the number of students; (iii) Disparity in curriculum; (iv) Irrelevant curriculum in many cases; (v) Sub-standard facilities; etc.

This situation is quite disappointing and calls for ensuring and maintaining proper academic standards in at least such areas as the strength and qualifications of the faculty, admission procedure, enrolment, curriculum, finance, library-cum-workshop facilities, building, non-teaching staff, equipments, etc.

The need for creating a proper system of accreditation is being felt in the profession quite earnestly for some time now, but unfortunately a suitable mechanism for this purpose has yet to be devised. It has been a matter of wide discussion to select a body which may be entrusted with the job of accreditation. If for one reason or the other the accrediting work can not be done either by the UGC, or the ILS, or the IATLIS then a new body such as Indian LIS council may be created to check the proliferation of substandard courses and maintain academic standards. This issue has been discussed at a recent IATLIS Seminer held at Andhra University, Visakhapatnam during 26-28 August 1991.

12. Some Suggestions

In order to improve and maintain the quality and standard of LIS education in the country some concrete measures need to be taken. These measures, as suggested below, should form part of some phased programme to be taken care of by some national body.

1. LIS education programmes at the post-graduate level, i.e., B. Lib. Sc., M. Lib. Sc, MPhil and PhD should be conducted only at the university level with clearly defined objectives while those at the undergraduate level may be conducted by the library associations, women polytechnics, state central libraries.

2. Every LIS school should have adequate infrastructure required for a particular programme.

3. Minimum teaching staff when both B. Lib. Sc and M. Lib. Sc courses are offered should be 1 Professor, 2 Readers, 4 Lecturers, at least one with training in computer applications.

4. There should be a minimum standard and parity in duration of the courses, curriculum, method of evaluation, physical facilities, teacher-student ratio.

5. In view of varying standards of general education at graduate and post-graduate level, admission to LIS schools should be based on previous educational record but on the Entrance Test centring round the aptitude for library and information work.

6. An accrediting agency be set up at the national level in order to maintain minimum standards of LIS education.

7. All LIS courses be restructured and updated to include information science, information technology, areas. However, requirements of various types of libraries be kept in mind.

8. Seminars, role playing, simulations to be given importance in the teaching techniques.

9. Each student should be required to undergo a minimum period of one month's internship/apprenticeship in libraries recognised for the purpose.

10. Periodic surveys should be conducted to assess the manpower requirements in the libraries, for more reliable data, and establishing definite trends in manpower supply and demand. A Roster of library and information personnel maybe set up at a suitable national organisation with regular updates.

11. There should be cooperation and coordination amongst the various LIS schools to bridge the gaps by facilitating exchange of faculty. This could be achieved through a national body.

13. Conclusion

To try to make prediction is quite an unrewarding activity, but at the same time it is difficult to resist the temptation too, though fully aware that the likelihood of its being wrong may be greater. The technological advancement is so rapid that it is difficult to look into the times to come. Our library professional perhaps have not changed their attitude fully and in the past they had been vacillating in addressing themselves to the change in society and technology and their impact on library and information profession during the current decade and the next century. The chip technology, communication technology, printing technology, etc which was round the corner a decade ago has now already entered the threshold. This is now putting greater responsibility on us, on LIS educators, planners, library and information science managers to go and see beyond the present library objectives. This calls for immediate change in the quality of education and training of the professionals so that they could be prepared for increasingly technology-driven information systems and services of tomorrow.

REFERENCES

1. India, Ministry of Human Resources and Development, Committee on National Policy on Library and information Systems, *National policy on Library and information systems: A presentation*, New Delhi: The Author, 1986.
2. Isaac, K.A., Library and information science education in India: Sinning or sinned against? *In* Sewa Singh (Ed.). *Librarianship and library science education*, New Delhi: Ess Ess Publications, 1988, pp. 79-84.
3. Kumar, P.S.G., *Hundred years of library education and its future: Seminar papers*, Nagpur : Dept. of Library and information Science , Nagpur University, 1987.
4. LIS manpower needs in India: An assessment, *NISSAT Newsletter* 10(3) July-Sept. 1991:16-17.
5. Mangla, P.B., *Homage; Ranganathan memorial lecture* (10. 1982), Ujjain: Dept. of library and Information Science, Vikram University, 1982.
6. Mangla, P.B., Levels of training in library and information science: Admission requirements and duration, *Library Science with a slant to Documentation* 15, 1978;125-131.
7. Mangal P.B.. Library and information science education in India, In B.M. Gupta (Ed), *Handbook of library, archives and information centres in India, v* I, New Delhi: Information Industry Publication, 1984, pp. 229-256.

8. Mangla, P.B., *Library and information science education in India : Papers and recommendations*, New Delhi: Macmillan, 1981.

9. Mnngla, P.B., Library and information in India: Trends and issues, *Granthana* 1(2) July: 29-44.

10. Ramakrishnan, M.N., et al, *eds, Library and information science education in India; New perspectives*, Trivandrum : Dept. of Library and Information Science, Kerala University, 1989.

11. Rajan, T.N., Manpower needs for information work in India, *In* B.M. Gupta (Ed) *Handbook of libraries, archives, and information centres in India*, v 1, New Delhi: Information Industry Publication, 1934. pp. 303-315.

12. Seminar on Curriculum Development, held at SERC, CSIR complex, Taramani. Madras, 20-22 Feb 1990, *Papers*, Madras: Institute of Information Studies, etc, 1990.

13. Sewa *Singh, Indian library literature, 1981-85: An annotated bibliographic guide*, New Delhi: Ess Ess Publications, 1988.

14. Sewa Singh, *Indian library and information science literature (1986-89)*, New Delhi: Ess Ess Publications, 1991.

15. Sewa Singh, Library science as a carrer, *Careers*, Punjab Government Chandigarh, June 1987:1-7

16. *Survey of public library services in India*, conducted by the Planning Commission's Working Group on Libraries, tabulated and analysed by D.R. Kalia, Delhi: Indian Library Association, 1965

17. University Grants Commission (India), Panel on Library and Lnformation Science, *Recommendations*, New Delhi: UGC, 1982 (mimeographed),

18. University Grants Commission (India), Inter-Agency Working Group, *Development of an information and library network: Report*, New Delhi UGC, 1988.

19. Zorkoczy, Peter, *Information technology ; an introduction*, New Delhi Affiliated East-West Press, 1989.

13

USE OF INFORMATION TECHNOLOGY IN SOCIAL SCIENCE DOCUMENTATION SERVICES WITH SPECIAL REFERENCE TO NASSDOC

Among the objectives of social sciences, one is that of developing a body of knowledge contributing to our understanding of the problems that beset our society and help us to design ways and instrumentalities of overcoming them and improving the quality of life. The stress here is on development related research or applied social science research. This type of research got great impetus in India during 1970s. People engaged in this need latest information to keep their knowledge up-to-date for formulating alternative plans of development. There is thus a great need to maintain an uninterrupted flow of information from the generation end to the user end. There are however many hurdles in-between.

COMMUNICATION OF INFORMATION

The size of social science community is increasing at a faster rate resulting in the growth of volume of social science knowledge and information. Any information by itself has no value. Its value comes from its communication and use. Communication involves the transfer of information from one person to another and is affected by the variables of time and space. Generation and application of social sciences knowledge requires an easy access to available knowledge. According to Dr. Yogesh Atal "In order to generate new knowledge and new information, it is necessary to have easy access to information that already exists. New knowledge is built on the foundations of existing stock of knowledge.... Without knowing where we are, we cannot move forward, we cannot chart out our path. Information provides the contours of our cognitive map."

But the process of communicating information or information transfer is rendered difficult because of certain problems like increase in number of users of information, information explosion, interdisciplinary nature of information, information scatter in numerous sources, increasing role of information in shaping the economy of society, geographical, language and other barriers. And unlike other commodities "Information is a peculiar commodity. When transfered from source to recipient, or from seller to buyer, it remains available to both. Moreover, information is rarely required for itself alone — it is usually only wanted because of its potential contribution to some human activity".—B C Vikery and Alina Vikery.

In order to overcome these barriers, there exists today a vast array of electronic tools and techniques for accumulating, storing, organising, retrieving, communicating and interpreting information on a world— wide scale. "We are experiencing now what might be called 'the push of technology' and its impact on every facet of information handling". - M N Seetharaman.

ROLE OF ICSSR - NASSDOC IN INFORMATION COMMUNICATION

In order to promote social science research and its better utilisation by administrators, academicians and scholars, an autonomous national organisation, Indian Council of Social Science Research (ICSSR) was set up in 1969 on the recommendations of VKRV Rao Committee. Among its financial assistance programmes, it at present provides maintenance and development grant to 26 research institutes which are engaged in research activities in social sciences and are not affiliated to any university.

ICSSR in an endeavour towards dissemination of information to social scientists set up Social Science Documentation Centre(SSDC) in 1970. SSDC has been renamed as National Social Science Documentation Centre.

The paper will focus on development of machine readable bibliographic databases in National Social Science Documentation Centre and services offered with their help.

NATIONAL SOCIAL SCIENCE DOCUMENTATION CENTRE

NASSDOC like any other constituent organisation, strives to meet the objectives of its parent body (ICSSR), that is, assistance in development of social science research. With the result NASSDOC has designed its services, products and supporting infrastructure accordingly. Here only those services / products of NASSDOC will be described which are supported by computer technology.

Hardware and Software With NASSDOC

NASSDOC has five PC-XTs, four printers, one Modem, and one CD-ROM drive. Each PC-XT has 640 KB RAM, and one floppy drive. Four PC-XTs have single hard disk of 20 MB each and one has 2 hard disks of 20 MB.

These PC-XTs operate under MS DOS ver 3.2. NASSDOC has computer software namely dBase III, Wordstar, Akshar, CDS/ISIS and IDAMS. In addition to the above, hardware and software in ICSSR — Data Archives is also available to NASSDOC for use.

Development of Local Databases Based on Locally Available Materials

Current Awareness Service

(i) Current Contents of Indian Social Science Journals

The Current Contents of Indian Social Science Journals reproduces edited table of contents of more than hundred important journals received in NASSDOC. The arrangement is alphabetical by the title of journals. When more than one issue of a journal is covered, issues appear in chronological order. Each article citation includes title, author(s) and page number(s) if available. Articles cited are numbered sequentially.

The subject index contains multiple subject headings for each article. The author index lists each author and cites the article number. Corporate authors are omitted. Both indexes help in quick retrieval of articles on a desired topic.

The database is maintained on floppies and its printed version is brought out quarterly.

(ii) Conference Alert

It is a quarterly calendar of forthcoming conferences, seminars, training courses, etc. in social sciences and penumbral fields.

In this database/publication, entries in chronological order give date, title, venue and address of the contact point/sponsoring body of the forthcoming conference, seminar etc. Appended are subject and location (Geographical) indexes.

The objective of this publication is to furnish advance intimation about the programmes to enable the interested scholar to plan participation, and to submit or request papers.

Bibliographic Database of Research Project Reports

NASSDOC receives reports of the research projects funded by ICSSR. Bibliographic database of near about 2000 and abstracts of 1500 reports have been created. For simplification of use author, subject and title indexes have been created. This helps the researcher to retrieve the desired information through multiple search keys and helps the staff in providing quick reference service and in compilation of short bibliographies on demand. Many problems were faced while creating its subject index.

Area Study Bibliography

The "Area Study Project" aimed at bringing together all social science research material excluding articles pertaining to the different states/ union territories of India. The databases on Bihar, Karnataka, Maharashtra, North East Region, and Orissa have been created and are being maintained in PC. The data is arranged authorwise and subject and title indexes are given for different approaches.

Interlibrary Resource Centre (ILRC) Catalogue

ILRC was set up in 1975, inviting local libraries to deposit their non-current, infrequently used but important for research serials with this Centre. Recently, due to lack of space, the acceptance of the deposits has been suspended. A bibliographic database of this collection has been created. It gives title, year of start, place of publication, history of journal and holdings of the journal in ILRC. Multiple approaches for retrieving information is possible.

Updation of ICSSR Directory of Social Science Research Institutes in India

NASSDOC is maintaining a directory of Social Science Research Institutes in India in machine readable form. The proformas were sent to 325 institutes. In all 162 proformas duly checked/updated have been received. The information for 162 institutes is available in NASSDOC's database. It gives information about institute's name, address; type of organisation e.g. national, international, etc.; type of activity indicating research, research promotion, policy making, research projects under process, publications etc. Eight indexes have been provided to approach an institution. Besides the benefit of manipulation of data, it helps a social scientist to have information of so many institutes at one place only.

Union List of Social Science Periodicals

Database on Union List of Current Social Science Periodicals in Delhi Libraries, 1989 was created to facilitate resource sharing. It records the availability of near about 4000 current titles of periodicals being received in 48 libraries in Delhi. The database is being maintained on floppies and a mimeographed version has also been brought out.

Database of Core Journals in Social Sciences Available in Major Libraries in India

Near about one thousand titles are listed. Each journal has been given subject descriptors, maximum upto four. Information about country of the origin, its frequency and language of the journal is available.

Messages Transmission System

Electronic mail (E-mail) is a computer based Electronic document delivery system. It is used to create and transmit messages electronically addressed to an individual or a specified group of individuals.

Libraries and information centres participating in DELNET transmit their messages through E-Mail. NASSDOC is one of the participating members. Requests for interlibrary loan and other messages are being sent to other participating libraries. The messages are routed through PCs, modern telephone, host computer (at NISSAT) and acceptor. Delivery of documents has quickened with it.

Concept of electronic mail or any other LAN activity for that matter is a novel idea. But in Indian conditions it is difficult to work with them. The problems arise from telephone networks, and the Indian environment in which computers are made to work.

Databases Acquired in NASSDOC

On CD-ROM

NASSDOC has acquired so far two databases viz Population Information On Line (POPLINE) and AUSTROM.

POPLINE provides information on population, family planning and related health issues. It consists of about 1,60,000 published and unpublished records with detailed abstracts and in-depth indexing. The majority of items date since 1970, but some sources date from as early as 1827.

AUSTROM is a compilation of eleven Australian social science and education databases. It contains detailed information from published and unpublished material. The coverage starts since 1978.

NASSDOC provides bibligraphic service from these two databases. A printout of citations sometimes with abstracts on requested subject is supplied to the scholar.

Current Contents on Diskettee

NASSDOC has acquired Current Contents on diskettee: Social and Behavioural Sciences. It is a weekly service from Institute for Scientific Information Inc. Searches are conducted on requested subjects covered in it and results downloaded or printed.

Being current service, there is no provision of cumulation of data for more than one week. This service could be of immense help for bibliographic service if there were at least bi-monthly or half yearly cumulations.

Documentation Services From Other Libraries and Information Centres

CD-ROM Based SDI Services

Agricultural Research Information Centre of Indian Council of Agricultural Research has started providing an SDI (Selective Dissemination of Information) service using databases available with it on CD-ROM. The databases are: AGRIS (International Information System for Agricultural Sciences and Technology), SESAME (French Agricultural Bibliographical Database), and CA (Chemical Abstracts). A scientist has to bring or send a floppy diskettee for searches which are to be downloaded in the disk. A maximum of 250 references are supplied at a time. However, if the searches are few, the same could be given in print output.

Index of Articles on Agricultural Economics

It is a computerised index of more than one hundred journals pertaining to agricultural economics, rural development and allied subjects. NASSDOC receives this index on floppies as well as its print out. The information can be retrieved from several access points.

DEVINSA

Development Information Network for South Asia (DEVINSA) is a cooperative information network of six South Asian countries — Bangladesh, India, Maldives, Nepal, Pakistan, and Sri Lanka — represented in Committee on Studies for Cooperation in Development in South Asia. DEVINSA database consists mainly of unpublished literature like conference reports, theses, research reports etc. produced in these countries. But relevant published documents are also included.

Main purpose of this database is to provide to users information on current socio economic developments activities in South Asia. The cummulated database is held online in a computer in Marga Institute, (the Coordinating Centre), Sri Lanka.

Two by-products (i) DEVINSA Bibliography and (ii) DEVINSA Abstracts are published from this database.

(i) DEVINSA Bibliography is a bibliography of about 250 entries and is published monthly.

(ii) DEVINSA Abstracts contains all the entries published in six previous monthly bibliographics.

Both these publications are cumulated annually under the names DEVINSA Annual Bibliography and DEVINSA Abstracts Annual.

Besides these two published services, retrospective search on request is conducted by the Coordinating Centre. Moreover, user can obtain a copy of the document from user's country focal point.

In Indian Jawaharlal Nehru University is national focal point for CSCD.

Artha Suchi

It is computerised index to government reports, journal articles and newspaper write-ups in the field of Indian economics which are being received in NCAER library. Artha Suchi is available online besides in printed form. The information retrieval is quick, easy and is possible from various access points like keywords, author, name of serial etc.

Parliament Library Information System

Parliament Library Information System (PARLIS) was computerised with the assistance of National Informatics Centre (NIC) in 1985, the database is stored in main computer at NIC. The information is available online and relates to (i) Indices to selected parliamentary questions (ii) Parliamentary debates (iii) Parliamentary bills (iv) Bio-data profiles of members of Parliament (v) Socio-economic background data in respect of MPs (Lok Sabha) (vi) Data regarding Presidential elections in India from 1952 to 1987 (vii) Statistical information system containing information tables relating to economy of India.

Fortnightly Docplan Abstracts

The mimeographed publication is brought out by Planning Commission Library. The records appear alphabetically subjectwise subdivided geographically. Author index and specific subject index is given at the end.

IMPEDIMENTS AND SUGGESTIONS

Social Sciences except experimental psychology and econometrics are considered soft sciences; attitudes of funding agencies towards social sciences is also soft but in a negative sense. Comparatively less funds are sanctioned for its research and study. And for their libraries and information centres funds trickle further though many filters, with the result, computerisation in these centres has got affected and social scientist is not getting proper stimuli for use of information.

Because of paucity of funds, it has not been possible for NASSDOC to get hooked up with any international online database.

To serve social scientist in a better way, one PCXT with CD-ROM drive could be kept in the reading room, so that with the help of reference staff, social scientist could conduct his/her search himself/herself from bibliographic databases acquired from outside.

NASSDOC has plans of computerising its documentation programmes like Union Catalogue of Social Science Periodicals in India and Retrospective Index of Social Science Periodicals. But because of inadequate hardware these activities are being delayed.

By and large social science libraries do not have library staff trained in information technology to undertake independently implementation of computerisation in libraries.

There is always a communication gap when untrained library staff and computer professionals communicate. This results in time lag to complete any information system. To overcome this problem library should either hire computer staff or should thoroughly train its already existing staff.

Our social scientist is not a demanding consumer of information industry. It may be due to lack of appropriate supply of information to stimulate the latent demand. The social science libraries/information centres should market their products/ services more vigorously so that social scientist knows and makes use of them.

REFERENCES

1. Agrawal, S.P. & Manohar Lal, Documentation activities and services in social sciences: Role of NASSDOC and ICSSR Regional Centres. pp. 78-108 *In* Handbook of libraries, archives and information centres in India. Delhi, Aditya Prakashan, 1990. Vol.8.
2. Bonazza, Abdelmajid, Information user studies. pp. 144-164 *In* Encyclopedia of Library and Information Science. Vol. 44 (Supplement 4).
3. CD-ROM based SDI service *APINESS Newsletter* Vol. 10,1991. pp. 2-3
4. Current Contents on Diskette: User Guide.
5. Electronic mail system in Delhi libraries. *APINESS Newsletter* Vol. 10, 1991. p. 2.
6. Haravu, L.J., Managing university library resources and services: The role of automation. *Journal of Library and Information Science* Vol. 7(1) June 1982, pp. 84-95.
7. ICSSR Newsletter. Jan-Mar 1991. pp. 11-12.

8. Lakshmana Moorthy, A. & Rajendran, V., Information technologies for libraries and information cent res. *AGLIS Journal* Vol 8(1-4) Jan-Dec 1990, pp. 6-16.
9. Lilley, Dorothy B. & Trice, Ronald W., A history of information science, 1945-85. San Diego, Academic Press, 1989. 181p.
10. National Social Science Documentation Centre Services and product brochure. 8 p.
11. Rab, S. Fazle., Managing information: Need for the planning of social science research institute's network (SSRINET) pp. 253-265 *In* Vashishth, C.P. *ed.* Computerisation and library network: Seminar papers-Thirty sixth All India Library Conference, Jodhpur, Dec 26-29, 1990. Delhi, Indian Library Association, 1991.
12. Roberts, Stephen Andrew, Social science libraries and collections, pp. 60-94 *In* Encyclopedia of Library and Information Science. Vol. 28.
13. Seetharaman, M.N., An introduction to online networks and services and a case study of an experimental project in NAL, Bangalore, pp. 279-293 *In* Khan, H.A. and Ijari, S.R. *ed.* Current problems and trends in library and information services: Prof. K.S. Deshpande commemoration volume. Varanasi, Indian Bibliographic Centre, 1990, 370 p.
14. Sirkin, Arlene Farber, Marketing planning for maximum effectiveness. *Special Libraries* Vol 82(1) Winter 1991. pp. 1-6
15. Vickery, Brian and Vickery, Alina, Information science in theory and practice. London, Butterworths, 1987. 384 p.
16. Yates Mercer, P.A. & Steward, Y.F., The marketing of internal business information services. *Journal* of *Information Science: Principles and Practice* Vol. 17 (4) 1991. pp. 221-233.

14

MEANING OF COMPUTING POWER

Introduction

To quote figures given out by M.G.K. Menon in the last decade, India registered an eight-fold increase in computing power between 1971 and 1979 alone and the growth has continued unabated ever since. This would mean that computing power had a compound growth-rate of 56 per cent between those years, thus doubling itself every fifteen months. It is no mean achievement for at developing country and the growth-pattern has shown no signs of abatement in the years to follow.

The Computer Brain

In order to understand the meaning of computing power (which can be defined as the measure of a few hundred thousand or more calculations done per second), one has to look into the computer as a device which carried out such computations in a sequence determined by human commands, without external intervention. All computations are carried out in the Central Processing Unit (CPU) resembling human brain, which comprises the arithmetic/logic unit and the control unit, for doing the actual "number crunching" and data manipulations, and directing their performance respectively. The set of instructions or commands (software), along with data, are stored into the memory from where CPU fetches them for execution. This improvement came only in the post-ENIAC computers, thanks to the mathematical genius of he Hungarian-born scientist John Von Neumann. The instructions as well as data are entered into the memory through the peripheral input/ output (I/O) devices which are connected to the memory through channels for dataflow. While channels take commands from the CPU for carrying out and I/O operation, they have enough electronics built into them to carry out the commands independent of the CPU.

For nearly two decades since the mid-fifties, the most popular memory of modern computers had been the magnetic core, comprising thousands of tiny soft-iron rings within a precisely designed grid. Any specific location can be "addressed" almost instantly for retaining or retrieving a "bit" (for "binary digit") of information is magnetised (I) or demagnetised (O) form. The expensive core memory has long been replaced by far cheaper semiconductor memory on chips. While cost per bit has been higher in small core memories than in the big memories, semiconductor memories provide "random access" with a steady cost per bit, since the supporting electronic circuits are built in solid'-state components.

Input and Output Devices

Semiconductor technology has not entered much in the field of storage (or auxiliary) memories in the form of magnetic tapes, discs and drums. These I/O devices have the advantage of large capacity and low cost, for storing information in bulk and having high speed of operation. Magnetic "bubble" memory has now entered the field as an improved technology, with the problem of "volatile" operation getting gradually solved. Optical technology is another contender giving risk to compact discs.

Input devices translate information from a variety of sources into a code that is understood by the computer. Key-boards are useful for data input of varying volume, although one can prepare an intermediate output on a taster medium (tape reel, floppy disc) for recurrent use. Other devices are touch-tone telephones, data-entry terminals (with keyboards and display units), optical scanners ("reading" characters at high speeds), electronics ears (recognising a limited number of spoken words), etc., all for specific applications. Processed data are translated into electrical impulses that can control a variety of output devices, such as, high-speed printers (using drum of chain), visual-display terminals, artificial voice or laser-operated printers.

Progress in Technology

It is salutary to comprehend at what rate improvements have taken place in the computer technology starting from the fifties. According to James Martin, the increase in number of logic circuits that can be packed into a given volume, has shown an expotential increase. At the same time, there has been a steady increase in the cost of logic circuitry in terms of millions of instructions per dollar, thus illustrating the gain in computer power per unit of cost over a very limited time-period. The increase in speeds of high-speed computers in terms of memory-cycles per second has been accompanied by the tremendous growth of the capacity of on-line data-files directly accessible by the computer. The dramatic rise in the computer capabilities over time is too evident to need elaboration.

Considering all factors, the computing power depends on the available hardware facilities. If the CPU is micro-programmed, the word-length (a group of bits which determines the characteristics of the micro-programming) is an indication of its power. Microprocessor-based systems come in 8-bit or 16-bit or 32-bit machines, with limited direct-address capability as well. In a large computer, instructions can be fetched from memory in a single reference, while in microprocessor-based systems several references to memory are required. Micro-computers including personal computers are thus small and slow with memory size between 640 Kilo Bytes (KB) and 8 Mega Bytes (MB) and suited ideally for simple business functions or a limited number applications at a low cost, where the hardware can be even pre-coded as per the user requirement. Mini-computers (32-bit) have memory-sizes varying between 4 MB and 16 MB, with the speed around a few million operations per second. Mainframe computers (64-bit and above) have a range of memory between 16 MB and 54 MB while super computers can go from 64 MB to a few hundred Mega Bytes — with increase in operating speeds, and more sophisticated and taster peripherals — having a wide range of applications.

Computer Operation

Each computer operation can be broken down into a series of sequential steps. If the hardware facilities are more, several steps can be converged to form a single step, thus reducing the time to execute an operation. Further, the speed and capacity of the CPU accessing memory also contribute to the computing power. If the memory is slow (like the earlier cote-memory), it may introduce a waiting stage in the CPU. Instruction execution time depends, in turn, on the CPU cycle time and varies from low, medium to high for mainframe mini to microcomputers respectively.

When I/O devices are resorted to for auxiliary memory, they reduce the power of the machine, since access to these devices is comparatively slow. I/O devices play a major role in the overall performance of the computer. Their speed should conform to the bus speed in a bus-oriented microcomputer or to the channel speed in larger machines. Electro-mechanical components of the I/O devices are the main hindering factors and have often an attachment of *cache* memory in order to appear fast to the CPU. In the cost hierarchy, cost per bit is the highest for I/O parts (for exchange of information between user and machine), followed by the main memory and mass storage memory.

Throughout, measured in terms of number of jobs processed per unit time, depends on the computer environment and the type of jobs. Some instructions take a longer time to be executed and some shorter. A particular mix of instructions, known as Gibson Mix, gives a specific number of thousand operations in terms of frequency of usage. In order to have a high throughout, multiple programming (or multi-tasking) is used by running a mix of CPU-bound and I/O-bound jobs, resulting in better utilisation of all the resources. Thus, maximum computing power available with the machine gets utilised for useful work in a balanced fashion. Another way of increasing throughout is by multi-processing where more than one CPU is used either for specialised job (e.g., array/matrix processor), or in a master-slave mode (e.g., remote processor), or in independent mode with shared resources (e.g., front-end processor).

With the advancement of integration technology the actual size of the machine is too deceptive for guessing its computing power. The latter depends entirely on the computer architecture and not on the size solely determined by technology. While a pure micro-processor (without peripheral devices) can remain embedded in a modern machine (like car engine helping its operations), a mainframe computer can come in a couple of cabinets running an entire factory through remote terminals!

In the world today, there is a growing lag between computer *hardware* (machine with the peripherals) and *software* (set of instructions to operate the machine) technology. The cost of computing power has come down by several orders of magnitude in the last one generation, and the unit cost of memory and storage decreased at a compound annual rate of 40 per cent during this period. On the other hand, the cost of producing software necessary to exploit the growing computing power has risen steadily, and the increasing complexing of systems and application software has been truly overwhelming. Boehm's diagram at Fig. 1 on hardware/software cost trends brings out vividly the concept of spending more on software than hardware today.

Software, as a sequence of commands (programme) used to achieve the desired output, is not limited to one particular job or application. Advanced categories of software tools include operating systems, language compilers, application packages and user-written programmes.

Operating Systems

It is a distinguishing characteristic of third-generation computer systems that the hardware is designed to operate under control of rather sophisticated software. Especially in a multi-programming and/or multi-processing computer, *operating system* allocates system resources and sorts out problems of conflict, blocking and interference among simultaneous users of the computer. In particular, scheduling of operations, functions of the input/output devices and management of main and auxiliary strong are software activities that are centralised and carefully controlled by operating system.

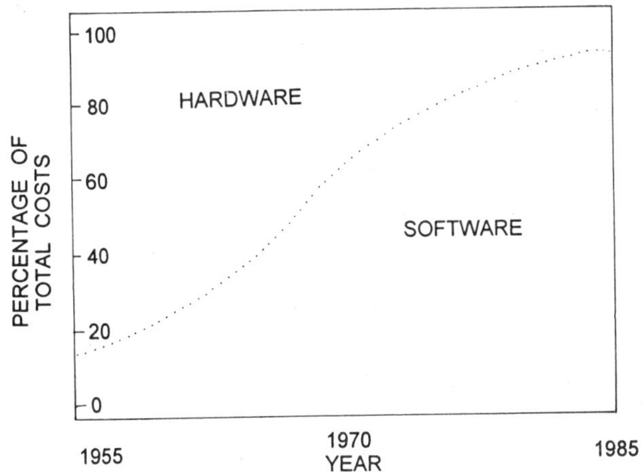

Fig. 1: Hardware/Software Cost Trends

Operating system aims at optimising the overall operations and achieving a comprehensive effectiveness, by supporting different modes of the user operation. For example, in *batch* mode, operating system supports running of a batch of programmes at a time. In multi-*programming* mode, many jobs are run concurrently, with one Programme carrying out the input/output operation while the other programme makes use of the CPU for computation. In *remote batch* mode, programmes are run from a remote site where the actual processing is done. A communication link connects the central computer with the remote site having intelligent or non-intelligent terminals. In *time-sharing* mode, operating system allocates computer resources to the users in a shared fashion so that a particular user gets time-slices for specific intervals without bothering about other users. In *real-time* mode, data are entered and enquiries made from remote sites as processing is going on.

Compilers

Language compilers are types of basic software with which a computer system translates programmes written in high level language into that of machine language. Now, machine language is the sequence of bits for which the machine is designed architecturally to operate. Assembly language is a step removed from machine language, using a set of mnemonics and translating them through assembler into machine code. Among high-level languages, FORTRAN (Formula-Translation Language) has been evolving since 1954 and is very suitable for complex calculations of scientific kind with little data. COBOL (Common Business-Oriented Language) came from US Departments of Defence in 1961 and has been found useful for simple calculations of commercial kind with large-volume data. PL/1 (Programming Language 1) came in 1965 and combines the features of FORTRAN and COBOL for being used in both business and scientific applications. ALGOL (Algorithmic-Oriented Language) came in 1960 and is quite, good in solving mathematical problems while RPG {Report Generator) is a powerful language for generating tabular reports. BASIC (Beginners All-Purpose Symbolic Instruction Code) is quite simple to use and fit for on-line interactive processing. The most recent powerful languages are PASCAL, C and ADA. Programmes written in the above languages are compatible with most available computer systems.

Other Software

A complete software system for a computer contains, besides operating system, a set of compilers for various languages as above, one or more system loaders, a filing system, a set of utility routines (for various input/output functions), special and general debugging systems, and generalised software for application, such as, sorting and merging, mathematical programming,, engineering design, report generation, simulation graphics, and so on. All these interface smoothly with operating system and its input/output conventions.

Until 1969, users were provided with all the general-purpose software by the manufacturer along with the purchased (or hired) machine at no extra cost. Since then, all manufacturers have followed IBM in "unbundling" of software: with the exception of operating system. All software products are now priced separately. Techniques of software development are also no longer *ad hoc* but use sets of modules that can be used "off the shelf" components for developing new software products or modifying the old ones. Structured programming use prior verification methods to eliminate much of the programme-testing activity.

Application Packages

Application packages are ready-made and well-documented programmes for performing specific functions. These software packages are available on certain computer systems or for a certain class of users. They are often made flexible enough to be portable to other machines or adaptable to other users. Examples of common application package. In India, for scientific as well as business application, cover Project Management System (PMS) for determining critical activities through project network and keeping up schedules of cost and resource allocation; Mathematical Programming System (MPS) for using linear programming to optimise given objectives subject to the constraints; General-Purpose Systems Simulation (GPSS) for discrete simulation of events; Vehicle Scheduling Package (VSP) for operating a fleet of vehicles with referent to route allocation and load distribution; Production Planning and Control System (PPCS) for planning production along with manpower and material allocation; Financial Accounting and Analysis Package (FAAP) for all financial functions of ledger-keeping, reconciliation and analysis, — apart from sales analysis, market research and survey analysis, electronic circuit analysis and numerical control programmes. Another package, called Statistical Package for Social Sciences (SPSS) has, in fact, been of very wide use.

In the conventional processing, the user accumulates data in computer files in his own format and utilises them for a specific application. In the case of data-base approach, prevalent now over two decades, data are organised in such a fashion that they can be used for many users for a variety of applications. This approach has considerabie data independence and reduction in data redundancy. Two applications of data-base management like Customer Information Control System (CICS) and Information Management System (IMS) are well-known IBM packages and similar versions are available with compatible machines, such as, Reyad, Hitac, etc.

User-written programme are generated in many applications where either application packages are too general-purpose to suit the specific user environment or just not available. Such programmes having the advantage of being tailor-made for the purpose can be easily altered to changed user-requirement, adapted to different machine organisations or made to satisfy different system constraints — although at a cost.

All software tools need good documentation for correct usage, wide dissemination and independence from the original creator. At least three manuals are needed: for the user, for the operator and for the maintenance programmer. Also, because of the complexity of large software systems, there are often errors (bugs and inadequacies in running them. Maintenance groups are needed to keep track of all needs for correction. In some cases; extensive changes require major revision in documentation, thus needing release of a new version of the software product.

SELECTION OF COMPUTERS

Computer is a highly complex device and a great deal can be made of the technical attributes of the individual machines in their actual usage. For instance, commercial data processing comprises reading data, printing out data, storing data and retrieving data from magnetic media. Computer performance for such work would be mainly determined by the speed and capability of input/output (I/O) and storage peripherals. Most jobs in government departments, industry, business houses and public utility systems are heavily I/O-bound. On the other hand, scientific, engineering and operations research problems require good computational facilities, such as, available core store and instruction speeds. Such jobs would be mostly found in academic institutions and R&D organisations.

The important factors to be considered for selection of computer for an organisation are: cost of equipment: availability of a suitable configuration; feasibility of upgrading the configuration to obtain more computer power; software availability and suitability; and quality of manufacturer's support-services, e.g., maintenance, training and systems support.

Alternative Approaches

After a proper configuration has been worked out in advance, appropriate computers should be looked for. Computers are not all alike in the market and the pricing structure varies from manufacturer to manufacturer. Some computers are rented out by manufacturers on a one-time installation charge and monthly rental thereafter. The rental covers a certain number of hours (prime shift) for which the maintenance is included. IBM in India used to follow this practice for their second-generation computer systems, all charges being extra beyond prime shift.

Alternatively, computer time can be hired from a service bureau. For this purpose, suitable service bureaus have to be explored in the neighbourhood and logistics worked out. One approach is to employ a few programmers and systems analysts for developing application programmes and purchase only computer-time from the service bureau for running the programmes. Typically, a regional computer service centre with a mainframe system would earlier charge Rs. 600 per hour for I/O-bound jobs and Rs. 2500 or Rs. 3000 or Rs. 3500 per hour of CPU time from academic community or business organisations or other consultants. The charges have considerably come down now. The other approach is to contract the entire job of designing, developing and implementing the application programmes to the service bureau on a turn-key basis. Once the job is ready, it can also be run on the service-bureau computer under a separate contract. Both these approaches permit shift of the job to an in-house computer whenever feasible.

The final alternative is to buy a computer system for in-house usage. This is the most difficult choice including heavy investment of capital with a substantial amount of foreign currency, if the system is of foreign currency, if the system is to be imported), employment of skilled people on a permanent basis and tying up with an available technology for considerable time especially when computer hardware is continually undergoing improvement

Available Variety

Availability of a suitable configuration can be from a variety of manufacturers. Indian government was earlier following a policy of letting medium to large computers to be procured from abroad against import licence or open general licence, with all large manufacturers from the West (and Japan) competing for the Indian market. The leading world manufacturers included IBM, AMDAHL, REYAD, CDC, ITEL, CDC, DEC, HONEYWELL, NCR, BURROUGHS (now UNISYS), HP, UNIVAC, ICL, SIEMENS, DG, CRAY RESEARCH, PHILIPS, INTERDATA, FUJITSU, HITACHI, NIPPON, TOSHIBA and many others. Many computer models follow IBM architecture, with the first five manufacturers above being even plug-compatible with IBM systems.

Micro, mini and mainframe systems are allowed now to be produced in India with gradually more liberal approach. Some of the manufacturers are ECIL, Hyderabad; BEL, Bangalore; HCL, Delhi; ICIM, Bombay; DCM Data Products, Delhi; ORG. Baroda; NELCO, Bombay; PSI, Bangalore; and several others. While microprocessor-based systems cost today around Rs. 15,000—5 lakhs, mini system can cost anywhere between 5-20 lakhs, mainframe system Rs. 20 lakhs—1 crore, and super system above Rs. 1 crore. Incidentally, REYAD computers (EC and SM series) available earlier against rupee payment from USSR and Eastern Europe, have fallen into disuse now. Even its costs are coming down everyday!

Expansion of Capacity

As computer load starts building up, the culture of date processing spreads within the organisation, leading to the need of expanding computer capacity by 3-4 years. The possibilities are either replacing the old computer by new machine or augmenting the computing power by adding more CPU and memory. The experience of wholesale replacement can be both traumatic and very expensive. For example many Indian users have passed from second-generation and third-generation to fourth-generation computers, with a new concept of organising files and generating reports by using direct-access files, database management and sophisticated operating-system environment. The simple expedient of converting all programmes from second and third to fourth generation machines can prove to be the least cost-effective.

Augmentation of computing power can also be difficult, as most micro-computers are virtually non-expandable in terms of CPU and memory. Even peripherals cannot be increased beyond a limit due to limited plugging capabilities. Mini and mainframe systems have, on the other hand, specified scope for expansion both for CPU and memory, and peripherals. Future augmentation needs have to be kept in view at the time of procurement itself. While the cost of I/O devices remain still high without the benefit of micro-electronics having much reached them, the cost of CPU and memory is going down everyday. A well-tried device is to configure the current computer around high CPU and memory, with only limited I/O capability, and to add I/O devices gradually as work-load goes up without drastically changing the CPU and memory.

Application Packages

Computer manufacturers supply hardware today supported by only basic utilities and systems software, while the remaining application packages (which used to come free with the computer before 1968) are supplied at a price. It is important to consider which of these packages can meet the user organisation's requirements and to what extent. Application packages usually include engineering packages (civil engineering design calculations, space-frame analysis, stress-strain calculations, load-flow analysis, traffic-lighting system); operations research packages (linear programming, network analysis, vehicle scheduling); management packages (inventory control, production planning and control, bill of material, employee services); specialised packages suited to broad patterns of industry and machinery (process control, numerical control) and so on.

There is a cost-advantage in buying the above kind of packages since they are general-purpose in nature. On the other hand, the user organisation may develop application programmes by its own team of analysts and programmers, in which case the cost would be high but the in-house programmes may turn out to be more specifically suited to the user and prove ultimately to be more cost-effective than the general-purpose package. There is the additional option available to the user organisation to engage an outside consultant or service bureau for developing application programmes rather than deploy an in-house software team. While acquiring a computer, it is advisable to work out the economics of firming out contracts for application packages against generating on one's own.

Support Services

Support services available from the manufacturer are often difficult to unwrap from the attractive package presented by him. Maintenance of the computer, after its installation and the initial testing, is the responsibility of the manufacturer during the warranty period of one year or so. Thereafter the Computer Maintenance Corporation (now the CMC Ltd.) is encouraged by the Indian government to take over the maintenance responsibility, with the other alternatives being: continued maintenance under a new contract by the manufacturer (usually accepted by the latter); employment of in-house systems engineers to do the maintenance; or entrusting maintenance to a third party. The last two solutions may be a little costly due to the stocking of essential spares and timely procurement of the rest of spares. Training is looked after normally by the manufacturer for a specific number of personnel from the user organisation. Both scope and quality of training should be carefully watched to ensure comprehensiveness. It is always salutary to look for an all-India presence of the manufacturer's representative for being able to do the critical trouble-shooting.

Conclusion

Since a large number of organisations are going for the purchase of single or Multiple PCs (in the range of PCs, PC/XTs and PC/ATs), if is worthwhile, to summarise the selection criteria they should look for. These include: (a) knowledge of performance (through comparative statements or bench-marks); (b) possibility of upgradation in future in the CPU and I/O devices; (c) feed-back on other users' experience; (d) availability of support services (for hardware, system software and application software); (e) provision of documentation in the form of manuals; (f) arrangement for practical training by the vendor/manufacturer, (g) feasible alternatives for future maintenance; and (h) arrangement for securing computer-time from the vendor/manufacturer in the event of computer up-time being less than what is stipulated during purchase.

15

EVALUATION OF COMPUTERS

The tremendous spurt in the growth of computer and calculation industry is reflected in its value of Rs. 18.50 crore in 1975 going up only to Rs. 30.00 crore in 1980 and reaching around a few thousand crore by 1990. It is estimated that the computer industry growth today far outstrips the growth of electronic industry as a whole. The microprocessor revolution has made the computer easily available to small industry and business houses. The large market competition that has ensued is due to the high rate of growth in a virtually limitless market, along with the simplicity of hardware design based on imported microprocessor chips and other peripherals.

While the computer manufacturers are so many and so eager to sell their products which are often deceptively similar looking to each other, it becomes an important task for the likely user organisation to make a good job at the selection and evaluation of the best computer suited to its needs. The first step is a simple survey to explore if computerisation is at all worthwhile. It is surprising how many times a preliminary study of this nature would diagnose whether a computer would be useful at all, depending upon the nature and turnover of the organisation, its general work-load and information environment. Following the *diagnosis* if in favour of computer, it is advisable to launch a detailed *feasibility* study to assess what the likely application areas are; what the information needs would be in each area; and how an information flow could be best organised based on computer. Users who are as yet unfamiliar with computers or are about to step up considerably their computing activities can certainly seek external expert assistance in this evaluation process. Existing base of systems, analysts and programmers may be all right for data processing management, but it seldom covers the experience of computer selection or of the scale and technology being investigated.

Feasibility study should lead on to determination of data-processing load and frequency, which should form the basis for assessing the likely configuration of CPU and memory, and the supporting I/O peripherals. It is at this stage that the user should start looking at the available computer systems and ask manufacturers to quote against a defined equipment specification. While saving some evaluation time in this process, the user may get some useful new ideas from one manufacturer that are still relevant if another is selected. The reaction from manufacturers to the specification also provides some idea as to his support capability. Further, timing the performance of the system by the manufacturer indicates his view of software overheads, simultaneous activity and so on.

Evaluation Points

The user should insist from manufacturer the total cost estimate associated with his equipment, including space and air-conditioning. Besides, a number of specific questions can be asked on such factors as availability and cost of support services (up to post-warranty maintenance, if needed); precise performance figures including reliability; maintenance terms with all shift-variations; variety of purchase and leasing terms; projected performance of the system against the specifications; upgradability without incurring upgradation or conversion costs; hardware and software compatibility across the entire series-range and with other systems; and versatility in operation due to a choice of high-level languages, a wide variety of "user friendly" utilities and application packages.

The obvious purpose of evaluation is to select the "best" computer for the user organisation. Definite costs should include such items as central computing equipment and later enhancements; communication equipment if needed; computer room and service; conversion cost from current systems; training cost for the user staff (less free services); user software cost (against manufacturers packages); un-bundled software cost; and programming cost (if language-dependent). While measurement of cost and performance (based on calculations, simulation, standard work-units like Gibson's mix or benchmarks) need not be precise, minor differences are best dissolved by holding discussions with manufacturers and taking reasonably pragmatic decision. Before the final selection, there should be a balance sheet of the short-listed systems drawn up over a period of years to get a true comparison of different machines.

An ingenious way of selecting a cost-effective computer is to go for an *integrated* system where a mix is obtained from Original Equipment Manufacturers (OEM) for the cheapest devices made by each. While this sounds simple and is also done by some manufacturers already (e.g., DEC series CPU and memory with memorex discs), the important criterion is to obtain full plug-compatibility in the OEM mix of devices otherwise the integrated system can land the user in no end of troubles, as it is difficult to establish fool-proof hardware and interfaces in the integrated system, even if it is cheap in cost. India has some useful experience in it, but not the full infrastructure yet nor any manufacturing facility for a proven integrated system.

For the very large variety of micro-computers (like personal computers), a few specific considerations arises in the matters of selection. First of all, there is inadequate knowledge of technology behind the hardware. While the hardware designs are simple (based on the manuals provided by the suppliers of the chips), the users are hardly ready with professional expertise to understand and evaluate the hardware impartially. As a result, there is the recurrent theme of buying hardware having either over-capacity or under-capacity *vis-a-vis* the needs of the user. Secondly, there from the beginning an inadequate involvement of the user who alone can understand their requirements in full and advise suitably the manufacturer while designing the software. Thirdly, there is inadequate understanding of the cost implications of hardware and software, with the latter going up to more than half the hardware cost with actual usage. Fourthly, there is often no proper definition of the user needs and what aspects of these needs would be precisely met by the microcomputer. Fifthly, there is no clear-cut provision of a minimum time-frame of, say, 3-4 months when the system should function without significant errors. Sixthly, there is often less than adequate after-sales service-support from the manufacturer due to either lack of precise knowledge of the new technology or sheer inability to sustain such services in the teeth of severe price-competition. Seventhly, the microcomputer is unable to add on future capability with change in technology. Finally, there is the "buy or hire" dilemma when the relatively low-cost microcomputer seems a suitable investment proposition straightway, although the volume of computer-load could easily be met by hiring that much computer-time.

Life of a microcomputer can be safely taken as 3-5 years, if proper maintenance to provided The latter is satisfactory in the metropolitan cities but not so elsewhere. There is also the nagging, question of reliability, particularly for peripherals like floppy discs. All in all, the total cost of setting up a microcomputer centre and its expansion needs later on, in keeping with the business-growth, remain matters of detailed analysis, on which time in the earlier stages must be spent and performance of various types of microcomputers evaluated, — rather than going for a machine on an imporomtu basis or, worse still, as a status symbol.

IMPORT OF COMPUTERS

The world computer scene showed up at least a dozen giants whose worldwide - revenue in the fiscal year 1980 had been above $ one billion. The related survey, whose results came out in late 1981, included such product areas as mainframes, minicomputers, microprocessors, small business systems and personal computers, terminals and peripherals, software and services, data-communication equipment but exclude word processors, electronic registers and switching equipment. Table 1 lists the 12 largest computer concerns in the order of their world revenue, and does not include the Japanese giants like Fujitsu, Hitachi and Toshiba which have all been going overseas outside their huge and highly protected home market.

TABLE 1

World's Top 12 Computer Concerns

Rank	*Name*	*Country*		*World Revenue (Base = 1980)*	
1.	International Business Machines	USA	$	26,213	mill.
2.	Burroughs (Now UNI SYS)	USA	$	2,902	mill.
3.	Sperry Univac	USA	$	2,800	mill.
4.	Control Data Corporation	USA	$	2,791	mill.
5.	National Cash Register	USA	$	2,525	mill.
6.	Digital Equipment Corporation	USA	$	2,368	mill.
7.	Siemens	West Germany	$	2,047	mill.
8.	Honeywell	USA	$	1,634	mill.
9.	Hewlett - Packard	USA	$	1,546	mill.
10.	International Computers Ltd.	UK	$	1,494	mill.
11.	Cif - Honeywell Bull	France	$	1,489	mill.
12.	Olivetti	Italy	$	1,221	mill.

It is heartening to note that while some 120 third and fourth generation computer systems from the overseas computer concerns were imported to India and made operational over the half decade between 1976-81 and the total number of computer systems increased from 120 in 1970 to around 600 in 1980, the figure went up to several thousand by 1990. The current computer scene in the country is marked by vastly greater number of wider range of computer-types, and higher overall computing capacity after 1990 than ever available in the 1970s and 1980s.

Import Parameters

Import of a computer system, irrespective of its value, requires the prior clearance of the Department of Electronics (DOE) in our government before issue of an import licence by Ministry of Commerce. This also applies to computer systems proposed for import by all R & D organisations, For clearance of import of computer systems up to Rs. 5 lakhs, a liberal procedure is followed. This includes determination of essentiality of the computer proposed for import, assessing whether needed computer can be procured from indigenous suppliers, drawing up — if otherwise — of specifications for the optimal system, floating of tenders, evaluation of bids and final approval for import.

Import of a computer system is allowed to only a few categories. First of all, an actual user who requires an imported computer for his own use, and not for business or trade in its given such a licence. Thus, in the case of an industrial undertaking (large-scale, small-scale or cottage-industries sector), the imported computer should be utilised for the manufacturing processes or operations conducted within its own promises. In the non-industrial category, such as, hospitals, R&D organisations, academic institutions, commercial establishments and individuals, the imported computer should be utilised for the specific purpose for which it was sought for import.

For importing a computer system over a value of Rs. 5 lakhs, the actual user draws up functional specifications, based on his current and anticipated applications. Help of outside consulting agencies used to be sought, if necessary, in earlier days. For instance, Central Government offices in Delhi (e.g., Customs, Income-tax, Audit, Insurance, etc.) could consult Department of Statistics whose computer centre they might be using. DOE then would scrutinises the given specifications in terms of national priorities laid down from time-to-time and would approve, in principle, the need for import with a specific configuration. The user was associated in deciding upon the functional configuration for the import of a computer, with changes wherever necessary. DOE thereafter called for competitive sealed tenders from various manufacturers and agents on a global basis. After the user had provided to DOE a ranking of his preferences for computer-types, along with reasons, DOE appointed a committee of experts (comprising hardware, software and systems specialists) to evaluate the tenders and make technical recommendations. The latter were put up to an approval committee comprising senior government representatives from DOE, Ministry of Finance (Economic Affairs) and the administrative ministry for the user organisation. The approval committees decision was deemed to be final, for placing contract by the user organisation for the computer finally selected. It is to be noted that clearance from indigenous angle for imported computers was handled by DOE and not the normal channel of DGTD. The system stand fairly liberalised now, with the stringency gone.

Labour Angle

For procurement of imported computers, clearance from labour angle is generally necessary from Ministry of Labour. The latter need *inter alia,* certificate from the concerned State Government that labour union for the actual user organisation has no objection to the computer system being installed; reasons why the work cannot be done through existing computer facilities; types of applications, with their periodicity, which are proposed to be handled by the new computer; benefits to be expected as regards improvement in efficiency, quality, cost reduction and economy, likely effects on the employment in the establishment, especially in relevant departments; likely effects on conditions of employment, promotion prospects, working conditions and wages of the concerned workers; methods of adjusting any employees rendered surplus; and safeguards to protect the workers, interests including the method of sharing possible benefits.

Import Against Export

Besides actual users, import of a computer system may be allowed for: (a) an Indian organisation intending to export software and requiring exchange (FE) for importing a computer for softwrare (b) an Indian national, settled abroad, setting up an export-oriented software firm and wishing to import a computer with his own FE earned abroad; and (c) an Indian organisation wishing to import a computer with a view to enhancing or modifying hardware and software against specific export orders and then to re-export the computer.

The applicant for undertaking export of computer software presents a detailed project proposal to DOE, covering background of the applicant organisation technical capability and nature of export proposal. A standing committee of computer specialists set up by DOE examines, in depth, the capability as well as credibility of the applicant to undertake software generation for export, whether the applicant could use a locally manufactured computer for this purpose and, if not, whether he could use imported computers already in the country. If the standing committee finds the project acceptable from technical and economic angles, the applicant is permitted import of a computer (and related data processing equipment) through the special import procedure administered by DOE. After clearing a proposal, DOE monitors the progress of the project based on six-monthly performance reports from the party and periodic site-reviews carried out by DOE. Progress on a project is evaluated by a monitoring committee comprising representatives of DOE, CCI&E, Ministry of Commerce and Ministry of Law.

It is important that the applicants for categories (a) and (b) above have on hand guaranteed software export orders covering at least 20 per cent of the CIF value of the computer proposed for import. While imported computer price does not exceed 50 per cent of the project export commitment over 5 years for category (a), the import price can be 100 per cent of the export commitment for category (b). For category (c), import is allowed without any extra obligation, except that the imported computer should not be used for any domestic purpose. Legal bonds are executed for software export commitment involving import of a computer system, stipulating 20 per cent of the total export commitment by the end of second year, 40 per cent by the third year, 60 per cent by the fourth year and full by the fifth year. This apart, at least one-third of the time of the imported computer has to be solely used for software generation for export.

Special Considerations

The above are fairly stringent procedures, trying to cover some loopholes discovered in the recent past Default in meeting the minimum export performance level could earlier lead to government instituting legal action for confiscation of the imported computer system. It is now possible that applicants from 100 per cent export-oriented software firms may be cleared directly by Ministry of Commerce within the above guidelines without reference to DOE, and all other cases of import of computer systems under export obligation will be cleared by DOE in any case.

The recent import policy seems not to favour import of computers export against software export, — the accent being heavily on use of indigenous systems. Another feature is the planning by DOE to put together the computer requirements of a group of similar users and then import systems that can serve them all. For education sector, for instance, it is possible to think of a few computers from the same vendor, — thus ensuring exchange of programmes among the educational users. It is a good idea which needs watching in application.

The CMC Limited has been normally recommended for maintenance of all imported systems, unless in-house maintenance is preferred by the user. CMC is often the designated procurement agency for spares, tools and test equipment for their maintenance. Others can import spares up to 3 per cent of CIF value of the imported system. The import duty on computers have undergone many changes from 40 per cent till 1978-79 to 178 per cent in 1982-83 and reduced again thereafter Government thinking towards liberalisation of computer import or reduction in the import duty has always been welcome by the users and appears to have finally gained ground today.

THE WORLD OF MICROPROCESSOR

Microprocessor has been hailed, since the advent of transistor in 1948, as the most significant technological development. This device first came into being for applications in calculators in 1971 when Intel Corporation of USA announced a new processor Intel 4004 at a very low price. The device is a simple monolithic Integrated Circuit (IC), employing Large-Scale Integration (LSI) in a Metal-Oxide Semiconductor (MOS) technology. LSI involves multiplying the number of electronic circuits squeezed on to a silicon chip from the 10,000 or more of 1980s to a million or more in the 1990s.

Application-wise, innovations have gone far ahead from the mere calculation kind. Within a decade, designs are in hand for systems that can understand instructions issued in ordinary speech to be used for controlling robots, that can automatically translate languages, or can automatically diagnose and correct their own faults, and for a myriad other purposes. All these fall into the genre of very large-scale integration (VLSI) finding applications in the factory, office, hospital or home with equal facility.

Structure and Function, Microprocessor to Microcomputer

A microprocessor needs some additional circuits to be capable of arithmetic and logical manipulation of data. It thus functions as a complete central-processing unit (CPU),—consisting of an arithmetic/ logic unit (ALU) and a control unit When the microprocessor is combined with memory and input/output (I/O) devices, a microcomputer is formed.

In a microcomputer, the ALU performs the arithmetic and logic operations on data received from memory or input devices. The control unit controls the flow of data and instructions within the microcomputer, — by fetching instruction from the memory, by decoding and executing instructions, and by properly sequencing events performed by the ALU and I/O devices. While the memory is used to store data and instructions, the I/O devices provide a mechanism for transferring data to and from the outside world.

Microcomputers, like larger computers, manipulate information represented by binary digits, called *bits.* Groups of bits are called *words* and word-sizes vary from microprocessor to microprocessor as 4, 8, 12, 16 and 32 bits (64 bits and 128 bits being still at the planning stage). The word-length determines the characteristics of different microprocessors. Binary information is manipulated in an organised sequence of steps (programme) where each step is termed on *instruction.*

Design Aspects

A microcomputer design is based on four building blocks: input devices, memory, a microprocessor (with a calculating section and a decision capability for selecting alternate courses of action), and output devices. The building blocks are interconnected by a group of lines (one for each bit to be transferred) called a *bus.* Figure 6.1 illustrates a microcomputer block diagram where the I/O devices share the same bus. It also shows various data registers for temporary storage and manipulation of data and instructions.

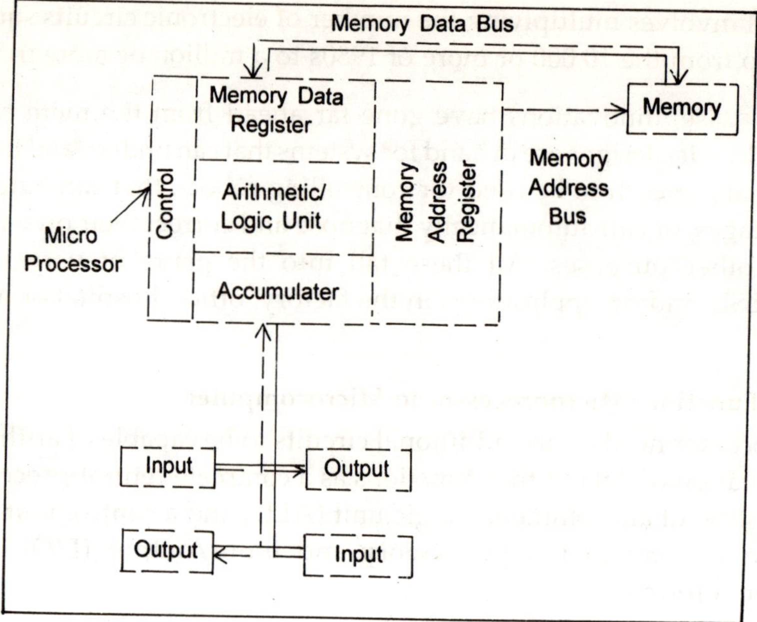

Fig. 1: Block Diagram of a Microcomputer

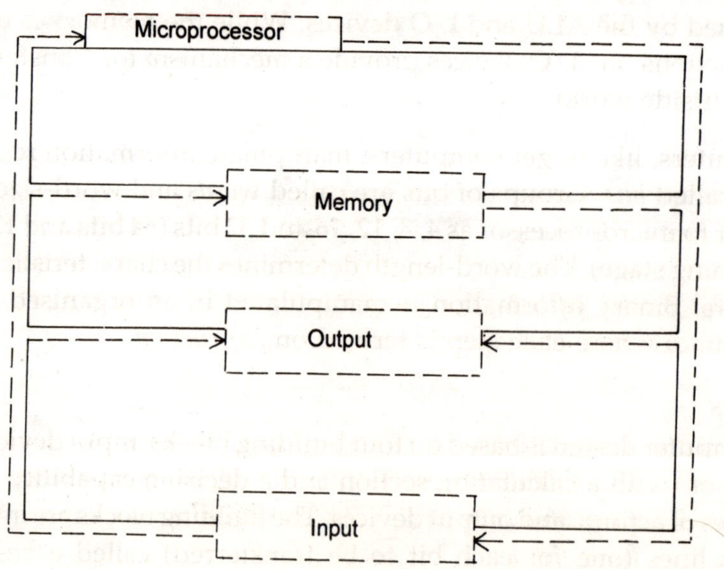

Fig. 2: Block Diagram of a Microcomputer with a Single Data Bus

Quite often the memory and I/O devices share the same bus in a microcomputer. In this case, the microprocessor may treat an I/O device as a memory element and gains the facility to add new memory blocks as and when needed. This is illustrated in Fig. 2.

ROM and RAM

A microcomputer needs to store programme steps and data, and recall them at the appropriate time, in order to perform its function. In situations where the memory values do not change, e.g., in dedicated systems, read-only memory (ROM) is used to store programme-steps and data-values. Read-write memory (RWM), also called random-access memory (RAM), is used to store data which changes during the operation of the system e.g., results of calculations or programmes which change frequently. In either case, the memory function is to store and provide on command a data-value or a programme-step.

Microprocessors are making an impact on the design of virtually all digital systems. They are increasingly finding applications in systems which formerly used random logic. In complex systems, a microprocessor is preferred to hard-wired random logic, because of the flexibility in programming simplified design, reduced cost and higher reliability. The microprocessor cost continues to diminish as integration moves up from a single LSI chip with 8,000 to 10,000 transistors to a single VLSI chip capable of incorporating 100,000 transistors or more.

Application Range

Typical range of applications, categorised by machine-size, can be as follows:

1. *4-bit devices:* Accounting systems, appliances, calculators, game machines, intelligent instrumentation, simple terminals;
2. *8-bit devices:* Control systems, intelligent terminals and instruments, point-of-sale terminals, traffic controllers, communication preprocessor (data concentrators), process control systems;
3. *16-bit and 32-bit devices:* Data acquisition systems, numerical control, process control, intelligent terminals, supervisory control (gas, power, water distribution), automatic testing systems.

Many microprocessor manufacturers provide prototyping systems for development purposes. These systems usually have microcomputers with extensive memory and I./O capabilities. They are particularly useful for designing microcomputers tailored to specific applications.

Types of microcomputers available fall under the categories of single chip microprocessors, single-chip analogue-signal microprocessors, and microprocessors with a family of co-processors and I/O processors to form a high-throughput computer. The last-mentioned can be multi-microprocessors with fibre optics support for distributed processing and network.

Applications in electronics are legion today, with a few mentioned below:

(a) *Domestic electronics:* Appliances such as automated cooking ranges, sophisticated audio-video equipment in cars, home do-it-yourself microcomputer hobby kits;

(b) *Entertainment electronics:* Television and video games, home microcomputers for many purposes using multi-channel television sets as output display;

(c) *Industrial electronics:* Front-panel control with oscilloscopes and other measuring instruments for displaying readings and time-based concessions, interface control for generating complicated protocols to match different interface requirements, machine-tool control with numerically controlled machines (using ready-made boards), real-time data-logging conversion and storing for later analysis or process control.

Manufacture and Import

The computer section of Bhaba Atomic Research Centre (BARC) had developed LSI chip in the 1980 and manufacturing units like semi-computer complex at Chandigarh have already started functioning. Still a large number of microprocessors in India are imported from abroad and are based on popular components available from the US industries as follows:

1. *Intel series:* 4004 (4-bit), 8080/8085 (8-bit), 8088, 8086 (16-bit); 80386 (32-bit);
2. *Zilog series:* Z80 (8-bit), Z8000 (16-bit);
3. *Motorolla series:* 6800 (8-bit); 68010 (16-bit); 68020 (32-bit);
4. *Texas Instruments series:* TI990 (8-bit); TI9900 (16-bit) onwards.

Out of 150-180 Indian firms licensed in the past few years to produce microcomputers about 40-50 firms have gone on stream. The total turnover of Indian microcomputers is nearly Rs. 750 crore per annum, in 1989-90 out of which nearly 30 per cent is exported.

To give an idea of speed and capabilities, Intel 8080 microprocessor has a set of 78 instructions, instruction execution speed of 2-9 microseconds, RAM speed of 500 nanoseconds, and ROM speed of 600 nanoseconds. As regards cost, while a microprocessor chip was priced at $ 160 in 1974, chips with new and improved performance are available in the $ 5-10 range all over the world.

Manufacturers of microprocessors have been trying to make their components suitable to a broad spectrum of usage by making, on the one hand, microprocessors specialising in low component count and useful for small applications and, on the other hand, microprocessor boards offering minicomputer capabilities.

Microprocessors can help in converting most hardware overheads into software (programmable) routines. Interface protocol controllers can be easily implemented using pre-assembled boards. Real-time data acquisition is made possible by these microprocessors for later test and analysis. A surprising amount of power is packed into an area as small as a thumb-nail!

Performance limitations (e.g., speed, shorter word-length, limited-addressing modes, fewer internal registers) reduce the competitiveness of first and second-generation microcomputers where minicomputers are now used. These limitations are fast receding as more sophisticated technologies appear on the horizon.

MICROPROCESSORS AND INDUSTRIAL PROCESS CONTROL

When any industrial process control system is looked at from closed quarters, its essential tasks appear to be monitoring of control variables, analysis of present values by processing these inputs and exercise of control using a pre-defined procedure. A spin-off product may be a reporting function which provides normal statistics and highlights alarm conditions.

Basic Characteristics

The industrial process control system should have the following characteristics:

(i) *Real-time response* — the control system should apply corrective action in a very short time often within seconds;

(ii) *Normal and abnormal control*-the variables should be kept within a pre-defined range through finer control. In addition, the variables should be monitored for detecting unusually high or low values;

(iii) *Statistical report* — the data collected should be translated into management reports, for being analysed to improve the overall performances;

(iv) *Reliability* the system should be as highly reliable as possible;

(v) *Ruggedness*—the system should be rugged enough to withstand dust, electrical motor noise, high temperature or high magnetic field;

(vi) *Fail-safe operations* — the system should be able to operate in such a manner that it has a safe operating mode through self-diagnostic provision) in the event of failure;

(vii) *Low down-time* — the system should be capable of quick and on-site repair, with the hardware and packaging of the system made in a modular fashion.

Application Potential

The above characteristics make out a strong case for application of microcomputers in industrial process control for the following plus points:

(a) *Real-time response*— the high speed of microcomputer enables it to provide response in real time while monitoring or controlling the number of variables;

(b) *Memory* — a large amount of historical information can be collected by using memory. The table look-up procedure can also be considered as an alternative to storing data in memory;

(c) *Processing power* — the microcomputer can' carry out elaborate control calculations by correlations and analysis of the inputs;

(d) *Decision-making* — the microcomputer can identify existing situations and alter the course of action accordingly through its dynamic logic capability;

(e) *Stored programme control* — the microcomputer, can be programmed to follow independent procedure in each case. This availability permits use of standard hardware in varied applications and achievement of complete control function through "customised" control programmes;

(f) *Flexibility* — since the control function is a part of software, changes in control calculations or refinements (as a result of analysis of calculated statistics) can be easily accomplished;

(g) *Command driven modes* — the microcomputer can be operated for different modes through manual commands passed via keyboard.

Other Considerations

It is a logical choice to use microcomputers for real-time control application due to their minimum logic hardware, system flexibility, low cost per function and minimum system development time and cost, apart from the ease in updating the systems, low maintenance cost a built-in protection of system know-how.

Minimisation of logic hardware is achieved by using the integral concept of system architecture with the four functions: data, address, control and supervision.

System flexibility is achieved through software-orientation. For example, temperature control in a furnace can be achieved by calculations passed on input parameters. With a little experience gained on the furnace, it should be possible to carry out better calculations for controlling the temperature to finer limits.

Low cost per function is feasible by increasing the number of functions in the logic of software for the same cost of the microprocessor. For instance, more input terminals can be added to the microcomputer with hardly any cost.

Minimum system development time and cost is a very important advantage for a microcomputer. The microprocessor-based controller can be initially designed by carrying out a simulation of the chosen microprocessor on an universal microprocessor development system. Emulation (run on the actual microprocessor type) has some advantage over simulation (run on some other processor). The programme errors can be corrected and the programme then re-assembled and tested. Such development systems make possible an orderly section-by-section check-out of the complete system when the hardware and software are eventually brought together. In India, ECIL's Micro-78 can be well used as a microcomputer development system.

Real Time Control Applications

There exist a large potential for applying microprocessors in cases where it is difficult to implement hardwired logic or where a computer is likely to be underutilised. The following real-time control applications with microcomputer are worth our attention:

(a) Programmable Logic Controller (PLC) — industrial process control by PLCs can include conveying systems, packing operations, palletising gauging and testing , transfer lines, machine tools, sorting mechanisms, pumping stations, material handling, filter cycling, batch sequencing and food processing. The stored programme concept of the PLCs permits to design virtually any control system by simply creating the stored programme in the standard PLC. The business potential in India has already reached Rs. 10 crores per year;

(b) Supervisory Control And Data Acquisition (SCADA) — this has enormous potential in power generation equipment. It replaces hardware dedicated logic devices by connecting each remote SCADA to a master SCADA under the control of a mainframe computer. This is illustrated in Fig. 3 with serial telephone communication lines.

Other control applications using microprocessors are scanners and data loggers, real-time co-ordinate mapping and conversion, power-plant reheat temperature control, torque measurement and control, billet mill control, and weight compensation for the moisture present.

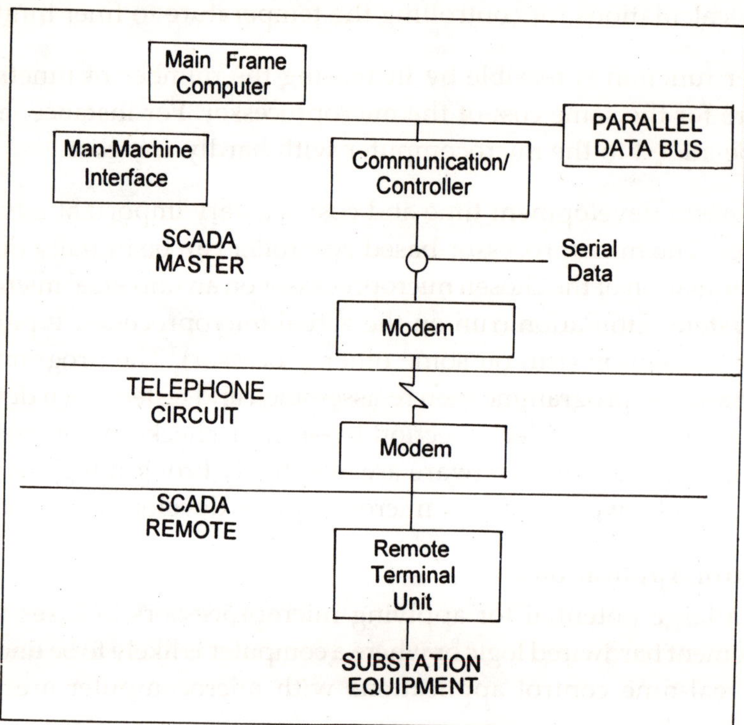

Fig. 3: SCADA System (Modulator—Demodulator)

Further Illustration

A few such control applications are mentioned below:

(i) Modular microcomputer expansion power system has been used in Europe to control rolling mills, transfer lines for automobile engines and cigarette-packing and bottling machines;

(ii) Microprocessor-based calibrator and thermometers are used in the USA to calibrate temperature of thermocouples with laboratory accuracy;

(iii) A microprocessor-based looking system has been used for safe deposit lockers in West Germany where each locker is scanned electronically every two seconds and any fault (by attempt to open the locker) starts an alarm on the control panel;

(iv) Microcomputers are used in the USA for a variety of car-driving conditions, including those normally sensed by automatic gear boxes such as load, engine speed and road speed. The microcomputer selects gear ratio and engine throttle opening, to match driver's demand with road conditions;

(v) Microcomputer-based washing machines are used in West Germany to control electrically the water temperature and the power of the wash drum This provides more effective wash and spin cycles for the clothing;

(vi) Microprocessors have been used for liquid milk processing depots in Europe to regulate the reception, storage, movement and processing operations;

(vii) Microcomputer-based display system is used for nuclear power station at Bhaba Atomic Research Centre in India, for its developmental work in text and word processing;

(viii) Microprocessor control data recorder is used by the British Gas in the U.K. to record gas flows and pressures relative to climatic factors at key points in the supply and consumption network;

(ix) Microprocessor control is used in Holland for standard draughting pens and different coloured felt-tip pens, for vector generation, absolute and relative plotting, and drawing of circles and arcs;

(x) Singal- chip microcomputer is used in Europe on any instrument panel for several functions : Time-of-day clock, current fuel consumption, average fuel consumption, average speed, range on fuel available, timer and outside temperature monitoring.

Essential Steps

In order to develop a microcomputer-based industrial process control system, the following steps are required to be followed:

(a) The process to be controlled should be studied for identifying all important variables;

(b) Desired relationships among the variables should be worked out for control;

(c) Control calculations should be clearly defined for each set of conditions, including condition and alerting schemes;

(d) The control system should be designed to translate the requirements into firmware package;

(e) Interaction between firmware designer and end-user should be carried out for identifying the system extensions and modifying system response where necessary;

(f) The control calculations should be fully tested by simulating the control conditions;

(g) Field trial should be carefully planned with cooperation from end-user.

The microcomputer-based industrial process control system is a cost-effective solution for India., industries. The system, when used properly, can result in higher production with improved quality, reduced wastage and finer precision. A significant fact is that besides applications in new plants, the microprocessor-based solutions are easily adaptable to existing processing machines.

QUALITY CONTROL BY MICROS

Imagine a large proscenium stage, on which a musical drama or a dance ballet is being performed, being lit up by 100 or so spot lights. Each "spot" is to be individually balanced against its neighbouring lights even during frequent changes. In a way, changes of lighting replace one stage picture with another. This is "cross-fading" often barely discovered by the audience, although a complete change has taken place in the lighting control.

Now imagine balancing of "spots" and control of "cross-fading" with complete accuracy night after night, when a play is being performed for many nights, — so that the "cues" are in full conformity with the altering emphasis and mood on the stage. The situation can be extraordinarily complex and the only answer is to use control systems based on a digital approach. Now the microprocessor technology has given rise to the "galaxy" console from where a lighting director programmes and controls the entire lighting sequence of the performance, — with his movements monitored and warnings given in the event of mistakes. "Galaxy" is already immensely popular in Europe and Australia, and has already appeared in the Middle East.

Closed and Open Loop Control Tasks

In the above application, the microprocessor continuously monitors the quality and intensity of light as two process variables, performs suitable calculations on these to generate control values and outputs these to the electro-mechanical units, which in turn control the process variables. This is known as *closed loop control*. If the microprocessor outputs the control values to the lighting director via video display units (VDUs being a given option), which in turn apply the necessary control values, then the control strategy is termed *open loop control*.

From simple-level controls to sophisticated instruments for quality control and process analysis, the trend is to incorporate the microprocessor into the instrumentation system. The tasks to be performed are four-fold: (i) closed loop or open loop control of selected critical loops; (ii) monitoring process variables for alarm conditions; (iii) calculating critical parameters like steam/gas ratio; and (iv) preparation of logs and management reports through printing attachments. For this purpose, basic data logging is done by sampling inputs at regular intervals and then storing each data in specified Random-Access Memory (RAM) locations temporarily, to be transferred later on to an external bulk-storage device, such as, magnetic tape or disc.

Advantages for Microprocessors

The advantages of the use of microprocessor for quality control applications are consistent and smooth operation, response to unusual conditions, avoidance of human errors and better utilisation of human skill. More sophisticated alarm techniques can be employed aiming at the prevention of upset condition in quality by predicting the alarm conditions.

Many vendors today have come up with "support chips" which add to the power of the microprocessor and hasten its entry to the "hybrid" environment of instrumentation. This is a welcome sign since such instrumentation systems are flexible (or, technically speaking, "programmable") because they are based on microprocessors "driven" by software. Very scanty changes in hardware are required even if the systems were to be used for different quality control purposes.

An important feature of microprocessor architecture is the "bus" concept This feature makes it all the more easy to add on "support peripherals" as need arises. A few examples of such peripheral chips available easily in the market are : (1) keyboard controller; (2) floppy disc controller, (3) printer controller; (4) standard parallel/serial interface; (5) instrumentation standard interface controller, (6) digital-to-analog (DAC) and analog-to-digital (ADC) converters to which microprocessor bus is compatible; (7) VDU controller.

Typically for quality control, the controller can be used as a fixed set-point controller, sequential controller or ratio controller and for relative-speed controllers. It is also possible to provide controllers for special applications using optional devices, e.g., an external comparator. The controller consists of three modules: a comparator assembly, a controller assembly and an operator communication and display assembly. The comparator forms a standardised signal for the control deviation from the signal for the controlled variable — supplied by a current or voltage sensor, a thermo-couple or a resistance thermometer and from the signal for the set-point The input signal formed by the comparator is processed in the controller assembly and indicated within +5 per cent of the set point. The output signal of the control amplifier can be switched to one of three operating modes (automatic, follow-up or manual). The light-emitting diodes (LEDs) indicate the control deviation according to magnitude and direction.

Serial Procedure

By way of an example, we can consider the application of a microprocessor-based system as a front-end test instrument used in quality control of a direct current (DC) servo motor. Characteristically, such a motor should have a steady rotation (rpm), should produce little vibration and should have very low inertia. Furthermore, its temperature rise should be within specific limits and the change in its rom should have a slope as required by specific standards. The first test can be devised as the rom test, where a microprocessor can be used in conjunction with a DAC and other power-electronic circuits. Changes in the input power can be hooked on through a tachometer to an ADC, which in turn can monitor the resulting changes in rpm through the microprocessor bus.

The above results can be stored in a floppy disc connected in the microprocessor bus through a floppy disc controller. Results so stored can be compared to the standard data for acceptance or rejection signals displayed on the VDUs. The second test for inertial requirements can use the same hardware, with the entire instrumentation now "oriented" by freshly loaded software programme for the new test. The motor can be operated in start-stop mode and the resulting inertia effect can be observed through the same rpm monitor (by virtue of the changed software). The third test is to check for temperature rise and can be performed by attaching a thermometer probe to another ADC. Such a switch-over is very simple with a microprocessor-based system because both the monitors are connected to the "address space" of the same microprocessor but at different locations. The address switch-over is done using only one macro-instruction. The final test is for check on vibrations. This time a pressure transducer is connected to the ADC hooked up to the microprocessor, or, with the address switch-over being similar to the previous case.

After all the above tests are performed, a final O.K. signal is displayed on the VDU. If any test fails, the test data is recorded on the floppy disc and its contents printed for subsequent re-checking. The entire quality control system as mentioned above is elegant for its compactness and reduced down-time, the contrast to a conventional quality control system. The compactness is achieved by making software changes as the only variable and by keeping the total hardware unchanged throughout The reduced down-time is due to the tact that only floppy discs have to be changed in between if separate test programmes are required.

Microprocessor-based instruments such as digital temperature scanners, dataloggers, etc., are in the process of manufacture, mainly by the small-scale sector. These equipments are being manufactured at Bombay, Baroda, Pune, Bangalore and Lucknow, etc. These sophisticated instruments are getting evaluated as regards their performance and accuracy, particularly in the chemical industries where the environment is not always favourable for the use of electronic instruments.

In selecting the proper type of microprocessor-based controller for an application, the prime factors to be considered are what precision of control is necessary and how difficult the process is to control. The desired result in some cases is precise adherence to the control point. In other cases, maintaining the temperature within a comparatively wide range is all that is necessary. For easier controller tuning and lowest initial cost, the simplest controller which will produce the desired result should be selected. A good method often used is to try a simple controller, e.g., proportional plus manual reset, and note the results compared to the desired system response. This will suggest what additional features are required or some that may be deleted.

SELECTION OF MICROPROCESSORS

Microprocessor industry in India, in common with the rest of the world, is one of the fastest growing one. New microcomputers, based on the microprocessor, appear in the market almost every week and the increasingly large displays of such equipment in metropolitan cities during the national computer conventions in recent years have been an instance in point.

Microcomputers can be made "flexible" or "programmable" to do a bewildering variety of jobs in industry—beginning from entertainment electronics up to sophisticated instrumentation. It is interesting that the engineers are involved in the programming of the equipment in as much as the programmers are involved in the electronics which they have to programme.

Choice Considerations

It is perfectly possible for a buyer to select a wrong microcomputer because it is a 32-bit device, because it is fabricated using a new technology or because it has topped in a benchmark test. On a further probe, it may appear that the 32-bit device is really unnecessary for the particular usage, the new technology is perhaps not fully tested out in the market, or the benchmark is relevant only to the context of performance for a particular repertoire of instructions.

The selection process involves the following topics of importance:

1. Functions to be performed;
2. Hardware and software: requirement;
3. Speed limitations;
4. Systems design aids including hardware and software.

Quite often it is the functions to be performed which determine the applicability of microcomputers to the task. First, microcomputers are economically more advantageous than the erstwhile microcomputers which were often underutilised. Secondly, microcomputers can apply to systems which formerly used random logic (combination and sequential networks). The resulting systems are relatively flexible, cheap and can often "customise" the system via software changes. Thirdly, the inexpensive computing power of microcomputer has led to many applications not covered before, such as, games, kitchen appliances and "smart" measuring instruments.

Hardware and Software Considerations

Hardware and software requirements include architecture, namely, word-length and speed, and programming flexibility. Word-length considerations include analogue resolution, computational accuracy, character length and width of parallel inputs or outputs. The larger the word-length, the better is the microprocessor in cases of calculation-oriented applications. The number of bits in address is important because the greater the number of bits the large is the "address space" of the microprocessor, This means more main-storage space or Larger-accommodation for I/O in a memory-mapped I/O environment The number of general or special purpose registers is also important because they provide easier and faster data handling. In cases of jump or call type of instructions, it is sometimes necessary to preserve programme parameter before the execution of such instructions. Such preservation can be done using stack-push type of operation. Another feature worth noting is the availability of hardware and software interrupts. Use of interrupts may be made to increase the throughout of system in that the CPU can wait for an interrupt from one source while it continues servicing an earlier one from another source. Most microprocessors have vectored interrupts and incorporate built-in priority among them.

The speed of the microprocessor is also an important criterion. The speed is measured by cycle time, state time, minimum instruction time, register-to-register addition time and interrupt response time. Register-to-register addition time is a popular estimate of the computing speed because nearly every processor has an add instruction. These measures should not be the only criteria used in timing estimation since they do not measure the power of the instruction set.

The degree of programming flexibility can be assessed by an examination of the processor instruction set. Multiple addressing modes conserve memory, simplify-programming and increase speed by using one-word memory reference instructions. Other important capabilities include arithmetic instructions, and logical and I/O control instructions.

Another important consideration is the ease with which the microprocessor can support the peripheral chip which the designer may want to use. There are some very powerful peripheral chips which can unfortunately be used with a few specific microprocessors. In some fields of application, other considerations like temperature range of working come into picture. The availability of a good range of support peripheral chips is also important in many applications.

Manufacturer's Support

Hardware and software support from the manufacturer are both important considerations. Software support includes documented manuals and applications literature. Both of these are an important measure of the manufacturer's commitment to servicing the needs of the user. Another system design consideration is the availability of a prototyping system which is essential to develop and debug hardware and software for a given application. Such a system usually includes a microcomputer system with extended memory capability and interface for an I/O device, such as, teletypewriter, a control console, ROM programming capability and software support The software support should include, as a minimum, a monitor, an editor and an assembler.

Most of the systems from the semiconductor vendors are, despite individual, claims of superiority for certain features, quite similar. All generally have resident software — monitor, assembler, editor and debugger — and the latest models are appearing with an in-circuit emulation capability, so that users can debug programmes using their actual prototype hardware. The software resident in the development systems-monitor assembler and editor — may not be an absolute necessity to the design of microprocessor-based systems, but the debugging features would be difficult to do without. The software tool sophistication has become similar to that of minicomputer software. The basic software tools are executive programmes (also called operating systems), text editors, assemblers, compilers and interpreters for programmes, linkers and debuggers. High-level language is an increasingly fundamental consideration. In general, a high-level language for Microprocessor applications should have several characteristics. Foremost of these is block structuring which allows several design layers to work independently on programme modules of a large project.

Taking into account all the above requirements, the following microprocessor checklist (prepared by *Electronic Products Journal)* could be found very useful in the evaluation of the minicomputer:

A. Cost Considerations

Normally chip cost is not the largest factor, but it could be in a simple system. The major cost is usually in the circuitry needed to support the microprocessor. The engineering cost to put your system together, however, can be greatly influenced by the amount of quality of support the chip supplier has available.

1. *Support Circuitry*

   Clock circuitry and clock drivers — how many phases? Power supplies — common or special? Memory — standard or special? Power of instruction set (a good instruction set can reduce memory requirements by 40%); Support requirements (the larger these are, the more expensive the printed-circuit board (PCB) or the greater the number of PCB's required); Base of checkout (test vs purchased card); Processor card availability (small production and preproduction will use off-the-shelf cards).

2. *Support from Supplier*

   Hardware Support — prototyping systems; mechanical hardware; processor cards; memory cards; interface cards and cables.

   Software Support — high level languages; assemblers; utility programmes — debug and edit; loaders — absolute and, relocatable; peripheral drivers (teletypewriters, card reader, line printer, floppy disc, etc.); special sub-routines.

3. *Literature*

   How well written the hardware and software manuals are determines how much time is spent in learning the system — Technical manuals; Software manuals; Application notes; Special interfaces — D/A, A/D peripherals.

4. *Technical Support*

   This can reduce the engineering time and cost required to get the new product designed and into production — Area system specialist; Field application engineer; Plant applications and engineering groups.

B. Performance

1. *Speed*

   Efficiency of the instruction set — how many instructions are needed to solve a particular problem (a mathematical problem, a process control problem, data handling, etc.)? Execution time of each instruction; Microprogrammability — can the instruction set be changed?

2. *Interface*

   Input/output flexibility and capability — How many peripherals can be handled? How many commands to each peripheral? How large is the subroutine to handle any of the peripherals? How much logic is required?

Interrupt flexibility and capability — Can vectored interrupts and/or polled interrupts be handled by the processor? How many interrupts can be handled by the processor?

Special control features — Enable signals (single line control where fast response or ease of interface is important); Sense inputs (test a single input and respond accordingly).

Conclusion

Selection of microprocessors for specific types of jobs can be based on criteria which are divergent from the general selection criteria of computers discussed in Chapters 4 and 5. The feature brought out above have special relevance to the burgeoning use of microprocessors in our country.

16

ADVENT OF PERSONAL COMPUTER

A personal computer is a microcomputer designed and installed exclusively for use by an individual. As a desk-top computer, it appears to be a typewriter-type keyboard with a television monitor sitting on top of it. Responding to the programmed instructions and executing the desired jobs, it has become an electronic consumer durable product in the West and is vastly popular already in the Indian metropolitan cities.

Genesis and Structure

1975 saw the first use of hobby computers, thus ushering in a personal computer industry. The dramatic growth began in 1977 when Apple II was introduced by Apple Computers, Pet by Commodore and TRS-80 by Radio Shack. Others to join the ranks soon were Exidy, Bally, Video Brain, Processor Technology, Cromemco, Ohio Scientific and Southwest Technical Products. Table 1 indicates some of the current personal computer types.

A personal computer, like any microcomputer, has three sub-systems of *hardware, software* and *firmware. Hardware* comprises the electronic circuitry, power supplies, memory, central processing unit (CPU) and peripheral devices, such as, video-display unit (VDU), audio-tape cassette, alpha-numerical keyboard, etc. *Software* is a set of instructions (programme) written in a language acceptable to the personal computer by an individual who can instruct the computer to execute his assigned job. Often manufacturers, too, supply pre-programmed software (in the media of floppy discs of magnetic or paper tapes) for executing specific jobs. *Firmware* is a system programme in read-only memory (ROM) which comes in hardware occupying some space in the personal computer memory and is supplied by manufacturers. The remaining portion of memory can be used by an individual for storing of his programme.

TABLE 1

Connect Personal Computer Types

Microprocessor	*Personal Computer*	*Manufacturer*
Intel's 8080 or 8080A	MMD-1	E & L Instruments
	BYT-3	Byte Inc.
	8080	IMSAI
	Altair 8800B	MITS
	Poly 88	Poly Morphic System
	H-8	Heathkit
Zileg's 7-80 or Z 80A	Alpha Z-80	Alpha Digital Systems
	Various	Cromemco
	Horizon	North Star
	TRS-80	Radio Shack
Motorola's M-6800	Altair 680B	MITS
Rockwell's 6502	Apple II	Apple Computer
	KIM-I	MOS Technology
	PET 2001	Commodore

Personal computers can run programmes written in machine language using strings of binary codes. Some operate in assembly language which uses specially defined characters to assemble instructions and converts the latter to machine language with one-to-one correspondence. A few popular ones use English-like languages, such as, beginners all-purpose symbolic instruction code (BASIC), common business-oriented languages (COBOL), formula translation language (FORTRAN) and 'C' language, in that order.

Personal computers have grown in the USA alone at a spectacular rate of 200 per cent and more between 1977 and 1991, and constituted 40 per cent—50 per cent of the total computing power against a mere 8 per cent in the earlier year. Business-wise, it has crossed the multi-billion mark, i.e. much above Rs. 1,000 crores. Priced between $500 and $12,000, a personal computer can cater to any of the seven market segments hobbyist consumer very small business, technical or professional, business, executive, educational and industrial. Table 2 given an idea of these market segments.

Variety of Usage

In brief, hobbyist was the first customer of personal computer to use it for creating, learning and experimental purposes. Mass consumer and very small business user, on the other hand, need it for personal enjoyment (entertainment games), learning (educational games), personal management (record-keeping, cataloguing or computation), and monitoring and control of other equipment (appliances, security devices, lights, furnace or water-heater). For business executives, available application programmes include payroll, inventory accounting, project costing, cash management, hire-sales and income-tax calculations. Technical or professional user is primarily an engineer or scientist who uses the personal computer as a professional tool to help in design analysis (computer-aided design (CAD) or to monitor and control experiments. Business executives may include such users as business analyst, operations and market researchers, and accountants. In educational sector, personal computers are used both to teach programming and to aid in other kinds of instruction. Industrial sector comprises primarily manufacturing organisations who use personal computers for process control, data logging or production monitoring.

TABLE 2

Market Segments of Personal Computer

Segment	*Application*	*Current Price ($)*
Consumer		500-1,000
Adults	Education, Personal	
Children	Management Entertainment	
Technology-based user		1,000-4,000
Hobbyist	Hobbies, experimentation, creation	
Technical or Professional	Professional solution of individual application	
Business executive	Profession problems	
Very small business	Business Management Operation	4,000-12,000
Educational		600-1,500
Schools	Programming	
University	Computer-aided instruction	
Industrial		600-2,000
Plant engineers		
Electronic-equipment supplier	Process control, monitoring Quality control	

The most important sector of applications is for the business computation, rightly termed *executive computing* or *managerial computing,* which has brought a revolution in the end-use of personal computers. This has been possible for the availability of a few software packages which are based on the 'C' language and have been made very friendly to the users.

The electronic spread-sheet is the first facility that provides visible tabulations on the computer screen and can change the rows or columns many times more in the table in order to assess the significance of the changes. LOTUS 1-2-3, VISICALC, SOFTCALC, etc., are the commercial packages for this purpose.

The second facility is that of graphics which can be combined in the form of graphs, bar-charts,. pie-charts, block diagrams, venn diagrams, etc., along with the tables of the spread-sheet.

The third facility is that of word processing which provides total secretarial help in composing, modifying, deleting, adding, editing, spell-checking, right-hand or left-hand "justifying" (margin adjustment), etc., for all letters, reports, memos and other correspondence: in full or in parts. WORDSTAR, WORDPERFECT, SOFTWORD, etc., are the relevant packages.

The fourth facility is of data-base management for engendering queries and getting responses. This is an apposite facility for eliciting data and information for business purposes and is widely used through such packages as dBASE III+, dBASE IV, FOXBASE, SYBASE, SOFTBASE, etc.

Overseas Use

Combining the latest technological advances with economic pricing and aggressive marketing, personal computers are catering today to many specialised users, such as, doctors, automobile-dealers, hospitals, real-estate brokers, construction companies, insurance agencies and small factories In Indonesia, for instance, personal computers are being marketed with VDUs and operator-oriented language, where computer "talks" to an individual in English or Bahasa Indonesian. Even people with no previous computer experience learn the fundamentals of computer operation literally within a few days.

Personal computer is a cost-effective, professional, productivity-improving tool which a manager — operating alone — can use to create, manipulate and analyse information. Computer-aided analysis has always been considered worthwhile for better decision-making, with benefits justifying the investment. Now analysts, line supervisors and middle managers are taking to personal computers for being more productive with own facilities, — 100,000 of them in the USA by early 1981.

It is remarkable how personal computers have invaded the Indian market. To realise its potential, it is understandable that personal computers have moved from a luxury market to a utility one, from entertaining to functional uses, and from high-cost, limited-application products to low-cost, broad-application products. In order to be really useful in India, there must be a few universal applications, the price must come done to Rs. 5,000 or less, and marketing must fit the existing distribution outlets. At the embryonic stage, the primary users for personal computers were hobbyists for whom a high operating performance for a low dollar-value was essential. With users like business executives and scientists, availability of application software and service has become increasingly able to consider today providing total system solutions — hardware and application software — for mass consumers and business users both of whom provide large markets. Such systems solutions can be developed internally or in partnership with indigenous or overseas hardware or software producers, — for business consultants, issue-house managers, educationists, architects, civil engineers or electronic design engineers, to name only a few.

DISTRIBUTED DATA PROCESSING

Data Processing (DP) has come into being to provide accurate and timely information to assist the operation of a business. Data Processing as a function can and does exist in a manual fashion with the same objective. Usage of computer can help to achieve the objective at a fast pace and using a large volume of data. If one considers how DP can be made more effective, the idea of distributing this resource and managing the data being processed is a natural direction to take.

Basic Definition

The term *distributed data processing* is used to describe computer systems with multiple processors either at the same computer centre or in geographically separate locations. Rarely, the term is applied to the use of multiple minicomputers which are not connected at all. The degrees of dispersion for the distributed components can include interconnection to form a single computer complex; interconnection by cables in a computer room; interconnection by in-plant wiring; interconnection by permanent carrier telecommunication (e.g., a dedicated telephone line); interconnection by intermittent common carrier telecommunication (e.g., a dialled-up telephone connection); or some physical connection in one form or the other.

If telecommunication lines were fast enough, there would be no difference in function between a distributed computer system in one room and a geographically scattered system. Today, the telecommunication links used for data transmission are much slower than the channels which interconnect the devices within a computer room. Consequently the functions distributed geographically are different from those distributed within one machine room.

Aspects of Distribution

There are generally three aspects of systems that may be distributed: *processing, data* and *control*. Where interlinked processors are geographically scattered, the data they use may be scattered as well. In many systems, it is the structure and usage of the *data* that determines what is practical in the distribution of processors. Again, a system may have much of its *processing* geographically scattered and yet the overall management and *control* functions may reside separately at a central location.

Data can be stored either as straightforward data-files or as data-bases. A file is designed for data to serve a particular application or related group of applications. A data-base is an application-independent collection of data from which multiple records can be derived by software. There are major advantages in employing data-base software, but the software is complex and usually operates on data stored at one location. Distributed data are, therefore, organised often in the form of *data-files* (usually on-line) rather than as a data-base, although multiple data-base systems may also be interconnected.

Nature of Data

Different forms of data distribution involve central data with single lost computer; central data with multiple host computers; dependent hierarchical data (data in the lower-level machines often a sub-set of the higher-level data); independent hierarchical data (all the processors being self-sufficient DP systems); split data (the same data-structure at different locations); separate data (different data-structure at different locations forming an integrated system); replicated data (multiple copies of data stored at different locations); and heterogeneous data systems (independent computer systems). Figure 1 shows a typical corporate configuration containing most of the above, as visualised by Martin.

DP exists to provide accurate and timely information to assist the operation of a business. If management places its emphasis on DP with all its attendant complexities, the concept of distributing this capability becomes one step in an overall plan for supporting a business through information system. A major US financial institution went ahead in eighties for a complete distribution of the DP function, resulting in a significant decrease in the DP effectiveness. This could be attributed to three factors: endorsement to distributed DP without careful technical analysis and design; placement of DP and responsibility for it in areas that were not prepared for either, and the lack of an overall plan for DP that magnified the first two issues.

Users and User-Load

Selecting a computer system to serve a number of users spread over a wide area is a tricky problem, involving identification of user-groups (varying from inquiry-response systems to batch operations and even including real-time operations);

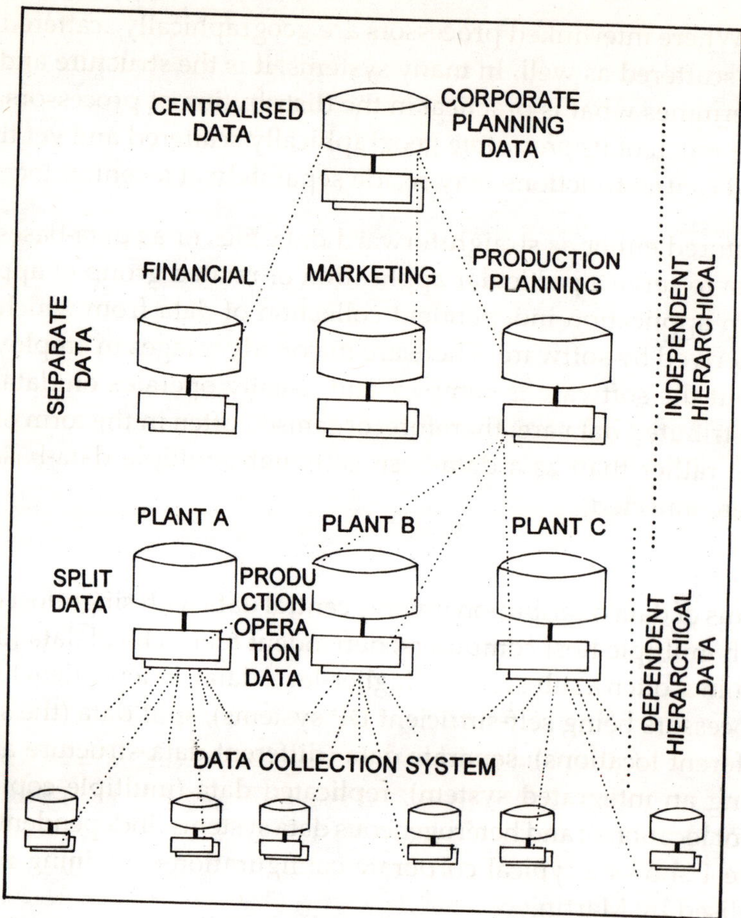

Fig. 1: Categories of Data Distribution

assessment and merging together the different needs of each user-group (for instance, most inquiry-response system users would have common needs); and summarisation of responses into a form suitable for system specification.

Before drawing up a realistic profile of expected user-load, certain standard terms to describe users is necessary to be explained. Among the *interactive* applications (which "interact" with the computer with each transaction), *conversational* users come first with varying applications, but with the common characteristic of input-output being single line each (with less than 100 characters) and being balanced as well, and the expected response-time being 2-5 seconds. Then come the *inquiry-response* customers characterised by short input-messages and long responses (dependent on design, size and access-time for large data-bases), and expected response time rising to 20 seconds or so (for extensive querying). The third category is the *remote job-entry* (RJE) users who enter jobs for subsequent processing, and response-time can be quite long. The last category is the *data-entry* users with, long inputs and short response-time (say, for generating database). Data entry may be done in conversational mode, with response-time less than 2 seconds. Among non-interactive applications come *batch-users*, with large volume of data in put and large amount of output, who may need large processing power and can be conveniently scheduled, often in off-shift hours.

The above standard terms can be illustrated from the distributed DP concept made operational at TISCO and TELCO. These two giant private-sector enterprises had each gone in for *Burroughs* 6806 computer as the host system at the plant, connected through high-speed line to Burroughs 1955 minicomputers as RJEs with 20 video-terminals each 4 RJE minicomputers for TISCO and 3 for TELCO satisfied 70 to 80 per cent inquiries on the spot regarding production and inventory, with long-term production records and the historical data going to the central computer once in every shift (i.e., thrice daily). *Conversational* usage was for program development through command and editing languages, debugging logic-flow: in short for improving productivity of programmes. *Inquiry-response* usage was partly on 1955 and partly on 6806 systems on the extended data-base. *RJE* usage for starting such jobs as stock-movements and daily stock-status on 1955 systems. Lastly, *data-entry* usage was for updating store-stocks, entering part-numbers, etc., with some peripheral capability, adequate character-display and a few hard-copy attachments (or dot-matrix printers). The above description does not include such real-time applications as process control, where local interaction is often within microseconds. Interactions with other components in such a system may require a response-time in milliseconds.

Check-list for Users

The following check-list has been compiled in order to draw up a user-profile:

Interactive General

How many times per day does one log? When in the day and how does one log? What are average and maximum sizes of input? What are average and maximum sizes of output? What are average number of inputs in a 10-minute period?

Conversation

What applications are used and each how many times a day? Does one use specific applications at specific times? What are storage requirements (in characters) for each application?

Inquiry-Response

What applications are used and each how many tunes a day? Does one have specific applications at specific times? What data-bases are accessed and for which applications? What are percentage-uses of video-terminals?

Data-Entry

What databases are accessed and for which applications?

Batch

How many jobs (with descriptions) are submitted daily — types, formats, number of records, typical form and amount of output. run-time of jobs, required resources (memory, storage devices, slow peripherals), required turn-around time, modification of data-bases, best run-times?

Management Questions

What is the impact of the system not being available? Do expansion plans exist? Can access to the system be scheduled? What is the impact of undetected errors on users? Can the number of simultaneous users be limited?

Answers to the above questions need careful integration and balancing to arrive at a proper user-profile. In assessing available systems and letting the vendors, interpret the user-needs, emphasis should be laid on capacity, performance, availability, reliability, flexibility, security and accountability, — each an important parameter in its own right.

DATA COMMUNICATION

Data communication involves flow of digital signals with the help of telecommunication devices, mainly between computers or terminals or both. Its impact extend to the fields of education, industry, banking, government and business, involving such applications as on-line reservation by the airlines, buses and hotels; freight loading and wagon movement; checking of bills in industry; on-line transactions in banks; order-processing and inventory control in manufacturing industry, and so on.

Need for providing data communication in India emerged a few years ago and a beginning was made to introduce it in telephone-type circuits in the seventies. The speeds realised were up to around 2400 bits per second (BPS) for intra-city and inter-city links without resorting to any special conditioning. The number of computers in India has been increasing rapidly and quite a few are capable of supporting remote terminals. Concepts of new services, such as, digital fascimile, teletex, videotex and possibility of providing a variety of tele-processing applications make it necessary to have a close look at the data communication methods to meet both the short-term and long-term needs of the users.

Transmission Parameters

Communication lines provide a single signal path from transmitter to receiver, information being sent serially bit by bit. Due to the serial nature of the path, message control information has to be sent along the same path as the message The direction characteristics of the line are described by such terms as simplex (one way only), half-duplex (both ways alternately) and full-duplex (both ways simultaneously). While information can be transferred in a simplex path only in one direction, half- and full-duplex lines transmit information in both directions. Care has to be taken with the half-duplex lines to avoid *contention,* i.e., both ends transmitting simultaneously and *lock-up,* i.e., both cads expecting each other to send the next message.

Asynchronous and synchronous are two main types of data transmission. In asynchronous communication, the data are sent with one character (composed of a fixed number of bits) at a time, preceded and terminated by start-bits and stop-bits for control. Such communication is commonly used with slow-speed manually operated terminals, such as, MECON terminal at Ranchi connected earlier for remote job-entry (RJE) to Regional Computer Centre, Calcutta. In synchronous communication, the message is sent as a continuous string of fixed length characters and is started with a string of synchronisation characters used by the receiver to synchronise his clock with that of the sender. Synchronous transmission is normally done in inter-computer communication. The advantage of synchronous over asynchronous communication consists in sending more useful data-bits in a given time

The parameters of the message transmission are the direction characteristics (half-or full-duplex), the line-speed, the transmission Type (synchronous or asynchronous), and the message control and code conventions expected by the receiver. These conventions are dependent on applications and manufacturers. The unit for measuring line-speed is "baud" which is the "umber of information-units transferred in one second. For biliary information units, the baud rate is equal to the number of bits transmitted per second and can range from 110 to 50,000.

Message Switching

The 'receive' function is generally more difficult than the 'transmit' function, since the receiver decodes and interprets the bits and characters (which may have errors) received, whereas the transmitter knows the precise character-sequence sent The ability to detect and correct errors is determined by the code-set and the transmission-discipline. The simplest error-detection available at the character level *is parity checking* obtained by including an additional bit in each character. *Message switching* logic is used if the source and destination points are not physically connected by a communication path. The message is first transmitted to an intermediate point (usually a communication computer), and then re-transmitted to another intermediate point or the final destination.

Computers are used in communications either as switches or to control switches. In the first case, each switching computer accepts messages from data terminals and holds the records until a communication channel is available to the computer serving the message destination. In the second case, the computer controls the equipment which physically connects the origin with the destination. The subscriber then uses the end-to-end communication-channel capacity to transmit his informations voice or data.

Stored Program-Control

Switching systems, used in the exchanges, provide the user with the facility of connecting telephone, teleprinter or any communication device, to that of another user, as and when necessary. Message-switching minicomputers: perform as the core of efficient communication systems and are an important in the Indian context. According to Ramani, while earlier telephone exchanges were entirely electro-mechanical, today's stored programme-control (SPC) exchanges incorporate a computer and the exchange-functions are largely determined by instructions given to the computer. An SPC exchange, for instance, has been installed at Prabhadevi in Bombay. In this exchange, a computer performs the control function, but continues to make and break ("analog") electrical paths for making connections, using relays. On the other hand, fully digital SPC exchanges convert signals to digital form and use digital circuits to set up calls between pairs of subscribers. The digital SPC exchanges have several advantages, including easy connection to digital transmission media, such as, satellite links or high-speed microwave links. An example is the SPC telex exchange in the Overseas Communication Service in Bombay in full operation for a long time.

SPC exchanges hold out many promises to Indian subscribers, such as, accurate and detailed recording and billing of calls: "tele-conferencing" (i.e., three or more people sharing a group-discussion over a distance via telephones); telephones in cars; coded control of STD calls; automatic testing of telephone equipment; abbreviated dialling for frequently used numbers; and so on.

Similar to the switching side, integrated circuits (ICs) have helped the transmission side as well. Major strides have been made in transmission by the communication satellite which can provide as many as 10,000 telephone transmission channels. A satellite can receive and re-transmit "broad-band" signals, i.e., signals carrying a large amount of information, say, for 1,000 voices. Ground equipment can combine ("multiplex") 10,000 voice signals into a broad-band signal for transmission and again separate them out ("demultiplex") on receipt Among other advances in transmission with broad-band communication are microwave system between Bombay and Trivandrum carrying thousands of simultaneous telephone conversations, and co-axial system between Bombay and Pune for hundreds of such conversations.

User Benefits

For the common user, improved data communication means low cost, easy availability and high reliability of long-distance communication. The 'space segment' itself costs less than Rs. 10,000 per year for voice channel between two places visible to the communication satellite, that is, about eighty paise for three minutes for places separated by a few thousand miles.

In data transmission, a user's objective is to transfer and access data which are error-free, almost instantaneous and at the lowest possible cost. An optimal approach demands that incompatibilities in computer architecture, communication protocol (i.e., hardware and software linkages), peripherals and devices are to be kept to a minimum. At the same time, unplanned duplication of data-banks, uncoordinated demands for data-terminals, and circuit-terminating equipment and computers should be controlled as well. Aspects concerning reliability, availability and acceptable error-rates have also to be carefully balanced and defined within the available financial resources. All such parameters can be broadly classified as follows (according to the size of message and response time):

(a) Conversational applications, such as, airlines, bus and hotel reservation;
(b) Information retrieval, such as, bank accounts, insurance policy status and hospital information;
(c) RJE or batch processing, such as, remote card reading and access to computer at a distant end;
(d) Message switching, such as, "electronic mail" (transmission of text, office-letters using own computer terminals and data-communication channels to a computer at the destination);
(e) Process control, such as, numerical control of machines and remote meter-readings;

(f) Inter-processor working, such as, communication between computers, programme and file sharing;

(g) Source data-entry, such as, inventory and payroll data preparation.

Looking into the future of tele-processing demands, Department of Electronics estimated that the data-link requirements would rise to 1600 around 1200 BPS, 325 around 2400 BPS, and 60 around 4800/9600 BPS, in 1983 from 200, 90 and 40 respectively in 1980. The actual demand has gone up much more since. The above data-channel demands do not include need of infrequently used data-links, with dialled data services. With the basic infrastructure available, the need for realising much more improved data communication services through Department of Telecommunications public-data networks is of paramount importance today. Their packet-switched public data network (PSPDN), under the name of VIKRAM Project, is gaining popularity in a large number of metropolitan cities and townships and fulfills a positive need of data transmission in the public domain.

COMPUTER NETWORK

The purpose of most computer networks is to allow a fairly distributed community of users to share computer resources. The technology of distributed processing and computer networks has made it possible for computer to cease to be isolated machines, and use programmes and data stored by computers in other locations. There are quite a few types of computer networks, — caused by different types of distributed processing, different needs of users, different kinds of organisations operating the networks, and so on.

Categories of Networks

Nature of distributed processing makes for four categories of computer networks. First, geographically remote terminals and remote job-entry (RJE) stations can be connected to a central computer. Secondly, geographically remote small computers can be used for minor pre-processing tasks and input data are transferred through magnetic tapes off-line (by post or by hand) to a central computer for main processing. Thirdly, a central computer can perform major computing tasks and can have connections to smaller computers with specialised functions, such as communication, facilities and graphics. Finally, dependent large computers (as "hosts") can communicate with one another, and share programmes or data. The last category of resource-sharing network of similar-computers is today the most prevalent one. Such a network was initially demonstrated in Bombay in 1980 with host systems at the Indian Institute of Science in Bangalore and the National Centre for Software Development and Computing Techniques (NCSDCT) in Mumbai, among others; a number of users at these two centres utilised each other's computer with great ease for remote access and electronic messaging. The system has now caught on.

Different organisations create computer networks for meeting different needs. Some networks are built in a single corporation for a single need, such as, airlines reservations. Some corporate networks are designed for multiple applications which can share a common data-base for being cost-effective. Some large corporate networks may be designed as a general-purpose network, integrating separate networks used by the member-groups for purposes of economy and better-service. Some networks are constructed to serve groups of similar-organisations, such as, banks airlines, universities, etc. These may be either general-purpose like ARPANET (connecting around 50 American universities and research institutions having dissimilar computers) or special-purpose like SWIFT electronic fund transfer network (connecting around 15 American and European banks having similar computers from UNISYS) or SITA airlines passenger reservation networks connecting all the major airlines of the world. A value-added computer provides a commercial network with leased lines to serve many customers in selected geographical areas. TYMNET and TELENET are examples of private corporations offering competitive service in the USA. Common carriers, such as, telephone companies, can provide nation-wide data-networks of different types, designed to move packets of data between subscribers in a fraction of a second. For instance, digital PCM trunks operate at speeds of millions of bits per second in North America. Multiple common carriers can also interconnect their data-networks. Finally, networks capable of carrying high band-width (i.e., a group of consecutive frequencies constituting a band) traffic are coming into existence for copying machines transmitting to copying machines, tele-conferencing, etc.

Proliferation of Networks

Computer networks are proliferating at a high rate throughout the world and becoming a powerful force in both private and public sectors, nationally as well as internationally. This recent upsurge of activity is due to three main technological trends: greatly increased reliability of computers; availability of low-priced minicomputers suitable for carrying out most functions needed to operate a network; and major cost saving improvements in communications technology.

Many specialised computer networks have come up, operating more economically than the general-purpose networks described above. This is due to the fact that the variety of large computers, minicomputers, microcomputers, terminals and peripherals — needed to be connected into distributed systems — is too great for any general-purpose network. Again, some systems demand fast response-times or brief interactive transmission, while others can accept delayed but cheap message delivery or batch-transmission of lengthy records and files. Most computer manufactures have network architectures for their particular equipment, such as, the architectures of the Digital Equipment Corporation (DECNET), International Business Machines (IBM-SNA), and Sperry-Univac (DCA). Some networks are designed for specific applications, such as, international electronic funds transfer or airlines reservation. Some networks handle only messages shorter than a certain length, thus considerably simplifying their mechanism.

Some networks are designed to interconnect computers but not terminals, with correct protocols programmed into the software. Some other networks handle specific types of terminals, such as, telex-machines or inexpensive machines which conform to definite protocols. An example is AT & T's Transaction Network System, permitting deployment of telephone devices along with a small display, keyboard and magnetic card-reader. Another example is the British Prestel network (originally called Viewdata) using conventional television sets at home for broadcasting data (comparable to Teletext in Europe).

Network Structures

Computer networks may be viewed as in Fig. 1, composed of nodes, — with circuits, channels or links connecting them. A node may vary from a small amount of fixed hardware logic to one of the major computers. Nodes are used to support network connections as "store and forward" computers (i.e., to receive and store messages, and to despatch them along one of the several different routes); as concentrators" (i.e., to take input characters from a number of slow terminals and assemble them into blocks); and as attachment points for major computers. Physical details of circuits, channels or links ''comprising lines, microwave-links, radio-links, cable television or satellites) are of little consequence for computer networks. Relevant parameters for a channel are its maximum data rate;—error" characteristics and direction-limitations.

In each computer network. there is a control mechanism by which the connected computers and terminals share the use of the band-width. A simple control method is multiplexing, i.e., transmission of a number of messages simultaneously over a single circuit. While data-rate in earlier networks using space-division multiplexing was limited to 9600 bits per second (BPS) or so, modern systems with high band-widths employ frequency-division multiplexing (FDM) as well as time-division multiplexing (TDM). In the former, there is a portion of the frequency spectrum of the medium assigned to each point-to-point connection, whereas in the latter, a time-interval is so assigned. Both FDM and TDM techniques are widely used in long-distance transmission.

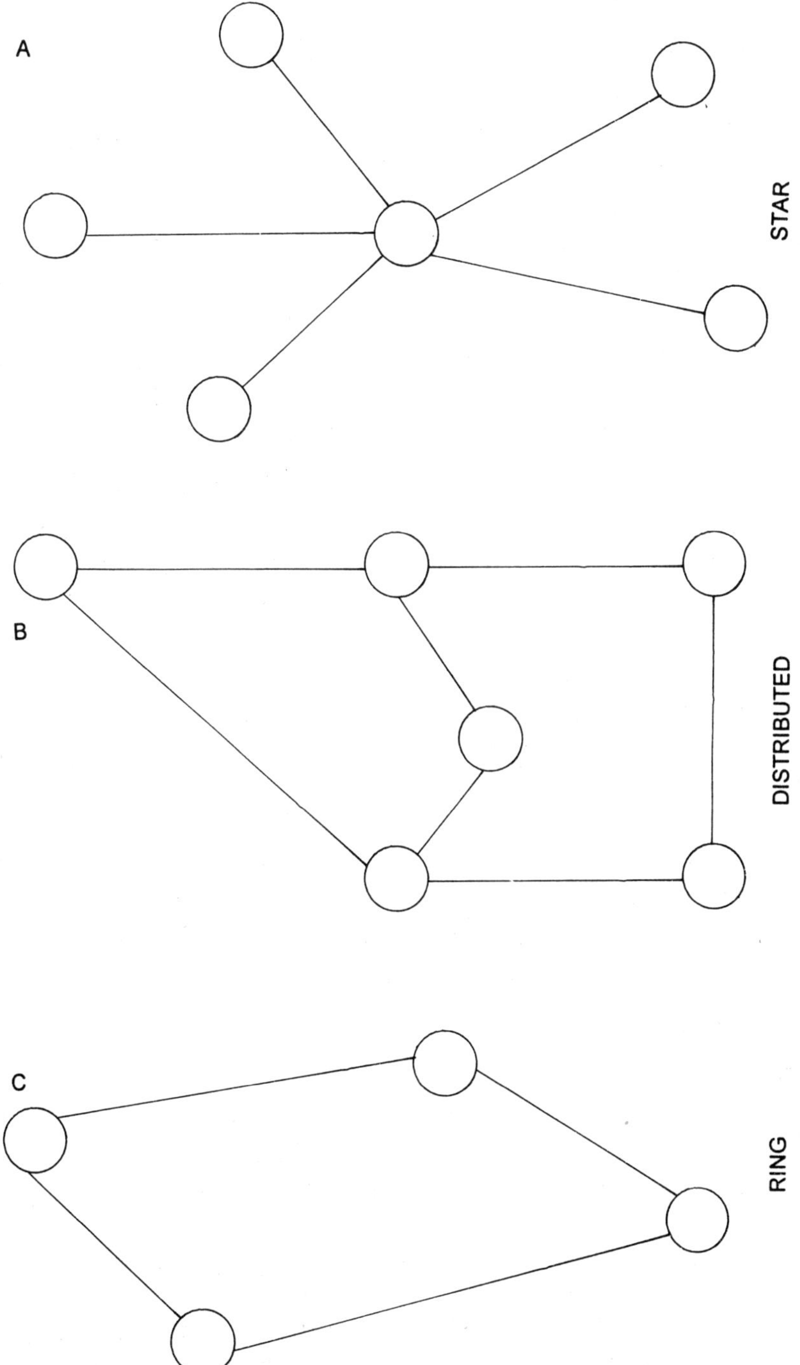

Fig. 2: Network Configurations

Early Efforts in India

A local area network (LAN) is a data communication system for interconnecting computers and terminals that are within one building or in several. buildings in close proximity (up to a few kilometres). LANS are desirable for the same reason as distributed networks are: they make possible locally the sharing of resources (such as, computing power, data-bases and switching services) by users at LANS are locations. The advantage is that it is feasible to implement band-width or data-rates of several megabits per second (MBPS) in local networks. These higher data-rates are realised in paired, twisted or coaxial cables and in fibre-optic media. Examples of early local "'star" networks were the clusters of B-1955 minicomputers around the large B-5806 system as the host computer in TISCO and TELCO (at Jamshedpur and Pune). Here the data and file transfers could take place in any job-operation from any computer.

NCSDCT has earlier developed a close-coupled network (CCN) using a few TDC-316 computers located at IIT, Bombay for further development of software. Another important effort was to develop a "star" network at IIT, Kanpur, with the IBM-1800, TDC-316 and DEC-1090 as the three outer nodes and a microcomputer MICRO-78 (based on INTEL-8080 chip) as the switching centre. The advantages derived by linking all the machines in a computer network were an all-round increase in the computing facility. In particular, the IBM-1800 devices of a card-punch and 7-track magnetic tape unit were made available to DEC-users over the network and old 7-track tapes could be easily converted to 9-track tapes used in the DEC system. Further, the IBM-1800 provided extensive real-time control facilities and hybrid computing, and these resources were available to a wide class of users over the network. Again, the TDC-316 was used as a RJE station for the DEC system. Finally, the TDC-316 was also used as "Concentrator" for terminals, thus allowing for easy system expansion.

Current Status

Networks, involving similar or disparate computers, have come a long way in India. CMC Ltd., has introduced INDONET which operates with IBM clusters or VAX/PDF clusters at Bombay, Delhi, Calcutta, Madras and Hyderabad, along with many extended terminals for distributed processing in other cities. This is typically a wide-area network (WAN) and provides regional software services.

There are a number of other WANs in operation today. The principal one is the National Informatics Centre Networks (NICNET), having regional centres at Delhi, Bhubaneshwar, Pune and Hyderabad; State and Union Territory capital centres at 32 cities; and district centres in some 461 districts. This is the premiere hierarchical network for the Centre, States and districts for improved information exchange, uniformity of data structure, use of mathematical modelling and, as a whole, efficient Central and State planning.

The other WAN is ONGCNET with the nodal centre at Dehradun, and regional centres at Bombay, Baroda, Calcutta, Nazira (near Jorhat) and Madras. The regional computer centres do routine seismic processing of the data gathered from the line-kilometres of the off-shore and on-land survey ships and survey-teams respectively, leaving the non-routine processing to the Dehradun IBM Computer.

The metropolitan area network (MAN) is confined within a city, such as, NIC's Computer Centres networked for the ASIAD games at different stadiums in and around Delhi city, or, Neyville Lignite Corporation's Computer Centres networked within the Neyville township.

Conclusion

India today is seeing the emergency of a large number of computer networks of varying capacity for resource-sharing (mostly disc-space and printers) and spread over long distances, starting often with LAN.

Indian banks are joining the SWIFT (Society of Worldwide Inter-bank Financial Telecommunication) network, and Indian Airlines and Air India are already members of the SITA (Society for International Traffic in Airways) network on a global basis. The education field has received a filip with the education and research network (ERNET) operating among the five Indian Institutes of Technology, Tata Institute of Fundamental Research, Indian Institute of Science and National Centre for Software Technology. Most of widespread networks are operating through INSAT 1-C satellite whose available channel capacity seems to be one of the limiting factors for the growth of networks.

17

THE USE OF COGNITRON FOR NATURAL LANGUAGE ANALYSIS

1. Introduction

The application of neural networks to higher-level cognitive tasks such as natural language processing has posed interesting problems that attracted the attention of scientists working in the area of neural networks as well as computational linguistics. Natural language processing involves the analysis of the text according to the norms of syntax and semantics, in addition to being interpreted by considering extra-linguistic pragmatic and world knowledge influences. Natural language understanding is a complex tusk because it is influence by a large and varied amount of interdependent knowledge, and its interpretation is constrained by a number of mutually non exclusive constraints imposed by linguistic resources, social interactions and the intuitive knowledge of the participant. The cognitive modal of understanding can be explained as the formation of a mental model of the information conveyed by the text. Natural language understanding by a computer can be viewed as a mapping from the text to a target internal representation where this internal representation is the parsed and interpreted meaning of the text conveyed by the producer.[1] In this view of natural language understanding, the formation of a syntactically analysed sentence is an important step towards further processing. In this work we consider syntactic analysis as a method of matching preprocessed input; sentences with already trained and formed syntactic patterns and hence determining whether the sentences are syntactically valid. If they are valid, the system also outputs the matching structure in order to form the syntactic representation. The major phases discussed are the preprocessor, the prepositional phrase clipper and the cognitron used for pattern matching.

The use of the neural network approach to syntactic and semantic processing aspects of natural language processing has also been considered using the perceptron approach but the basic problem of convergence of the perception was propogated to the system designed using it.[2] The use of a parallel distributed approach to syntax analysis was considered by Fanty but the localised approach used imposed a constraint that the number of processors used had to be specified in advance and this in return meant that the parser could handle only fixed length sentences.[3]

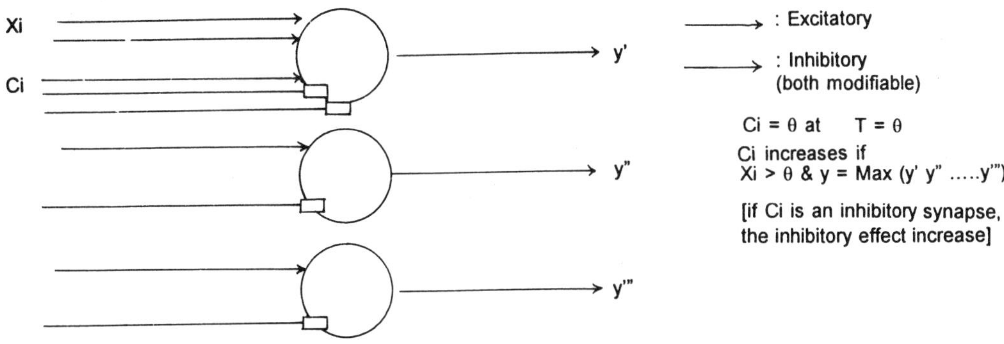

Fig. 1: A New Hypothesis on Synapse Modification

2. Neural Network — The Cognitron

One of the general approaches of neural networks is to incorporate the regularity in the input samples (in this case the grammatical knowledge) during the training or learning phase by giving appropriate training samples and allowing the knowledge to be incorporated incrementally. As new patterns arrive, the network organises itself to recognize that new pattern also. In this system we use the neural network model called the cognitron. The rest of the section describes the self-organising mechanism of the model.

The cognitron is based on the idea that synaptic connections between neurons in the brain are not completely inherited, but are plastically modified by learning through experiences. The self-organization of the cognitron progresses favourably in the unsupervised mode , i.e. without the aid of a teacher. In this model, the hypothesis used is as follows: It is believed that three are two kinds of neurons, excitatory and inhibitory types, considering figure 1 the synaptic connections from x to y is reinforced if and only if the following two conditions are simultaneously satisfied,

- Presynaptic cell x fire, and
- None of the postsynaptic cells situated near the cell y fires stronger than y.[4]

Here it is assumed that a cell is influenced only by a group of cells situated in a particular predetermined area for each called its 'connectable area'. The second condition ensures that among a group of post synaptic cells situated in a small area only one cell has its afferent synapses reinforced. This area is called 'Vicinity area.' The neighbouring cells have approximately same connectable area. But because of the second condition of the hypotheses it is ensured that only one cell which happens to have yielded maximum output in the vicinity area is reinforced. In essence an even slight difference in property exhibited by cells will grow further, culminating in each cell having its own characteristics. This type of reinforcement also works for inhibitory synapse where such a synapse is made more inhibitory.

Another important aspect of the cognitron is its ability to perform self-repair where even if one cell is damaged its function is taken over by reinforcement of another cell in the vicinity area; which had been previously prevented from reinforcement by the damaged cell.

3. The Basic Structure of the Cognitron

The Cognitron is a multilayer structure consisting of a number of neural layers of a similar structure cascaded one after the other, given two layers i and i+1, this section discusses the equations used to derive the output of a neuron in layer i+1 considering the influences of both the exitatory and inhibitory neurons of layer i as well as inhibitory neurons of layer i + 1 itself [Figure 2).

U_{ij} → output from neuron j in layer i

a_{ijk} → weight of synapse connecting j^{th} excitatory neuron in layer i to k^{th} neuron in layer i+1

C_{ijk} → weight of synapse connecting j^{th} inhibitory neuron in layer i to k^{th} excitatory neuron in layer i+1

b_{ij} → weight of the synapse connecting j^{th} inhibitory neuron in layer i to j^{th} excitatory neuron in layer i+1

V_{ij} → output of the jth inhibitory neuron in layer i

The first step is calculation of the inhibitory output for inhibitory neurons in layer i

V_{ij} → C_{ijk} U_{ik} (for fixed i + j C_{ijk} = 1) for all inhibitory neurons in layer i.

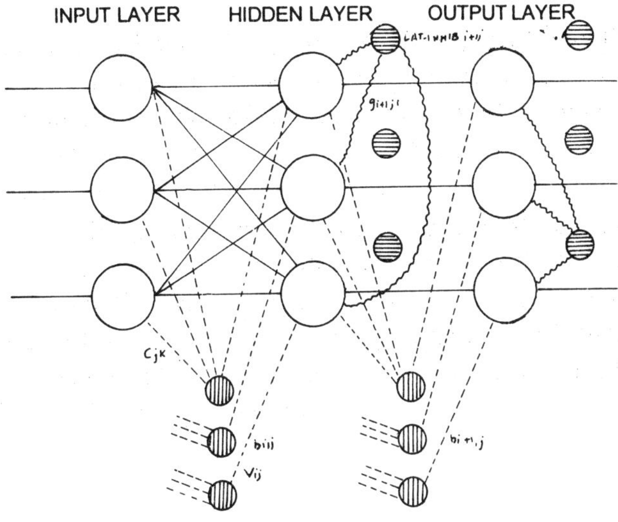

Full connection not shown

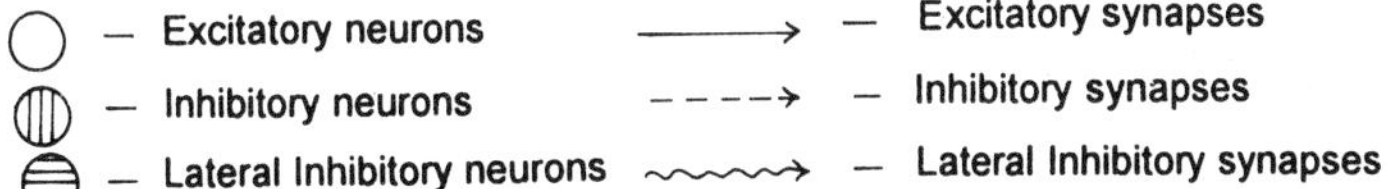

Fig. 2: The Cognition

The next step involves the calculation of the excitatory and inhibitory sums for all excitatory neurons in layer i + 1.

$E_i + 1, j \quad = \quad a_{ijk}\ U_{ik}$ excitatory input to neuron j in layer i + 1.

$I_i + 1, j \quad = \quad b_{ij} * Vij$ inhibitory input to neuron j in layer i + 1.

Now we find the output of each neuron in layer i + 1 as:

$$NET_{i+1,j} = \frac{1 + E_{i+1,j}}{1 + I_{i+1,j}} - 1$$

$$\text{if } NET_{i+1,j} = 0 \text{ than } OUT_{i+1,j} = NET_{i+1,j}$$

$$\text{else } OUT_{i+1,j} = 0$$

In case all the outputs are zero then all weights of all neuron are adjusted as:

$$a_{ijk} = Q_o * C_{ikj} * U_{ij}$$

$$b_{ij} = QP_o * V_{ij}$$

In case a particular neuron called the winner gives the maximum output then weights of the neuron alone are adjusted as

$$A_{ij} \text{ winner} = Q_1.C_i \text{ winner j. } U_i$$

$$bi \text{ winner} = (aij \quad \text{winner}) \ / \ (2{*}V_i \text{ winner})$$

where $0 < Q_o < Q_i$

This procedure is repeated on some set of training patterns till the output gets stabilised. In the cognition, lateral inhibition is also included where excitatory neurons gets inhibited by neighbouring excitatory neurons of same layer.

let g_{ijk} = lateral inhibitory weight connecting j with neuron k in layer i

$$LB_{i+1,j} = g_{i+1,j,k} \cdot OUT_{L+1,k}$$

$$\text{Then } U_{i+1,j} = \frac{1 + OUT'_{i+1,j}}{1 + LB_{i+1,j}} - 1$$

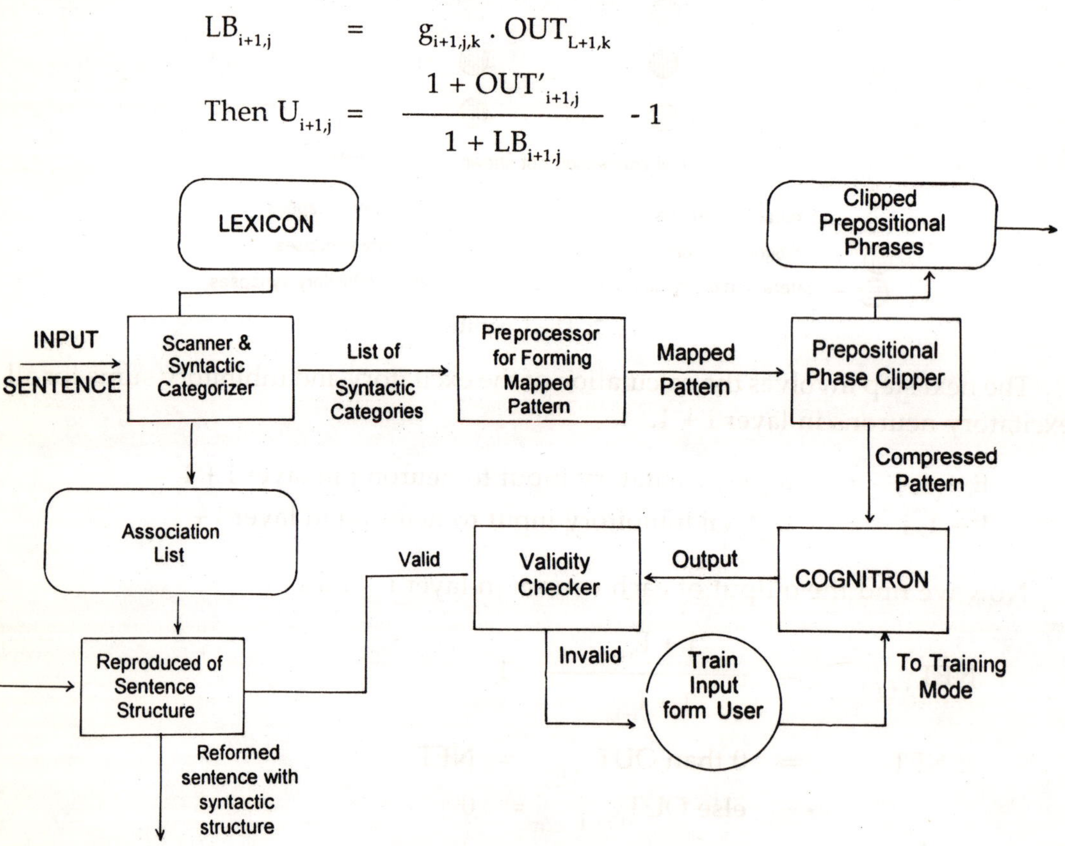

Fig. 3: System Flow Diagram

The main advantage of cognition is that due to ratio consideration of excitatory inputs E and inhibitory input 1, the output of the neuron never overshoots but coverage to a definite value. Due to the inclusion of lateral inhibition, self-organisation of the model becomes more reliable since adjacent neurons have some influence on the neuron. Thus after repetitive training of several sets of patterns the cognition self-organises in such a way that receptive fields of the cells becomes relatively larger as it progresses form layer to layer. Each cell in the final layer integrates or combines information form parts of first layer and selectively responds to specific characteristics or pattern of the training set. This self-organising property of the cognition is used for checking grammatical validity of input pattern (sentences).

4. Natural Language Processing and the Cognitron

In this system the patterns given for training the cognitron are the syntactic constituents of the grammatically valid sentences after they have been appropriately preprocessed. The major components of the system is as shown in Figure 3. The three phases of the system are the learning phase, the processing phase and the reproduction phase. In the first step of the learning and processing phase in the system, the scanner scans the sentence, separates the words and searches for the word and its syntactic category in the lexicon. The words are of no consequence in further processing and the association list of words and their corresponding syntactic categories are stored for reproduction during later phases of processing. The next step is a syntactic preprocessor which converts the pattern of syntactic categories associated with the sentence to a compressed syntactic constituent pattern. With each such constituent pattern is associated a number that uniquely defines that constituent. The division into constituents does not strictly follow conventional syntactic parsing constituents but are rather grouped according to uniqueness of number patterns. A one step look- ahead and a set of rewriting rules are used to obtain this number pattern. Partial verbs like will, shall etc. are given unique values. Similarly the verb and its tense derivatives are also assigned, different values. At the end of the preprocessing phase we get an interger sequence representing the sentence. Only certain combination of these phrases are valid. These combinations are taken as input training patterns to the cognitron (as in figure 4).

The next stab is the prepositional phrase clipper. The mechanism of clipping prepositional phrases allows the cognitron to recognize grammatically close patterns that vary only in the position of their prepositional phrases. This technique adds a new dimension to the system in that it is able to recognize new patterns which are grammatically close to the already trained patterns but which it has not seen before.

After the clipper phase, is the actual cognitron. The cognitron can be set to two modes; the training mode where it learns new patterns and the processing mode where it checks the validity of the given input pattern. We use a three layer network which during the training phase self-organises to recognize the features of grammatically

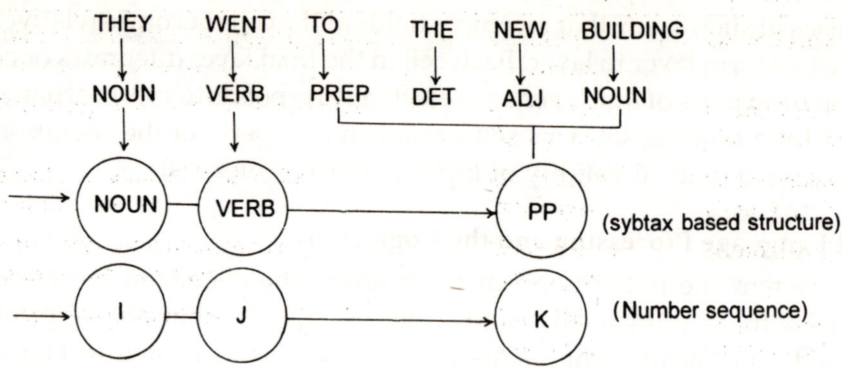

Fig. 4: A Mapped Pattern

valid sentences. During the processing phase the cognitron either recognizes (valid) or does not recognize (invalid) the pattern representing the input sentence. In case of valid sentences, we proceed to the reproduction phase which sends the valid pattern back to clipper where the original prepositional phrases are reinstated into the number pattern. This is then passed back to preprocessor where the original syntactic categories are associated with the pattern. Then the associated list created during the scanning phase is used to reform the original sentence and this is output along with the structure obtained from the preprocessor and the cognitron. In case the sentence is invalid the user is asked whether the pattern corresponding to the sentence is to be incorporated into the cognition and if so the cognitron is set to training mode and the pattern processed.

5. Conclusion

Unlike conventional parsers where the complete grammar has to be specified, this system treats sentences as being classified into different categories based on their grammatical patterns. The regularity of the syntax patterns in the sentences is used to incorporate the syntax into the cognitron. Since the cognitron is used, convergence of the network is guaranteed. The self-organising property regularity in the structure of the sentences is learnt from the training samples. Grammatically close patterns can be recognized since they are suitably clipped and input as an already learnt pattern as far as the cognitron is considered. The same structure of the cognitron can also be used to classify objects according to patterns of predetermined properties.

REFERENCES

1. M.W. Firebaugh, *Artificial Intelligence — A Knowledge Based Approach*, Burton: PWS Kent Publishing Company, 1989.
2. T. V. Geetha and R.K. Subramanian, "Natural Language Representation - A Connectionist Approach", *Proc. of the IEEE TENCON* 1991.
3. M. Fanty "Context-free Parsing in Connections Networks", TR-174, Rochester, NY: University of Rochester, Department of Computer Science, 1985.
4. Kunihiko Fukushirna, "Cogitron : A Self-organising Multilayerad Neural Network", *B Cybernetics* 20, 1975.

18

MANAGING THE TEST PHASE USING RELIABILITY MODELS

Software reliability modeling is of increasing interest to software developers and managers. The key to long-term competitive advantage lies in managing software quality effectively and economically. One of the most difficult phases during software development is the system test phase. During system test it is difficult to decide when testing is enough. Also resource allocation during testing is to be planned. Reliability modeling can be applied to manage the test phase effectively. This paper describes the results of the use of reliability models during testing in a project at TCS.

Choosing the Reliability Model

There is considerable literature on reliability models and their use in software projects. See[1] for a survey. Most of the models measure the reliability growth process of finding and fixing defects in a software product. While some models use the residual defects per 1000 lines of non - comment source statements as a measure of quality, users never perceive a product in terms of number of lines of code. Some of the newer models use defect arrival rate as a measure of reliability. These models differ in their use of time Calender time, execution time or testing hours is used as basis. While some have argued that the models on execution time give the best estimates (see[2]) it is very difficult to measure execution time without the use of tools. Moreover measuring execution time is difficult due to practical considerations. On the other hand estimates from models based on calender time are often coarse and managers are reluctant to base their decisions on those estimates. Hence we chose the Goel - Okumoto model which is based on measuring defects per hour of testing.

The Goel-Okumoto Model

The Goel-Okumoto model assumes that between software changes the number of defects observed during each hour of testing will follow a Poisson distribution with a constant mean. This defect rate includes the new and repeat defects. If the observed defects are fixed immediately, then the parameter will be decreasing. In this case we have a non-homogeneous Poisson process and the defect arrival rate tends to decrease exponentially as the test progresses. However the correction of defects is done in batch and the ideal state of instantaneous fixing is not attained in practice. But if we count only the new defects found each hour, then the assumption of instantaneous fixing is simulated and the model becomes applicable.

The functional form of the model can be stated as fellows:

If D(n) denotes the defect arrival rate after finding n defects then

D(n) = DO exp (- cn)

where DO is the initial defect arrival rate.

Using the Model

We applied the Goel - Okumoto model to a 80,000 lines of code product developed at TCS. This product was expected to have a large user base and due to the user characteristics a very low failure rate was desired. The development process was closely monitored, but due to market pressures the requirements changed substantially. When the system test phase started the test process was monitored using reliability models. The test was planned very meticulously and elaborate procedures were set up to capture the defect arrival data. The data capture was the responsibility of the test team. The development team analysed the defects thoroughly and classified them by severity and type. For the most severe defects causal analysis was also done and the observations from causal analysis were used during the fixing of defects. This considerably minimised the defect introduction due to fixing;

Setting the Release Criteria

The release decision must be based on

— functionality completeness
— performance specifications met
— no serious defects and
— defect arrival rate.

It is difficult to estimate a reasonable defect arrival rate for a product with a large user base. For the product under discussion, a defect arrival rate of 0.05 defects per hour was set as the release criterion. The system test phase concluded with an arrival rate of 0.04 defects per hour and the product proved extremely reliable in the field. An analysis of the field defects also showed that most of the defects were due to environment reasons and were reported by only 2% of the users.

Applying the Model

Once the release criterion was set, the model was used to manage the test process. Fitting the model to the most recent data, the defect arrival rate for the next few hours of testing was estimated. Sometimes the test team found less number of errors than estimated. But when the test team was reassigned the defect arrival rate improved and matched closely with the expectations. This reassignment was done frequently to keep the test process efficiency at optimum levels.

GOEL-OKUMOTO MODEL

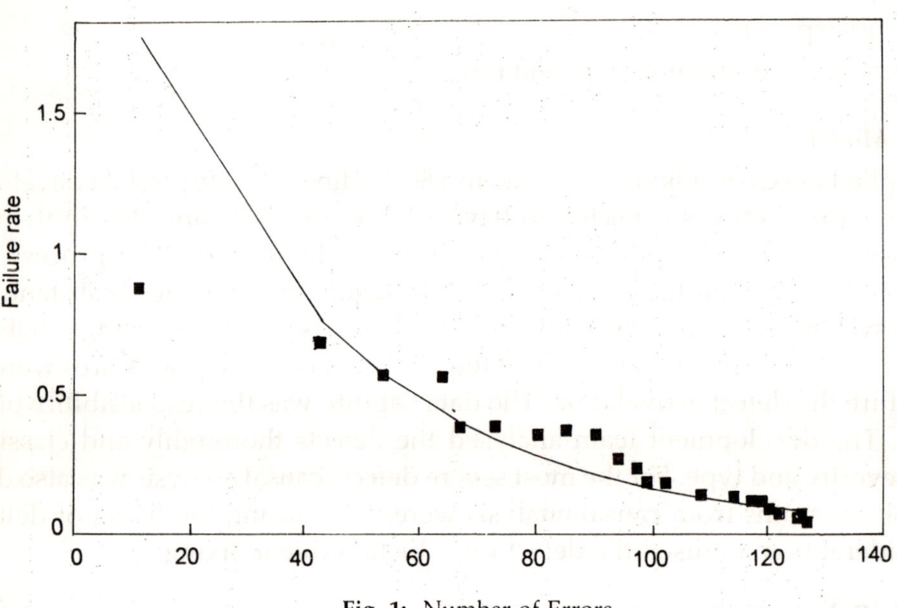

Fig. 1: Number of Errors

Even when the actual defect arrival rate matched with the expectations, care was taken to analyse the defects found to ensure that a sufficient number of high seventy defects are found.

The management could take decisions on resource allocation for the testing process using the estimates from the model. Setting a target for the test team also helped to measure the effectiveness of testing and take corrective action when the effectiveness was below expectations.

Fig. 1 shows the plot of D(n) for system test data. We have used nonlinear least squares to fit the model to the data. The closeness of fit was found to be 86%.

The model also helped to estimate the support requirements. The support team was just sufficient to meet the field requirements.

The number of defects found per hour of testing during the system test phase has proved to be a good metric and is useful for managing the test phase. It also gives valuable input for estimating resource requirements for testing and support.

A REUSE FRAMEWORK FOR ORGANISING SOFTWARE DEVELOPMENT EXPERIENCE

In all kinds of engineering application it is a well-know fact that the use of experience gained from earlier development is an important asset in the development of new systems. Domain experience boosts productivity. No application development or afford to have the luxury of starting every time form the scratch. But in case of software development, the reuse of experience is still confined to individual programmers or analysts. Most often reuse occurs by accident rather than by design. The transformation of this coincidental reuse into an institutionalised concept will be the key to improve software productivity.

A software component is considered reusable if the effort required to reuse it is much smaller than the effort required to implement a components with the some functionality.[3] The software reuse can be realised in the following levels of increasing complexity as:

- Package Level
- Library Level
- Source Code Level
- Design information Level and
- Analysis information level.

Package level reuse is the most established kind of reuse, in the form of compilers, editors, database packages and so on. Library level reuse also is in existence for a long time in the form of mathematical routines, graphics library etc. Source code reuse is also becoming popular. The concept of reuse should not end with code. The exploitation of design information, and in certain cases analysis information, associated with the code is very important. This is possible only through a judicious organisation of an integrated repository containing this information.

There are certain technical and managerial problems restricting the practicability of organised reuse. The following discussion addresses these problems and suggests ways to improve its current status.

The Effect of Reuse on Productivity

This section reports the data derived from the experience of using reusable modules Table - 1 shows the details of three sets of reusable modules developed during the course of the development of simulation software. Table - 2 describes the details of some full fledged pack ages developed using the reusable code.

The language used for the development of all these systems is Turbo Pascal. The unit feature available with turbo pascal helps a great deal in packaging the reusable modules and it provides some amount of data abstraction. The systems mentioned in Table 2 were developed for the simulation of different aspects of defence applications.

TABLE 1

Reusable Modules

		Reusable Modules	
	User Interface(l)	*Graphics(2)*	*Numeric(3)*
Total No of Modules :	19	45	10
Lines of Code :	1507	1050	250
Number of Global Variables :	6	17	2

TABLE 2

Systems Developed with Reuse

		Resuble Modules		
	System 1	*System 2*	*System 3*	*System 4*
Components invoked from User Interface 0) :	11	13	10	12
Graphics (2) :	37	34	31	28
Numeric (3) :	1	3	3	4
Lines of Code	2005	2140	1872	2024
User defined functions Lines of Code :	2689	3305	968	2663
Percentage of code from reusable sets :	42.71	39.30	65.91	43.18

Planned Reuse against Accidental Reuse

A comparative study was made to check the difference between code designed for reuse and coincidental reuse.

Experiment

The experiment has made use of the following sets of codes:

1. Code derived from a graphical user interface package developed as part of a - project.
2. User interface modules of Table - 1.
3. Graphic system modules of Table - 1.

The set 1 contains all the features available in the latter, but was developed as a stand alone package with little thought for reuse. Modules mentioned in sets (2) and (3) are specifically designed for reuse. The source language used for all the three sets was Turbo Pass. Two simulation systems with same specifications were developed, one using the code in set 1 and the other using set 2 and set 3.

Results

The study has led to the following conclusions:

1. Extensive modification was required on the code extracted from set 1.
2. The identification of reusable components has taken additional effort which is not required in the case of code designed for reuse.
3. The code which was not designed for reuse lack memory efficiency and shows side effects due to non functionality.
4. Code not designed for reuse contains implementation dependent features which affects the generality of the Code.
5. Programmers do patch work on the code to remove the bugs when the project completion time approaches. This affects the functionality of the modules and leaves mysterious code. This phenomenon is called deadline effect.
6. The understandability of the program may be jeopardised due to lack of documentation.

From the results of the experiment; it is evident that the code identified from existing systems must be scrutinised and modified to suit reusability. The advantages of this activity was found worth the effort.

A Cataloging Scheme for Reusable Experience

How does one know that a reusable component exists for meeting the goal? If a component exists which meets the goal partially, how to decide the amount of modification required to make it useful? Answers to these questions will be very important in improving the practicability of software reuse. A hypertext based cataloging system presented here solves many of the practical problems restricting the software reusability.

The domain experience is organised if the hierarchical fashion with the top level consisting of the category of the module like user interface, file management, graphics, numeric and so on. The second level contains the module names included in each category along with its input-output details. The third level stores the specifications for each module. The fourth level stores the different kinds of module complexity metrics which gives an idea of the complexity of the module and the amount of testing needed if it is redeveloped. The fifth level stores the links from the module names to the source codes.

The category index helps in reducing the search for a particular reuse information required for a particular application. there is facility to access the second level directly which provides a list of all modules. This helps in identifying and recovering from any error made in categorisation.

Once the programmer is slightly familiar with the system, the second level is found to be the most accessed one. This level provides module names and their interface details. With The interface details available, the module can be used as a black box.

Reengineering and maintenance of systems as well as software reuse require more information than what is available in the code. Generally code has become synonymous with reusable object because it is the most visible one. But all kinds of software development experience can be reused if it can be organised properly. The third level of the proposed representation scheme provides for the archival of domain experience other than code. This level stores the requirements, specifications, test cases and related features.

The designer is more concerned with the third and fourth levels. The complexity metrics can be used as a metric in deciding the advantage of reusing a module. A very low complexity shows that the module can be reused if the specifications are matching, or else the redevelopment time may not be considerable. A high complexity shows that the advantage of reuse will be very high in terms of development effort. Also if the module is redeveloped, the testing requirements will be very high.

There is a widespread belief that source code is the most important form suitable for reuse and if the specifications match corresponding code can be automatically reused. This notion is correct in some cases, but not always. The implementation of a specification can be done in several ways. The parameters, affecting the efficiency, to be optimised depends on the application. Some applications may have critical objectives of optimising the execution time, memory efficiency or both as in the case or real time systems. In case of such applications, the examination of code also may become important. The fifth level along with the complexity metrics helps in analysing the code for required optimisation.

Identification of Reusable Components

There has to be some guidelines for identifying reusable components from an already existing system. Caldiera and Basili [3] describes a way to automate the process of extracting reusable components from an existing system. This method is helpful in reducing the manual effort required for analysing large chunks of text containing source code.

One of the criteria they suggested has been found misleading in certain cases. They have suggested that for a component to be qualified as reusable, its frequency of invocations in the system should be more than a particular threshold number of times. But this has been found unacceptable in the case of most of the numerical routines. No method could be identified to surpass this criterion other than manual inspection, once the components are identified through the application of software metrics.

The use of software complexity metrics is a rationale approach to identify the reusable components in a system. The modules identified for reuse should follow certain guidelines of reusability metrics[4] or should be modified to meet them. The general reusability metrics are:

- The components should be general and the use of global variables and implementation dependent static values should be minimal.
- It should avoid the use of hardware and operating system dependent features.
- The module should be well-documented and the specification and test cases should be available.
- Its coupling with other modules should be very tow.
- The module cohesion should be very high.

Impact of Object Oriented Paradigm on Reuse

The data-based-decomposition of objects, resulting in class hierarchies and inheritance promotes far more than the top down approach followed in structured methodologies[2] the empirical study described in[2] shows that the object oriented paradigm substantially improves productivity mainly due to its particular affinity to reuse. The study concluded with the help of statistical data that reuse promote higher productivity and object oriented paradigm provides incentives to reuse above those of the procedural paradigm.

The major features in object oriented programming which promote reuse are encapsulation, polymorphism and dynamic binding. The encapsulation sees that there is no side effect due to accidental modification of data contained in a class. This together with polymorphism enhances the modifiability without side effects.

Role of Management in Promoting Reuse

Human being by nature is possessive. The very idea of reuse centres around sharing of information and experience to improve the productivity of the organisation. Hence this idea must be more attractive to the management than the individuals concerned. The organisation must have a well planned strategy to promote the development of software with reusability in mind. There should be incentives to promote reusable designs and code as well as for using it.

Conclusions

The idea of reusability is a well known concept. But this is not being utilised in a well planned manner in the case of software development. The best way to improve the productivity, quality and reliability of the software is the reuse of development experience. Some of the practical problems limiting reusability are discussed.

An integrated framework, for organising and representing all phases of software development experience is presented. This representation scheme is helpful in understanding, evaluating and planning all aspects of software reuse.

REFERENCES

1. V.R. Basili and H.D. Rombach, *Software Engineering Journal*, Sep. 91.
2. J.A. Louis et al., *An Empirical Study of the Object Oriented Paradigm and Software Reuse*, OOPSLA '91.
3. G. Caldiera and V.R. Basili, Identifying and Qualifying Reusable software Components, *IEEE Computer*, Feb., 1991.
4. C.V. Ramamoorthy et. al., *Programming in the Large*, IEEE Trans. on Software Engineering, July 1986.
5. R.G. Lanergan and C.A. Grasso, *Software Engineering with Reusable Designs and Code*. IÈEE Trans. on Software Engineering, Sep. 1934.
6. P. Freeman, *Reusable Software Engineering: Concepts and Research Directions*, ITT Proceedings of the workshop on Reusability in programming, 1983.
7. B.W. Boehm, Improving Software Productivity, *IEEE Computer*, Sep., 1987.

19

AN INTEGRATED FRAMEWORK FOR INFORMATION RESOURCE MANAGEMENT

Business management has traditionally involved managing four resources—capital, personnel, facilities and materials. In the last two or three decades, a fifth resource, namely information, has gradually gained importance in the industry and sharpened the competitiveness of many firms in the market place.

While definite advances have been made in Information technology and to some extent in information planning also, successful information resource-management calls for equal advancement in all the factors/dimensions that together enable effective employment of the resource. Lack of such an integrated approach has often stopped us from channelling our efforts to those areas where the least advances have been made, for instance, in the development of Information Managers.

This chapter suggests a framework for analysing the state of information Resource Management and delineates the progress industry has made in the usage of this resource. It further identifies the areas where future efforts have to go in.

A Framework for Resource Management

The framework would consist of three basic dimensions — Resource Identification and Acquirement, Resource Employment Facilitator and Resource Manager, which together would define the resource system and a feedback mechanism, Resource Effectiveness Measure.

(a) Resource Identification and Acquirement

Identification of the resource is the critical first step in the entire process. It is also required to identify the part of the business that requires this resource and decide as to how this resource can be used to further the business. One also needs to examine the cost and source of the resource and as to how it can be acquired.

(b) Resource Employment Facilitator

This includes the tools/techniques required to employ the resource productively.

(c) Resource Manager

Trained personnel are required to manage the resource effectively. The resource manager would be expected to play the role of the resource sourcer, resource employer and resource auditor. He/she has to understand the potential as well as the limits of the resource.

(d) Resource Effectiveness Measure

It is required to measure the contribution of the resource to the business i.e., the effect of the resource on the business.

The indicator should be able to illustrate how/where exactly the resource is adding value to the product/service.

The above framework can be applied to any type of resource, be it capital, personnel or information. Figure 1 illustrates the framework using the example of "facilities" resource in an automobile plant.

Frame work Dimension	*"Facilities" Resource*
Res. Identification & Acquirement	What Machine is required for Manufacturing? Who has the technology? How can it be acquired and used? What would be the cost etc.
Res. Employment Facilitator	Environment Support to run the Machine — space, power etc.
Res. Manager	Skilled workman, shopfloor supervisor Maintenance engineer etc.
Res. Effectiveness Measure	Number of automobile parts produced/unit time Raw material consumed per unit part production.

Fig. 1

The rest of this article examines information resource management based on the above framework.

Information Resource

Information can be broadly defined as data that has been analysed and which is actionable or which facilitates decision making. Any transaction or process in the business world has a physical content as well as an information content. Generally the importance and the percentage of the information and physical contents would vary with the industry, for example, majority of the transactions in the bank industry would be information intensive whereas opposite would be the case in the automobile industry.

While a major part of the information used by the firm would be generated within the firm, there are a lot of extraneous information which also becomes an input to the business process. Information becomes a resource when it can be fed into the business chain at some point where it can add value to the final product/service. The value addition may be achieved through cost reduction, quality improvement, improved distribution or any other factor, if the consumer perceives added value in the product then the information becomes a resource.

With respect to the framework described earlier, the four dimensions of information resource would be:

(a) Information Planning (Resource Identification & Acquirement)
(b) Information Technology (Resource Employment Facilitator)
(c) Information Manager (Resource Manager)
(d) Information Effectiveness Measure (Resource Effectiveness Measure)

Information Planning

A brief examination, of the definition of information given earlier, would show the reader that this is one resource which is almost limitless. The amount of data that is generated by a modern business organisation is very huge indeed. It could range from raw material procurement data to end-consumer behaviour data.

However, all this data that is generated cannot, obviously, be termed as resource. While it would seem that any data could be used in improving the business effectiveness and efficiency, the difficulty would be in identifying that data which is readily available and easy to capture, cost effective and gives accurate directions for decision making.

In the case of a consumer product marketing firm, for instance, any information on consumer behaviour/tastes/needs would be invaluable in tailoring the product to the consumer and thus increasing its value. But often, such data is either just not easy to capture and where it is easy, it may be too costly to be effective.

Often the value of data is multiplied manifold when it can be combined with other data to produce information i.e., when data is integrated. To demonstrate this point, let us take three different market data — relative price, market share and percentage of retail outlets stocking the product. These three data taken separately do convey some message to the marketing manager. But considered together, they become a powerful tool to analyse the market and identify the reasons for the product's performance. It may indicate that the sales has been low not due to overpricing but due to lower product availability/exposure. While in practice data on more market variables may be required for making a good market analysis, it only goes to prove the point that the rewards of data integration are bound to be enormous.

However, it is not an easy task to achieve this data integration especially in large organisations with data collection systems of all hues and colours. If proper planning is not done at the initial stages itself when the transaction systems are built, later on costly bridges may need to be built to integrate the data.

Thus it is critical to plan which data has to be acquired and how it has to be used so that the business is served and the information generated becomes a resource rather than a sunk cost.

The application systems that would evolve from the information planning would fall into two broad groups : Operational, and Planning.

Operational systems are these which directly support the day-to-day business operations. In most industries the first step in computerisation has been taken in building these systems. However, most of these systems have created information islands due to lack of integration, reducing considerably their effectiveness. Further the planning systems depend primarily on the data collected through the basic transaction systems, to plan the future business operations. If the data coming from the various systems are disparate and cannot be analysed together, then the planning systems would be as good as non-starters.

With the availability of powerful Relational Data Base Management Systems, with flexible data extraction facilities like SQL and the ability to maintain integrated databases, future efforts would be directed in integrating these data islands. The first step should be in defining the data architecture for the entire organisation and ensuring that all future systems follow this data plan. Only such a co-ordinated cross-functional effort would result in integrated databases, which would then form the foundation stone for all future planning systems.

Information that is generated by Operational and Planning systems could have strategic or non-strategic value. Information is said to have strategic value when it directly supports the business strategy of the firm and provides clear-cut competitive advantages in the market place.

But how does one identify the information that would be of strategic value and the systems implications of this? There are several schools of thought proposing different information planning methodologies. Most of these methods try to define the systems by identifying the information which directly support the business objectives of the firm and improves the value of the product.

The more popular among these would be Porter's Five Forces model & Value chain analysis, Rocket's Optical Success Factor method, Wiseman's Strategic Option Generator and Ives and Learmonth's Customer Resource Life Cycle method. A brief description of each of these methods[1] is given below.

(a) *Porter's Five Forces Model*: This method—follows from the five forces of industry competition as identified by Porter —bargaining power of suppliers/ buyers, threat of substitute products/new entrants and industry rivalry. This model could be used to identify the information that would yield competitive advantage by defending the firms against these forces or influencing them in its favour.

(b) *Value Chain Analysis* — Porter & Millar's value Chain Analysis divides a firm's activities into the technologically and economically distinct activities it performs, called value activities, which add value to the final product/ service. This model can be used to identify the information that can help perform, support or manage value activities, optimise or co-ordinate activities across linkages.

(c) *Rockart's Critical Success Factor:* As a first step the factors that are crucial to the success of the business objectives of the firm are identified. The information implications of these CSFs are then derived and systems planned to meet those information needs.

(d) Wiseman's *Strategic. Option Generator-* This model identifies five generic market thrusts (differentiation, cost, innovation, growth, alliance) and there strategy targets (customers, suppliers, competitors) and provides a check list of analytical questions that would clarify the firm's business strategy. More than pin-pointing the specific application for development, this method enables defining the direction of IT-Strategy connection.

(e) *ives & Learmonth's Customer Resource Life Cycle method:* This model focuses on the right hand end of the firm's value chain i.e. on the linkage between the firm and its customers. It splits the life cycle of how a customer acquires a product/service into four phases : Requirements, Acquisition, Stewardship & Retirement. The objective is to see in which of these phases information can be harnessed to improve the customer service.

Of late, many organisations have undertaken information planning exercises based on one or more of the above methodologies. However, the involvement of functional management has been limited and to a great extent these efforts have revolved around the Information Systems Department If information is considered as important a resource as say, capital or personnel, then should not the planning of this resource also be the concern of the top management and the functional managers?

Considering the fact that the business conditions are changing continuously, information planning has to be an on-going exercise rather than a one-off effort. Only this could ensure that the information plans reflect the changing business objectives of the firm.

Thus the information plan should be integrated into the annual business plan of the firm. While the details of the plan could definitely be worked out by the IG dept., the top management should insure that the overall information plan is synchronous with the other business plans every year.

Information Technology

The facilities required to capture, store, manipulate and distribute data and information, could broadly be called as Information Technology. Contrary to popular misconception, I.T, is not just computers, although they form a major part of it. I.T. consists of the following:[4]

(a) *Computers*—this is a central component of I.T. and ranges from microchip based personal computers to supercomputers. It also includes minicomputers, mainframes and workstations. Revolutionary technologies like RISC are making computers more compact and power packed.

(b) *Telecommunications*—With recent advancements in the digital telecommunication, field, this has become a critical partner in the I.T. area. By networking company across geographical and organisational boundaries and linking customers suppliers with the organisation, the power of the computers is multiplied manifold. State of the technology includes digital switching and equipment which rely on fibre optics and satellite for actual transmission Electronic Data Interchange, Integrated Digital Services Networking and video-conferencing.

(c) *White collar productivity tools*—Personal productivity software tools like word-processing s/w spreadsheet, project management s/w, CASE, CAD eta. would be included in this category. They are basically meant to enhance the efficiency of the knowledge worker.

(d) *Blue collar productivity tools*—The most popular component in this category would be industrial robots which perform a lot of tasks on the shopfloor.

(e) *Smart Products*—Image Processing s/w, Interactive voice Response systems, etc. from this category.

The above classification is not the only way to categorise I.T.. However, it shows the range of products/services that together comprise I.T.

Till a few years ago, the two major factors restraining the widespread deployment of I.T. had been the high cost and the lack of standards among manufacturers. However with the arrival of powerful personal computers, workstations and RISC based minicomputers the cost of the computers have reduced considerably.

A study conducted in the US[2] has shown that 1 dollar worth of computing today would have cost 5000 dollars in 1970. In 2010 it would cost 2/100th of a cent!! Transmission cost is reducing at double this rate. In fact the price/performance ratio of computer technology has been reducing at an annual compound rate of 40% in the last five or six years.

In recent times, concerted efforts have been made at many forums like the OSF, ACE etc. to set standards for the computing industry. Adoption of UNIX as the standard operating system is in itself a major step in this direction. The move towards Open Systems Architecture is bound to make it possible for the user to move data and applications across different hardware and software platforms with ease. This in turn enables the user to adapt to a new technology as and when it is introduced and without sacrificing earlier investments.

In addition, many major vendors like IBM, Digital have introduced facilities management service which would further reduce the cost; facilities management refers to a service where the vendor undertakes to run and maintain a client's computer system either at the client's premises or at the vendors own place. This would help the client in avoiding investment in dedicated I.T. professionals, assuring the reliability of the service/systems and reducing the overall costs.

Thus with reduced costs and standardisation moves, the initial constraints no longer hold. But has the business been able to exploit the situation? Unfortunately, the answer is no.

We have reached a point where technology is improving at so rapid a rate that before the user could start exploiting a technology, a new and more complex technology is introduced by the vendor. This is especially true of computers and telecommunication facilities.

As will be evident later on, unless the development in I.T. is matched by progress in other dimensions of the resource management framework, the fruits of I.T. are likely to remain unexploited.

Information Manager

By definition, any person who collects/uses/distributes information would qualify as an information manager. As the information manager has the responsibility of identifying and acquiring the resource and employing it, he/she has to know both the business as well as information technology.

Traditionally, these two jobs have been carried out by different departments — the functional department personnel identify the information requirements arising from the business and the systems personnel manage the technology to meet these information requirements.

Although such a division of labour would appear logical, in practice the pendulum has swung too much to the extremes — the user does not know the technology and the systems personnel does not know the business, leading to a very damaging communication gap.

Various methods ranging from decentralising the IT. function, introduction of profit centre concept for IT., etc. to job rotation of IT. personnel have been proposed to overcome the above problem. Many firms have even implemented some of these solutions but with mixed results. The major drawbacks associated with the above methods include lack of data discipline & system integrity, lower motivation levels of IT. personnel, etc.

It would be relevant at this point to examine the following issues. What would be the common skills that should be developed in all information managers? How should the organisation create the atmosphere where the functional managers and the I.T. manager can leave their respective specialisations behind and work together as information managers? To what extent should the IT. manager get specialised?

An information manager should have the ability to analyse the business situation and identify potential information resource. Since by definition, a sales manager as well as an IT manager are both information managers, the above skill would also serve as the common ground for meeting. Traditionally, the methodology to develop information managers has been to recruit specialist and expect them to pick up knowledge of the business from their job itself. Educational efforts have been limited to conducting training programs on technology to user personnel.

Research work[3] has showed that efforts to develop an information manager would have to start at the recruitment stage itself. It would be impractical to expect every person to have a thorough knowledge of the business as well as technology. The need for specialisation cannot be simply wished away.

However, each business should be able to define the extent of specialisation required of its I.T. manager, based on the type of industry they are in. In general the profile of the I.T. manager should be that of a well rounded generalist with good: interpersonal skills, required specialised knowledge and the ability to understand the business well. Regular sessions should be conducted wherein the IT. managers and the functional managers sit together and analyse the business situation using structured tool/techniques. This would ensure that the business priorities are well understood by the IT. managers ar.d the information systems implications are derived keeping these in mind. Such an effort would also ensure that all information managers share a similiar perception of the business and communicate using the same language.

While there are no easy solutions to the questions posed earlier, it is clear from the above discussion that a lot more effort has to go in defining the role/skills of the information manager and developing the personnel with the required expertise.

Information Effectiveness Measure

As noted earlier, however appropriate and efficient the resource and its management be to the business if there is no good measure of its contribution to the business, future investments in the resource are likely to go astray. Having said this, one should also realise it is not always easy to measure resource effectiveness especially when the resource is personnel, information etc.

Some of the qualities of a good resource effectiveness indicator would be that it is easy to measure, facilities Uniform interpretation and clearly indicates areas of strengths and weaknesses of resource management. Unlike capital or machinery, information is one resource whose effect on the business is difficult to pin-point and me sure, and even if measured is prone to subjective interpretation.

A direct result of this has been that investments made in this resource have been termed as "acts of faith rather than rational choice. This situation was acceptable as long as the resource was used purely for operational purposes and the investments were not high. However, when we are looking for strategic advantages from information and when the investments made are relatively higher, any mismanagement is bound to effect the business adversely. Although research in this area has been by and large limited, some methods of measuring information management effectiveness have been proposed. It would not be within the scope of this article to examine each of them. However, we will briefly describe one such measure which has also become popular in the business community.

Critical Success Factor

First suggested by D. Ronald Daniel in 1966 and later modified by John F. Rockart in 1979, the CSF method aims at identifying those factors whose success is critical for the business to be effective. Although first applied by Daniel to industry in general, Rockart extended it to individual managers as well as organisations. While the CSF methodology has been extensively used in information Planning exercises, the use of this methodology for measuring the effectiveness of information management has not been well documented in literature.

Once the business objectives/strategies and its CSFs have been identified, the information implication of each of these CSFs should be defined. These should then be prioritised depending on the criticality of the information to the CSFs.

The effectiveness of information management is a function of three factors — the purpose served by the information, its timeliness & accuracy, and the cost of obtaining the information (technology, manpower etc.).

The CSF served by the information is a direct indicator of the purpose served. Since the linkage between CSF and business is already defined the effective of information on the business can also be found out. It would then be required to compare the cost of the information with the above benefit derived by the business. Although this certainly would lead to subjective interpretation, the merit of this method lies in being able to link the information with the business in a direct manner.

Conclusion

The resource management framework described above could be likened to a tripod (as shown in the figure 2) having the three basic dimensions as its legs, and upon which the business rests. If the tripod is to support the business, each of the three legs have to be equally strong. In certain business situations, the weakness in one of the dimensions may be complemented by the strength of the other two. However if the weakness in any of the dimensions goes below a certain threshold level, it is bound to result in the collapse of the resource system and hence reduce its effectiveness.

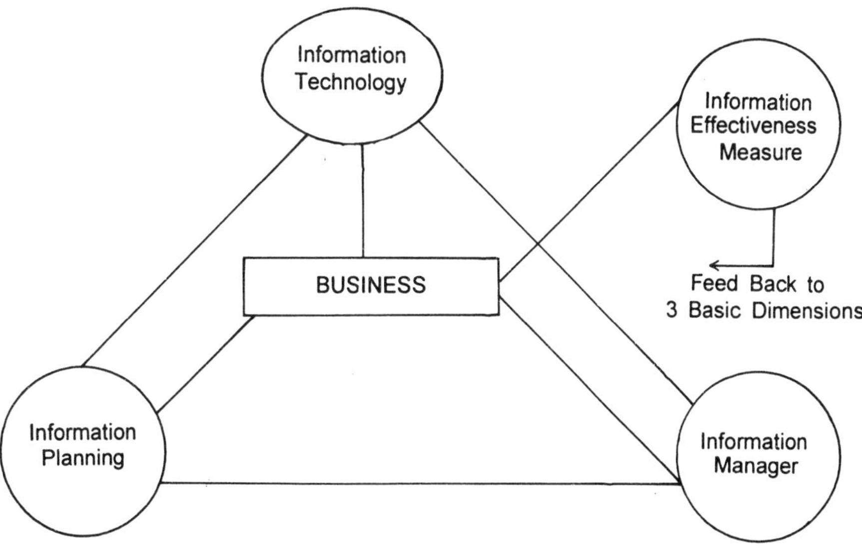

Fig. 2

As we have seen, the progress made by the industry in each or the dimensions of the information resource management framework vary. The last two decades have seen information technology growing in leaps and bounds. The 1980's also saw much detailed work being done in the information planning area. However, the importance of the information manager in the management of this resource has not been appreciated enough.

It would be fruitless to assume that we could exploit the information resource by just planning the systems properly or having the right technology to do it. The most challenging task in the next decade or so, in information management would relate to people and not technology. This would require combined efforts from top management, the IS department as well as the functional departments to promote an atmosphere where managers are motivated to exploit the potential of information resource and all skills required for this are imparted to them.

REFERENCES

1. Earl Michael, 'I.T. and Strategic Advantage : A Framework of Frameworks', *Information Management the Strategic Dimension*, pp. 33-53, Oxford University Press, 1988.
2. Hopper, Max. D., 'Rattling SABRE — New Ways to Compete on Information', *Harvard Business Review*, May-June 1990.
3. Lodahl, Thomas M. & Reddit, Kay Lewis, Aiming IS at Business Targets', *Datamation*, Feb. 15th 1989.
4. Morton, Michael Scott, 'Strategy Formulation Methodologies and I.T.', *Information Management - the Strategic Dimension*, pp. 54-67, Oxford University Press, 1988.
5. Porter; Michael E. & Millar, Victor E., How Information Gives You Competitive Advantage *Harvard Business Review*, July-Aug., 1985.
6. Rockart, John F. & Bullen C. V., *'A Primer on Critical Success Factors'*, Cambridge, MA.

20

INFORMATION TECHNOLOGY IN PRODUCTION MANAGEMENT

Computers have been in use in the Indian manufacturing scenario, especially in the engineering industries of the job / batch oriented type, for a long time. From time to time, there have been efforts to improve the extent and the scope of use of computers. In the beginning, computers were mainly used in factories to cover the more systematised areas and more understood areas like accounts, finance and other systems like shares, debenture issues etc. Oflate the production areas namely, Sales Forecasting, Bill of Materials (BOM), Materials Requirement Planning (MRP) etc. are being computerised. Also systems like MRPII (Manufacturing Resource Planning), factory systems like Identification of Items for Issue and Storage etc have been computerised.

In some factories, optimisation of metal cutting by nesting and NC/CNC machine input tape generation and to some extent quality control / inspection methods have been the areas where micro computers have been employed. In some cases these are interfaced with work stations and advantages have been gained.

In this article, we examine different aspects of the present level of computerisation and the scope of further areas of computerisation especially in the batch type of manufacturing industries.

Objectives

The objectives of this study are as follows:

1. To assess the extent of impact of computerisation in the production management area.
2. To assess the benefits of computerisation as felt by the production personnel.
3. To identify areas for further improvement in the use of computers in the production control systems.
4. To assess gaps at different levels of design and implementation.

The methodology adopted is by means of response to questionnaire and also by face to face interaction with some of the manufacturing personnel like production managers, engineering managers, purchase managers, engineers in the areas of sales, productions, shops, EDP and other areas. In some cases, discussions were held with senior management personnel in the production areas. This article reflects some of the findings that have come through in this type of interactions.

Major Findings

Looking at the responses and the comments of the respondents to the questionnaires and also based on interviews, the following major findings can be summarised:

1. As far as the scope and extent of computerisation in production management areas is concerned, generally there is good coverage of computerisation. This is as high as 80% in some of the industries where computerisation has been in vogue for more than 15 years. In the factories where computerisation process is on for less than 5 years, the finance and other related applications take more precedence. But once computers are in use for more than five years, progressively the total time spent in computerisation, management attention in the use of computers, as well as the coverage is more on the production management side.
2. The comparison between the coverage of financial & other systems and the production oriented systems also is interesting. It looks that there is very good percentage of computerisation in terms of the time spent on the financial applications in the initial stages. This is almost about 60% of the total computerisation time and computer resources. This also is true for factories where computers are in use for more than 5 years at the minimum.
3. As regards the benefits from computerisation, we find certain interesting facts. There is reduction in inventory, reduction in production lead time and improvement in work flow. These are the major benefits.
4. As far as the reduction of man power is concerned, people do not see this happening. This is also based on the fact that many computerised production applications are supplementary to the human effort and cannot replace the human effort.
5. One area where more implementation is required by using computers is Scheduling. In this complex area, results are not seen highly by the production engineers.
6. Also in improving capacity utilisation, the benefits are seen to be doubtful.

7. The improved work flow and reduction in the lead time seem to have been caused by good documentation, standardisation of procedures and timely release of shop orders and control of information and documentation in the production shops.
8. The areas where more computerisation is required are seen to be scheduling, shops, (information gathering as well as computerised data acquisition etc). Also in the areas of BOM (Bill of materials), stores, purchase and design; a lot of computerisation need is felt.

In addition to the above major findings, these are certain interesting comments that are made. Those are also indicators to the computerisation requirements.

9. It is felt that improvement in productivity can be obtained by going into the basics of manufacturing processes and improving the layouts, methods and training the people. Only then it is felt that Information Technology can help.
10. There is a strong feeling that MRP, MRPII type of applications need to be developed with more design inputs coming from the engineers and managers in the production area.
11. It is also felt that where there are more plants and more factories are under the same umbrella; if computerisation is done throughout covering all functions, the needs of production areas will be covered well.

    There is also a view that data collection must be made automatic as well as it is to be made the responsibility of the user. This means that the ownership is to be shifted to the user regarding the quality of the data.

    As the turnover increases, the number of products also increase and there is greater realisation that Bill of Materials and engineering data has to be of very good quality. The whole process of coding of part numbers, tools and other related standardisation processes has been realised to be the corner stone for success in computerisation.

    Though the above findings are of general nature, some of the items are felt to be more important in some factories, and some others in other factories. As we get more responses (as this is still an on-going study) the above findings may alter in their priority but the facts themselves may not undergo any radical change. In the next few paragraphs a few of the areas covered in the study will be discussed in detail.

Scope and Extent of Computerisation

When we look at the scope and extent of computerisation in the production management areas, two points come to the fore. They are that with more experience in use of computers in any factory, managers have shifted their emphasis from Information Technology in finance areas to the production areas. The second one is that both in the starting period of computerisation as well as after the stabilisation period (10 years to 15 years) the accent is on the standardisation of processes & methods and quality of the data. Also with the number of years of use of computers increasing, there is greater degree of level of implementation of production related systems. It looks as though around 10 years of use of computers, fairly the applications flatten out. The overall use of computers in production management looks to be quite high in almost all the organisations that have been studied and this is based on the fact that there is as high as 80% of the usage of computers in the production areas (Refer Table 1). This means; not many new applications get added. This is reflected by the fairly constant rating of the use of computers in production oriented systems compared to financial systems. This has been constant at 75% (refer Table 2) in factories where computers are in use beyond 10 years.

Though this may look to be too high a figure the very fact that production related areas cover from sales through purchase, inventory, production planning and control, material requirement planning, work order and shop order release, master production scheduling and load schedule of work centres, production documentation and production progress including finishing goods inventory etc., it can be seen that coverage is not unduly high. It is also a fact that some of the peripheral systems like costing, machine maintenance scheduling, vendor quotations processing are also viewed as production applications. As such other than conventional applications like payroll and personnel, all other applications appear to be, production applications. This in a way gives greater acceptability for computers throughout the factory and hence this high figure of coverage of computerisation of the production areas.

The coverage, in factories where computer usage is fairly recent may be less. This is likely to come out in the further study that is going on.

Table 1 gives the coverage of overall use of computers in production management areas. Table 2 gives the level of implementation of production oriented systems vis-a-vis the financial and other systems.

Benefits of Computerisation in Production Management Areas

1. Benefits Seen

When we look at the benefits that have accrued, there is reason for satisfaction for the computer professionals. Many production engineers feel that the reduction in inventory is a major benefit. This may be because most of the earlier production applications areas have started with stores and inventory control in the Indian industries.

TABLE 1

Overall use of Computers in Production Management Areas

S. No.	*Usage*	*% of Responsibilities in the Questionnaires*
1	High	37%
2	Medium	51%
3	Poor	12%

TABLE 2

Level of Implementation of Production Oriented Systems Compared to Financial and Other Systems

S. No.	*Usage*	*Computers in use in Factory for*		
		> 15 Years	*10- 15 Years*	*5-10 Years*
		% of Responses in the Questionnaires		
1	Very High	—	—	9%
2	High	25%	27%	13%
3	Equal	50%	45%	35%
4	Low	25%	28%	43%
5	Very Low	—	—	—

Next area where benefits are seen is reduction in overall lead times of product manufacturing cycle. This is to be seen vis-a-vis the benefits seen in the improvement in work flow. When the work flows smoothly through the sites/shops there is less waste of time in queues, in the search of documents and in making parts move as per the final delivery dates of the products. This improved work flow naturally leads to a reduction in the overall lead time of the products. This is reflected in Table 3 as the benefits.

2. *Benefits Not Visible*

For a long time both management and the workers held a notion that computers replace man power. It is seen that reduction of manpower is not there or is there to a very small extent (refer Table 4). This also is good, in that the manufacturing and production functions being highly critical, are normally supplemented by computerisation. This has not resulted in any heavy reduction of man power. The other area where benefits are not seen and improvement is definitely sought; are in scheduling and capacity utilisation. This may be due to the fact that the computerisation process itself has become complex especially in batch oriented industries where many products, many models and a lot of batches run in the shop floor at the same time. Though some attempts have been made at scheduling through the computer, there seems to be a gap at the shop floor level between the schedules prepared on computers and the actual work loading that is happening. This area needs to be studied further to arrive at any definite conclusions.

Table 3 gives the benefits seen and Table 4 gives the benefits not seen as per the respondents of the survey. The figures in % are the respondents who are deviating from a normal '3' rating in a 1 to 5 grading (1 = very high to 5 = very low).

TABLE 3

Benefits Seen

S. No.	*Benefits*	*% of Respondents in the Questionnaires*
1	Reduction in Inventory	38% — high to very high
		50% — medium
2	Reduction in lead time	35% — high to very high
		42% — medium
3	Improvement in work flow	33% — high
		44% — medium

Potential Areas of Improvement in Use of Computers

When we look at the potential areas where further improvements are both necessary and possible, we are in for a bit of education. This is because many feel that design, scheduling and shops need to be further computerised. Bill of Materials and stores put together (i.e MRP areas) also still are marked as areas where more computerisation is required. This is an interesting fact that even after large doses of computerisation in these areas, there is still potential for computerisation. This is both in coverage as well as use of more technology like bar code identification, direct data acquisition from the machines and automatic storage and retrieval of parts etc.

TABLE 4

Benefits not Seen

S. No.	*Benefits*	*% of Respondents in the Questionnaires*
1	Reduction of man power	36% — low of very low
2	Improvement in Scheduling	35% — low to very low
3	Improvement in capacity utilisation	35% — low to very low

When we look at the turnover and its relation to the demand for more computerisation, the Bill of Material and stores areas constantly demand more attention. Especially when the turnover is greater than 100 crores, the demand in these areas is quite high. This may be because with the number of products, parts, assemblies and operations, and inventory items, the whole complexity increases (with the turnover) and hence this demand. Also the areas of shops and design coupled with scheduling require more attention as can be seen in Table 6.

TABLE 5

Areas Where More Computerisation is Required

S. No.	*Area*	*Turnover*		
		< 50 crores	*50-100 crores*	*> 100 crores*
		% of Respondents in the Questionnaires		
1	Design	18%	20%	14%
2	Bill of Material	1.0%	10%	20%
3	Stores	15%	10%	10%
4	Scheduling	33%	30%	33%
5	Shops	24%	30%	23%

Conclusion

It is seen that computers have been useful and have found good acceptability in the production management areas. It is also a fact that more computer applications and IT applications are required in areas like scheduling, design and logistics management, on-line data acquisition & control and other production areas. Only with imaginative use of computers and automatic data acquisition processes and direct data acquisition from computers and networking across the factories of an organisation; the aspirations of the production professionals can be met successfully.

TABLE 6

Areas Where More Computerisation is Required

S. No.	*Area*	*Computers in use in Factory to*		
		> 15 Years	*10- 15 Years*	*5- 10 Years*
		% of Respondents in the Questionnaire		
1	Design	28%	14%	24%
2	Bill of Material	14%	22%	7%
3	Stores	14%	14%	11%
4	Scheduling	14%	29%	38%
5	Shops	30%	21%	20%

The questionnaire used in this survey is at Appendix I.

APPENDIX

PRODUCTION MANAGEMENT AND COMPUTERISATION SURVEY QUESTIONNAIRE

1.	Name (Optional)	:	
2.	Designation	:	
3.	Area of your work in the organisation (Please tick as appropriate)	:	Purchase, Production Control, Works, Engineering/Design, General Management, Finance/Accounts, Personnel, Marketing EDP.
4.	Approximate Turnover	:	Rs. > 100 Crores 50 — 100 Crores 50 Crores
5.	Kind of Product / Business (Please tick as appropriate)	:	Engineering Industry Automobile Electronic Goods Others (please specify)

Note: Please answer all questions. Kindly give your independent assessment.

Sl. No	*Question*	*Answer (Please tick as appropriate)* 1	2	3	4	5
1.	How wide is the overall use of computers in production management areas in your organisation?	Very High	High	Medium	Poor	Very Poor
2.	Compared to financial and other systems; what is the level of implementation of production oriented systems?	Very High	High	Equal	Low	Very Low
3.	How long have computers been in use in your organisation?	> 15 yrs	10-15 yrs	5-10 yrs	2-5 yrs	< 2 yrs
4.	How do the workers accept computerisation?	Very High	High	Satis-factory	Low	Very Low
5.	What is the extent of time consumed in computerising production management areas.					

contd..

Sl. No	Question	Answer (Please tick as appropriate) 1	2	3	4	5
	5.1 Computer hardware selection purchase/upgradation	> 5 yrs	3-5 yrs	2-3 yrs	1-2 yrs	< 1 yr
	5.2 Systems Analysis and design	> 5 yrs	3-5 yrs	2-3 yrs	1-2 yrs	< 1 yr
	5.3 Programming	> 5 yrs	3-5 yrs	2-3 yrs	1-2 yrs	< 1 yr
	5.4 Implementation	> 5 5 yrs	3-5 yrs	2-3 yrs	1-2 yrs	< 1 yr
6.	What is your rating on perceived benefits of computerisation of production control activities?	Very High	High	Medium	Low	Very Low
	6.1 Improved productivity	V.High	High	Medium	Low	V.low
	6.2 Improved quality	V.High	High	Medium	Low	V.Low
	6.3 Streamlined flow of work	V.High	High	Medium	Low	V.Low
	6.4 Optimisation of inventory levels	V.High	High	Medium	Low	V.Low
	6.5 Reduction of paper work	V.High	High	Medium	Low	V.Low
	6.6 Reduction of manpower	V.High	High	Medium	Low	V.Low
	6.7 Capacity utilisation	V.High	High	Medium	Low	V.Low
	6.8 Better scheduling of load	V.High	High	Medium	Low	V.Low
	6.9 Reduction of lead times	V.High	High	Medium	Low	V.Low
7.	As compared to expectations of the above factors what is your rating of actual benefits.	Very High	High	Medium	Low	Very Low
	7.1 Productivity improvement	Very High	High	Medium	Low	Very Low
	7.2 Quality improvement	Very High	High	Medium	Low	Very Low
	7.3 Improvement in work flow	Very High	High	Medium	Low	Very Low
	7.4 Inventory reduction	Very High	High	Medium	Low	Very Low
	7.5 Paper work reduction	Very High	High	Medium	Low	Very Low

Sl. No	*Question*	*Answer (Please tick as appropriate)* 1	2	3	4	5
	7.6 Reduction of manpower	Very High	High	Medium	Low	Very Low
	7.7 Improvement in capacity utilisation	Very High	High	Medium	Low	Very Low
	7.8 Improvement in load scheduling on work centres	Very High	High	Medium	Low	Very Low
	7.9 Reduction of lead time	Very High	High	Medium	Low	Very Low
8.	How strongly do you feel that the system design specifications need to be given by production engineers/managers.	Very High	High	Medium	Low	Very Low
9.	Will an easy to use tool for design of PPC system help production engineers/managers to specify requirements and design of PPC systems better?	Very Well	Well	Medium	Low	Very Low
10.	How wide is the gap between Master (long range) production plan and micro-level shop load scheduling.	Min. gap	Medium gap	Satis-factory	Large gap	Very large gap
11.	How strongly do you feel that a simple relative priority fixation on computer (without straight jacket dates) for jobs can help shop level people in loading jobs appropriately.	Very Well	Well	Satis-factory	Poor	Very Poor
12.	What is your rating on the effectiveness of					
	12.1 In-house EDP	Very High	High	Medium	Poor	Very Poor
	12.2 Consultants	Very High	High	Medium	Poor	Very Poor
13.	Has computerisation helped you to understand					
	13.1 How high is the utilisation (wastage) of raw material?	Very Well	Well	Satis-factory	Low	Very Low

contd..

Sl. No	Question	Answer (Please tick as appropriate) 1	2	3	4	5
	13.2 How difficult it is to arrive at product mix to get best mix of raw material cost, availability and market demand.	Very Well	Well	Satis-factory	Low	Very Low
	13.3 Cost of storage of raw material?	Very Well	Well	Satis-factory	Low	Very Low
	13.4 Cost of storage of finished goods?	Very Low	Well	Satis-factory	Low	Very
	13.5 Cost of storage of intermediate inventory?	Very Low	Well	Satis-factory	Low	Very
14.	Where do you want more computerisation?	BOM	Scheduling	Stores	Shops	Design
15.	Would you like to give any other comments.					

(Please attach extra sheets.
if needed or please write on this page)

21

MANAGEMENT OF LARGE SOFTWARE PROJECTS

Analysing the structure of large software systems is one of the most frustrating and consuming aspects of software maintenance. Brooks in his classic papers, "No Silver Bullet" has pointed out that as soon as we attempt to diagram software structure we find it to constitute of not one but several graphs superimposed one upon another and these graphs represent the flow of control, flow of data, patterns of dependency, time sequencing etc. Inspite of the progress in simplifying and the number of structures of the software they remain essentially unvisualisable. Adhoc ways or developing programs and rapid prototyping reduce the quality of large software systems and thus make software management cumber some.

Several problems arise in the management of large systems. The relevant problems from the software engineering point of view include [1]

(a) Fuzzy requirements
(b) Continual changes in the requirements during development
(c) Prediction of the resource requirements
(d) Feasibility evaluation and testing
(e) Managing large number of developers.

As the software grows larger, programmers need to understand what the code does and what it is supposed to do before implementing a change. Lot of effort is required to

(i) Maintain the quality of the software being developed.
(ii) Eliminate redundancy to increase productivity.
(iii) Analyse complexity at module level and redesign to reduce complexity to an appropriate level.
(iv) Identify reusable components to increase productivity.

A software information system for understanding large software and providing quality management is one of the major challenges of the decade. Several systems are designed which provide information about existing software. Some of those are:

(a) *C Information Abstraction system (CIA):* This uses a conceptual model to convert textual description of a set of C-source modules into a set of object relationships. CIA provides relational views and textual views through invocation of relational queries. The relationships can be used to generate graphical information that snows the internal structure of C-programs. CIA aids to a certain extent in subsystem extraction for component packaging .[2]

(b) *Large Software System Information Environment (LaSSIE):* This incorporates a large Knowledge Base (KB), a semantic retrieval algorithm based on formal inference, a user interface using a graphical browser and a natural language parser. LaSSIEs KB provides an intelligent index that is attuned to the programmers' view of large systems. LaSSIE captures descriptions of reusable objects along with the architectural constraints embodied in the design of a sizable body of software. Inference is used to answer the programmers queries about reusable components.[3]

(c) *Other systems:* Several other software information systems have been proposed and reported in literature. These systems fall into the categories of

1. Relational Code Abstractors (Cscope)[7], Masterscope[8] which derive certain code level relationships from source code.
2. Program Management Databases (SODOS, [3] ALMA) which are primary designed to serve as repositories to aid the generation of documents, test scripts etc.
3. Reuse librarians (CATALOG[3], ADT[3] which retrieve software components for possible reuse.
4. SOFTMAN[5], a Program Information Abstraction system, provides various levels of abstraction which aid the software manager.

PIA systems decompose the source code into high level information abstractions using reverse engineering techniques and also provide design recovery. Design recovery emphasises the recovery of application domain knowledge that helps acnieve informative higher level abstractions beyond those created by examining only the source code. These abstractions include module breakdowns. Program Description Language, Reuse information Abstractions, Redundancy Information Abstractions.

In the following sections, the quality factors of large software systems, charasteristics of PIA systems, components of SOFTMAN-a PIA system, and SOFTMAN's usability in large software systems are discussed.

Quality Factors — Large Software Systems Management and the Experience

As the software grows large, the influence of quality factors becomes highly significant with respect to costs and productivity. Some of the important favors are-visibility, traceable reusability and maintainability. At all stages of software development, attempt has to be made to maximize these factors for high quality software. The other factors redundancy, complete and deadcode are to be minimised for high quality software These quality factors are vital in problem-free management of large software systems.

Software visibility is the ease with which information needed can be found and obtain software projects. The information can be design methodology, algorithms implement or documentation. The structure of the software and the control flow should be visible project team. This characteristic of software systems helps improve some of the other factors like traceability and maintainability. Visibility promotes understandability and in uncovering errors during the testing phase. Especially, in large software projects, when the group of programmers and analysts participate in the software development, visibility greatly enhances the interaction and communication among them.

In software projects, the human element is responsible for the development, support and maintenance of the system.[11] Coordination among the group of people involved is essential for successful software development. In general, initial phases of software life cycle go week, but during the development and testing phases the difficulty in visualizing the software becomes apparent Changing customer requirements, project prototyping and not conducting reviews at various stages of development contribute to the invisibility of software.

Traceability refers to the ability to trace *a* design representation or actual program component back to requirements.[11, 12] Analysis documents, test data and knowledge of the source code help making the system traceable. By automating the process of tracing between the various sources of knowledge, the process of understanding the software and finding the necessary information becomes simple and makes the software management and maintenance easier. Non-traceability leads to maintenance problems. Maintainability is the ease with which software can be understood, corrected, adapted ana/or enhanced .[11.] Understandability of the system structure, standardization of methods, resources and documentation are important factors affecting maintainability.

Reusability is an important factor influencing the productivity and quality. In any software project there will be some amount of reusable information which can be used within the project or across projects.[9] During each phase of the development life cycle, the future software requirements should betaken into account keeping in view of software reuse. In large software projects, where the requirements dictate the development of millions of lines of code, a reusable component library influences greatly the project costs and time.

A common problem faced by large software systems is redundant code. Invisibility and non-traceability often lead to code redundancy. Addition of a new functionality to an exiting module is generally not preferred considering the amount of changes to be reflected in the existing code. This leads to multiplication of lines of code performing same functions as similar code is available elsewhere in the software. The testing and debugging time also increase due to redundant code. Reducing redundancy leads to quality software with testing and maintenance processes simplified.

Complexity is another factor influencing all software systems [11,12]. Program complexity can be measured using McCabe's cyclomatic complexity and other metrics. These measures quantify the complexity and also can be used to drive the testing process. Cyclomatic complexity and Essential complexity are often needed for identifying fragile software architectures and have been well-highlighted in McCabe's paper.[12]

Deadcode is the code which is designed but not used. There may exist modules which might have been developed in the earlier phases, but not used in the actual code. This unused cede increases the code length and makes software debugging and management difficult.

PIA system can be utilized in identifying the above problems and in achieving high software quality and better management of software.

PIA Systems and Reverse Engineering

PIA systems work on reverse engineering principle. Software reverse engineering is defined as the process of analysing a system to identify the system's components and their relationship, and to create representations of the system in another form or at a higher level of abstraction.

Normally, the input to a PIA system is a set of source code ana the output is information in the form of higher level of abstraction. The abstraction is normally in the form of

(a) Program Specification
(b) Control Flow Diagrams, Data Flow Diagrams, and Structure Charts
(c) Program Descriptions
(d) Program Complexity Metrics
(e) Program Interface details
(f) Hypertext Broosing
(g) Program Documentation

Tools having the above features help to understand the software system

The above components are integrated and controlled by a fixed query interface engine with a powerful graphical interface. The Conceptual Model builder builds information repository into a set of indexed files. There will be a set of files for each Project The fixed query system has been designed to meet most of the general requirements that are needed to manage large software systems. This fixed query system has its own merits and demerits when compared to a variable query system 2.

Managing Quality Problems with Softman

The set of quality factors mentioned in section 2 are required to be maintained for a healthy software system and are difficult to maintain in large software systems. SOFTMAN features can be utilized to identify and solve the quality problems. The methods to identify and solve the above quality problems and other management issues of large software systems are illustrated in the following paragraphs.

Software Invisibility and Non-Traceability

SOFTMAN analyses the source code and produces structure chart as the basic display. A relation to the source code, global variables, macros can be obtained instantaneously with SOFTMAN. This helps in solving invisibility and non-traceability problems. The occurance of any function in the project can be easily browsed and the details and corresponding relations with other objects can be easily analysed on-line. The variable explanation and function explanation features provided in the system will facilitate to extract information about the system. Software is invisible because of lack of knowledge about application domain and because code is non-traceable or not understandable SOFTMAN provides the program information and explanation of the system at any point thereby providing visibility. The cross referencing of variables, maces and functions, which are easily accessible through browsers, aids in software traceability, maintainability and understandability.

Identifying fragile Software Architecture

Abnormal complexity of a system often leads to fragile architecture. In large software prototyping emphasis is given to meet user requirements than to reduce the complexity of the system. If the system is complex it is harmful in the long run particularly during maintenance and testing. SOFTMAN provides complexity metrics-McCabe's Cyclomatic and Algebraic complexities, Nesting Level and Decision Count that aid in analysing the components. If the complexity measure is abnormal the modules can be broken into smaller components to bring down the complexities to a reasonable level.

Redundancy

Redundancy in code, is a pattern of code getting repeated at different places in the same system. Manually identifying redundancy is impossible in large software systems. SOFTMAN identifies redundant components of the system that have arised due to invisibility and non-traceability during development.

Identifying redundancy is a difficult task. This is mainly a pattern matching problem. SOFTMAN creates a node for each module along with its attributes like complexity factor, size, the interfaces of the function, and the flow graph. Each node is matched with rest of the nodes for size, then some of the nodes will be eliminated and the remaining nodes are then verified for complexity metric. The nodes of close complexity factors are considered as potential candidates of redundancy and rest of the nodes are eliminated. Then the nodes are verified for their module interfaces, the number of inputs and the number of outputs of a function. A match is made for a flow graph of nodes. By the above technique the search area is considerably reduced.-SOFTMAN generates a list of modules of similar functionalities and manual methods can be operated on them.

Component Packaging

The initial layered design of large software systems is conceived to provide a large number of reusable primitives. Software developed has two types of components:

(a) Domain, independent components
(b) Domain dependent components

The domain independent components can be used across different software projects and the domain dependent components can be used across similar projects under consideration. SOFTMAN provides an environment for the domain specialist to identify reusable components and package the components like that of in ADA language. Identification of components is by browsing subtrees of structure chart and packaging of the components is automatic. ADA package contains package body and package description. A reusable component library is generated and components can be retrieved for later use.

Design Recovery

SOFTMAN analyses the structure chart, data dictionary and its relation and provides an environment to frame Data Row Diagrams (DFD) as an add in Design Recovery. Though the facility is automatic, provision is made for manual override of Data Row Diagrams. Manual override is provided to dub two or more processes into a single bubble, to rename the bubbles and to redefine the sources and sinks.

Deadcode Identification

SOFTMAN generates the complete call structure as a tree and the unconnected components as separate trees. All these separate trees unconnected to the main tree are identified as deadcode and the nodes are listed.

Conclusions

PIA systems offer a variety of facilities in making large software systems understandable, traceable and visible. AT&T Bell laboratories. New Jersy, Software Productivity Consortium, HENDON, VA, Dept. of Computer Science, University of Maryland and University of California and others are doing research in exploring relational, knowledge-based, semantic models to represent the abstracted program information. In most of the cases, the theme of research is representing information in high level abstraction languages automatically, generating POL, identifying and cataloging reusable components for future reuse and the aspect of designing reengineering environments. The idea is to attain productivity and quality of large software systems through PIA systems and reengineering environments. The authors are presently working on updating SOFTMAN for generating reusable component library from components generated and coordinating different high level design abstractions like PDL and Data Flow Diagrams for design recovery from large software systems and finally to visualize a reengineering environment.

REFERENCES

1. C.V. Ramamoorthy et al., "Programming in the large". *IEEE Trans. on Software Engineering*, Vol. SE-12, No. 7, July 1986
2. Y.F. Chen, M.Y. Nishimoto and C.V. Ramamoorthy, "The C Information Abstraction System", *IEEE Trans. on Software Engineering*, Vol. 16, No. 3, March 1990.
3. Prem K. Devanbu et al.. "Large Software System Information Environment (LaSSIE)", *Communications of the ACM*, Vol. 34, No. 5, May 1991.
4. Eric J. Byrne, "Software Reverse Engineering: A Case Study", *Software-Practice and Experience*, Vol. 21 (12), December 1991.

5. R. Srinivasan, S, Ganesan and K.R.S. Iyyengar, "SOFTMAN-Software Management Environment-A Project Manager's Workbench", *Proc. of the Indian Computing Congress*, Hyderabad, Dec. 1991.

6. Paul Oman, "Maintanance Tools", *IEEE Software*, May 1990.

7. W. Teitelman et al. "The Interlisp Programming Environment" *IEEE Computer*, Vol. 14, No. 4, April 1981.

8. J.L. Steffen, "Interactive Examination of a C Program with C scope", *Proc. USENIX Assoc.*, Winter Conf., January 1985.

9. V.R. Basili and H.D Rombach, "Support for Comprehensive Reuse" *Software Engineering Journal*, September *1991*.

10. F.P. Brooks, "No Silver Bullet : Essence and accidents of Software Engineering," *IEEE Computer*, April 1987.

11. R.S. Pressman, *Software Engineering : A Practitioner's Approach*, McGraw-Hill International Editions.

12. C.W. Butler and Thomas J. McCabe, "A Clinical Approach to Reverse and Reengineering", *Reverse Engineering News Letter*, January 1992.

22

INFORMATION TECHNOLOGY IN CONTROL SYSTEMS

Control System Terminology

A control system is an interconnection of components to provide a desired function. The portion of the system to be controlled is called the plant and the part doing the controlling is the controller. In control system design a controller is developed which will control the plant acceptably. When the measurements of plant response are available to the controller (which in turn generates signals affecting the plant) the configuration is feedback control system.

Control system design has a whole gamut of applications. The few examples mentioned below indicate its various fields of use.

The first example is the automatic landing system of an aircraft depicted in Fig 1.

During the operation of this control system the radar unit measures the approximate software and lateral positions of the aircraft which are then transmitted to the controlling and the controlling unit calculates the appropriate pitch and bank commands.This information to the transmitted to the autopilot which in turn cause the aircraft to respond accordingly. Control system design also finds application in the altitude control of a satelite, antenna tracking system which automatically tracks an aircraft, and robotic control system. Further it is also used for numerical, control (NC) of machine tools, the temperature control of thermal processes and chemical process industries.

The different approaches of control system design are:

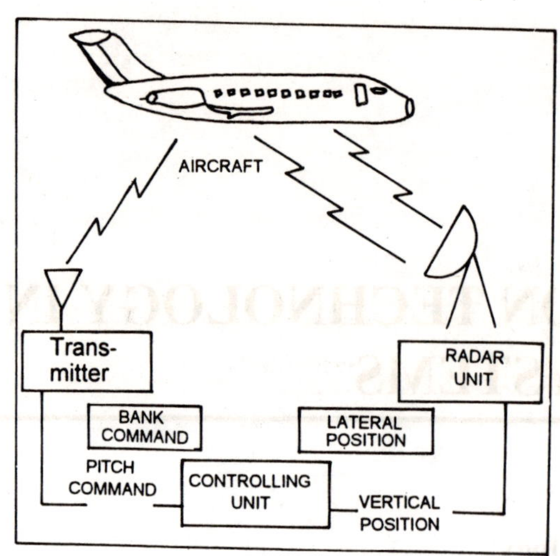

Fig. 1

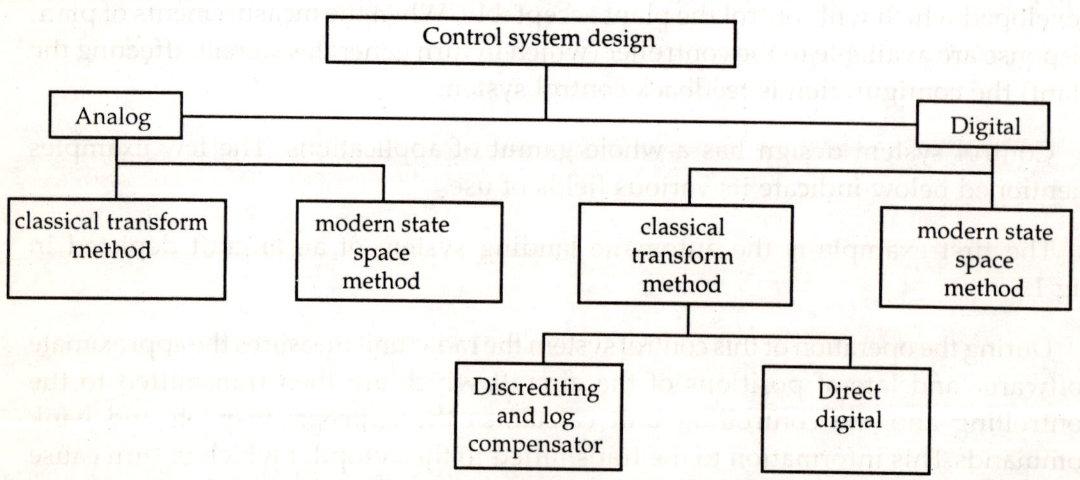

Fig. 2

Digital Control System

The rapid development of digital technology made possible by the invention of the transistor and integrated circuits has stimulated an increasing interest in the issues of digital control implementation. It is now routinely feasible to employ very complicated high order digital controllers and to carry out the extensive calculation required for their design.The advantages of digital control involve the scope of programmability and maintainability. Secondly, these advances in implementation and design capability can be achieved at low cost because of the widespread availability of inexpensive,powerful digital computers and selected devices. Thirdly, noise immunity can be achieved in digital control system.

Design Procedure

In a control problem generally a controller or filter is required to process the error signal in order that certain control criteria or specifications will be satisfied. The criteria may involve but not be limited to:

i) Disturbance rejection
ii) Steady state errors
iii) Transient response
iv) Sensitivity to parameter changes in the plant.

Solving the control problems will generally involve:

i) Choosing sensors to measure the required feedback signals
ii) Choosing actuators to drive the plant
iii) Developing the plant, sensor and actuator models
iv) Designing the controller based on the developed models and the control criteria
v) Evaluating the design analytically by simulation and finally, by testing the physical system
vi) Iterating this procedure until a satisfactory response results.

For the solution of a design problem methods based on both time and frequency domain are used. However, the frequency domain method is in general preferred.[1,2] In the present work, the techniques of frequency response, time response and root locus are investigated. First phase lag and phase lead controllers are considered. Then a particular type of lag lead controller called the proportional integral derivative (PID) controller is developed.[3]

Implementation

Each digital controller structure may be described by a unique set of difference equations. The equations require the operations of multiplication, addition and time delay.[1,2] These difference equations are implemented by microcomputers. The microcomputers are programmed in high level language to calculate the difference equations. In the present work, the implementation is based on the following combinations.

(a) An IBM compatible PC with PCL-718 card as interface.[4] The PCL 718 is a high performance, high speed multifunction data acquisition card for the IBM PC compatibles. The high end specification on the full size and complete software support from third party vendors make it ideal for a wide range of applications in the industrial and laboratory environment. The programming is done in Quick Basic in the present case.

(b) An IBM compatible PC with a digital signal processor (DSP TMS320C25).,[5] as a coprocessor [Fig. 3]. The DSP is a micro processor with an architecture that has been optimised for processing sampled data.[6,7,8] The optimised architectural features allow it to achieve high data processing rates. The key element of the architecture is a very fast array multiplier and accumulator that allow to multiply and accumulate instruction to be performed in one clock cycle.

Scope of the Present Work

The very objective of this work has been to design and implement a position control system. The system comprises separately excited D.C. motor [Fig. 4] fitted with a tachogenerator. Its Bond graph is shown in Fig. 5. It is actuated by a servo amplifier and preamplifier. Three different controllers namely, the phase lead, phase lag_lead and PID are designed using CC.[9] The controllers are implemented using an IBM compatible PC with (a) general purpose I/O card, namely, PCL-718 and (b) TMS320C25 Digital signal processor as the coprocessor.

In the first case, the programs are written in Quick Basic QB2 and in the second case, in the assembly language.

Conclusions

Salient Features of the Work: Results

The following relative advantages and disadvantages have been noted.

(a) The DSP is faster than PCL 718 I/O card

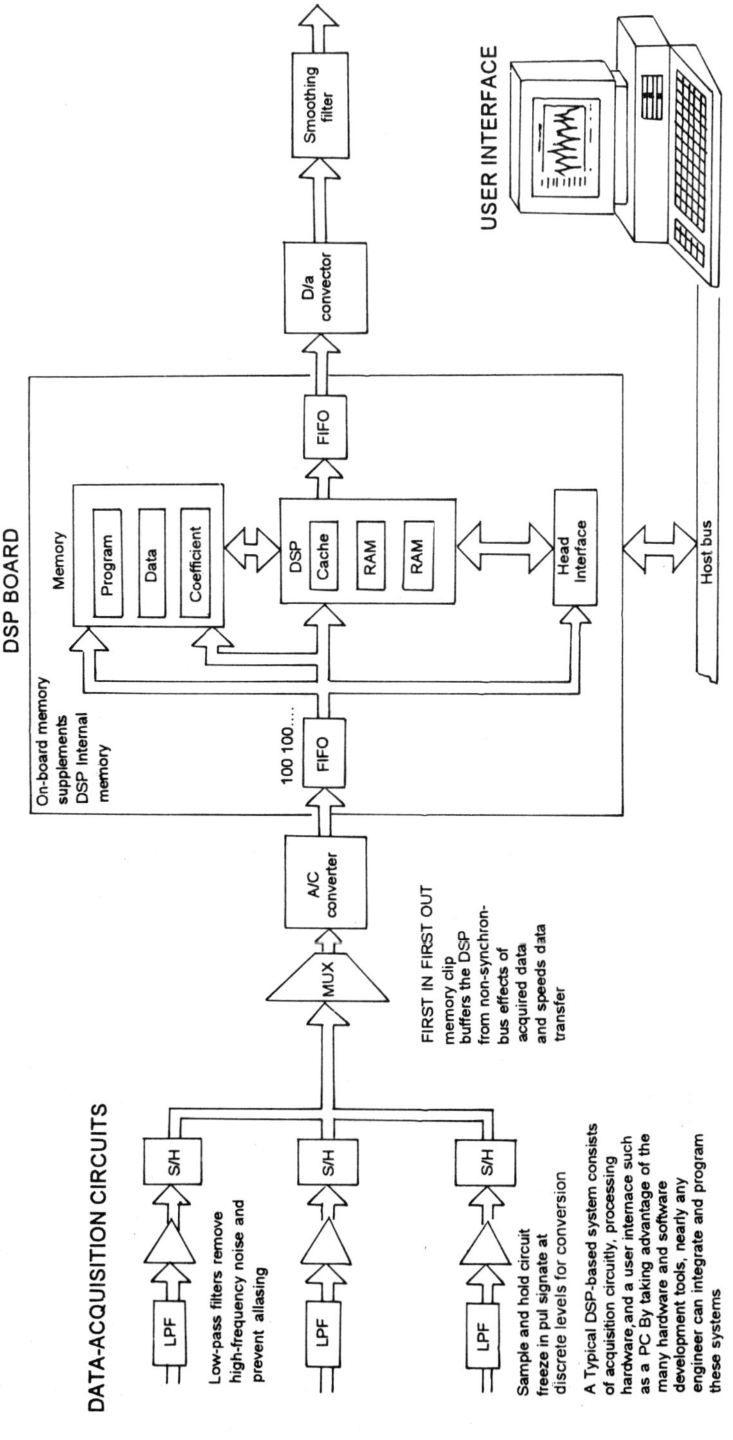

DATA-ACQUISITION CIRCUITS

LPF
S/H
LPF
S/H
LPF
S/H

Low-pass filters remove high-frequency noise and prevent allasing

Sample and hold circuit freeze in pul signate at discrete levels for conversion

A Typical DSP-based system consists of acquisition circuitly, processing hardware,and a user internace such as a PC By taking advantage of the many hardware and software development tools, nearly any engineer can integrate and program these systems

MUX
A/C converter

FIRST IN FIRST OUT memory clip buffers the DSP from non-synchron-bus effects of acquired data and speeds data transfer

DSP BOARD

On-board memory supplements DSP Internal memory

100 100....
FIFO

Memory
Program
Data
Coefficient

DSP
Cache
RAM
RAM

Head Interface

FIFO

Host bus

D/a convector
Smoothing filter

USER INTERFACE

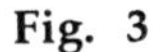

Fig. 3

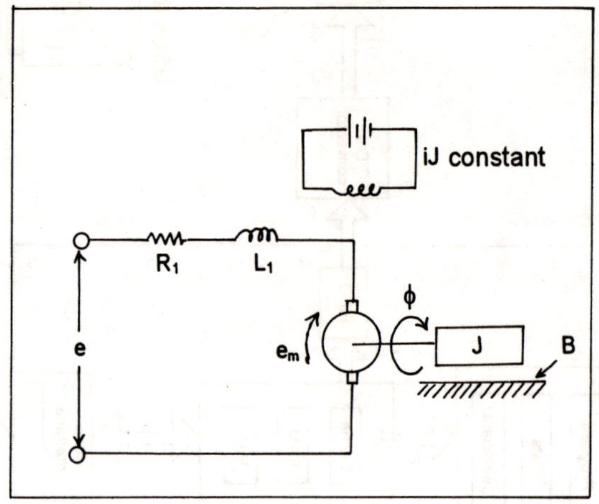

Fig.4

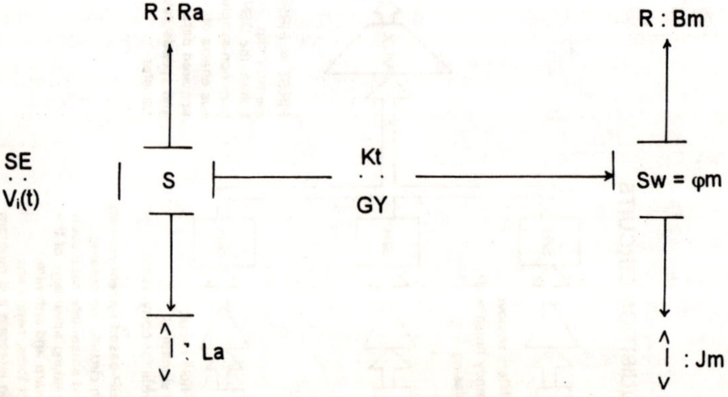

Fig. 5

(b) The PCL 718 is run by programs written in QB2 and is easier to program than the DSP. At present in the DSP the programs are written in the assembly language which is a bit tedious compared to the QB2 used in PCL 718. However one can use the TMS 320C25 'C' compiler (which is a bit costly) for programming the DSP which can make this task easier.

The control system setup used is quite slow and hence the PCL and DSP give comparable results. For faster systems where we need higher sampling rates, the DSP is expected to perform better.

Future Scope of this Work

Since the control strategies used here are linear the implementation is not so complex. For advanced non-linear control strategies like adaptive control, on line estimation and control like self-tuning regulator (STR), and variable structure control (VSC), the algorithms will be computation intensive. In such cases DSP will be preferred. These, algorithms can also be implemented to see the effect of change in process parameters on the system performance.

REFERENCES

1. C.L. Phillips and H.T. Nagle, *Digital Control System Analysis and Design,* Prentice Hall, New Jersey; 1990.
2. G.H. Hestetter, *Digital Control System Design,* Holt, Rinehart and Winstone, Inc. 1988.
3. Proportional Integral, Derivative Module PIDY, Feedback Instruments Ltd., Manual 150-6 ED B 1183.
4. PCL-208 High Performance Data Acquisition Card USER'S MANUAL, Dynalog Micro-Systems.
5. TMS 320 C25,USER's GUIDE; Texas Instruments, 1986.
6. Yogendra Jain, 'DSP Design Made Easy', *Machine Design,* July 26,1990.
7. Yogendra Jain, Tapping the Power of DSP's, *Machine Design,* June 7, 1990.
8. Herbert Hanselmann, *Digital Signal Processors in Motion Control,* Presented at International Workshop on Microcomputer Control of Electric Drives,Triest, Italy,3-4 July 1989.
9. *CG User's Manual.*

APPENDICES

APPENDIX - A

LOGICO-MATHEMATICAL MODELS

INTRODUCTION

Many information needs of an organisation can be met by establishing a common data base and from it, providing timely reports or online responses to the users, via remote terminals such as CRTs. An information system is also comprised of a number of information subsystems such as traditional accounting, inventory control, process control and production scheduling, shipping and transportation, sales analysis, and so on. The total information system is management oriented; thus, in addition to being a data processing center, it also uses logico-mathematical models to aid management in its planning, controlling, and decision-making functions. In addition to developing reports and systems for historical record-keeping and to satisfy business and governmental requirements, it is also the responsibility of the information systems analyst to select, test, and implement these models to provide alternative, predictive, optimising, and performance information. A systems analyst, therefore, needs a working knowledge of the various logico-mathematical models. In this appendix several models that over the years have proven to be valuable in converting raw data elements into meaningful information are presented.

TRADITIONAL ACCOUNTING MODELS

The traditional accounting function, in addition to handling routine data processing activities, also provides a great deal of information to both internal and external constituents. Much of the information provided by this function is historical, and is stated in terms of money. Traditional accounting, however, also provides information that is performance oriented. In the following subsections most of the traditional accounting models are presented.[1]

Accounting reports derived from models aid management (as well as others) in:

1. Planning, because reporting information on past periods helps the user to make predictions about future events.

2. Controlling, because budgets and standards are set, and performances are measured against these budgets and standards.
3. Decision making, because the reporting of possible outcomes based on alternative inputs allows the decision maker to select the best alternatives.

The accounting function also acts as an overall control device for external constituents such as stockholders. It provides performance measurement via position statements, earnings statements, and funds statements, which together help to indicate how management is doing. It also helps asset control (e.g., cash, securities, receivables, and so on) by promoting efficiency and internal control, which reduces loss through , error or fraud. Moreover, it limits needless expenditures by establishing a decentralised system of budgets.

Bookkeeping Model

The bookkeeping model is an equation which sets up a procedure for classifying, recording, and reporting financial transactions of an organisation. It can be stated as follows:

$$\begin{aligned} \text{Assets } (A_t) &= \text{Liabilities } (L_t) \\ &+ \text{Contributed Capital } (CG_t) \\ &+ \text{Retained Earnings } (RE_t) \end{aligned}$$

Each category represents some financial amount at some point in time. All transactions are classified and recorded in such a way that the total assets equal the sum of the liabilities, contributed capital, and retained earnings.

Retained earnings, at some point in time (usually stated at the end of an accounting period), is the algebraic sum of the retained earnings of the previous period, $RE_t - 1$, the earnings for the period, E_t and the dividends declared during the period, D_x. This equation is stated as:

$$RE_t = RE_{t-1} + E_t - D_t$$

Earnings are determined by matching the inputs for the period with the outputs for the period. In business organisations the inputs are measured in terms of revenue, *(R)*, and the outputs are measured in terms of expenses *(EXP)* required to generate this revenue. Income tax *(TAX)*, is not recognised as an expense, per se, but as a social cost of doing business. The equation for earnings is stated as:

$$E_t = R_t - EXP_t - TAX_t$$

Accounts

Accounts are set up which represent each[2] category in the above equations. These accounts are merely a place to receive transactional data, and to show increases or decreases where, at certain periods, the current amount balance of an item is available. All accounts can be algebraically summed, in accordance with the procedures dictated by the equations, to provide financial statements whenever needed.

These accounts take a variety of forms, depending on whether they are recorded on paper for manual data processing methods, or recorded on punched cards, magnetic tape, magnetic disk, etc., for computer processing. The basic procedures in classifying, recording, and reporting are the same whatever data processing method is used.

The essential features of an account can be shown in the form of a classical T-account, as follows:

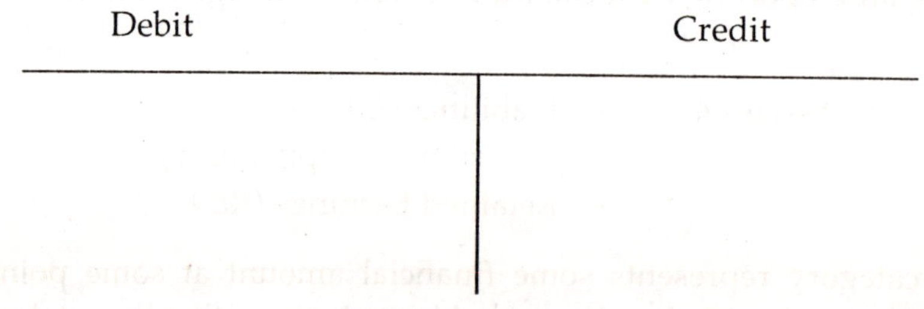

The rules of recording are as follows:

1. *Debits* increase assets, and decrease liabilities, contributed capital, and retained earnings.
2. *Credits* decrease assets, and increase liabilities, contributed capital, and retained earnings.

Retained earnings represent the "meter" for earnings (i.e., revenue increases retained earnings, therefore a credit increases a revenue account). Conversely, an expense decreases retained earnings, so a debit increases an expense account.

Accounting data can also be structured in the form of an m by n matrix with the following general notation:

$$A = \begin{vmatrix} a_{11} & a_{12} & \dots & a_{1n} \\ a_{21} & a_{22} & \dots & a_{2n} \\ \cdot & \cdot & \cdot & \cdot \\ \cdot & \cdot & \cdot & \cdot \\ \cdot & \cdot & \cdot & \cdot \\ a_{m1} & a_{m2} & \dots & a_{mn} \end{vmatrix}$$

Such a matrix is usually represented by the

following abbreviation

$$A = (a_{ij};) \qquad i = 1, 2, \ldots, m$$
$$j = 1, 2, \ldots, n$$

where i = rows and j = columns.

An accounting matrix, using 16 common accounts, is shown in Figure A.1. Notice that the increases and decreases in the accounts work the same as previously explained and that a current balance can be determined at any time. For example, look at Sales (column 10), a revenue account. It obviously has a credit balance (unless there were sales returns, which would be another account) and that balance is \$90,000 (row 19). But how were the sales made, cash or credit? Looking at the Cash and Accounts Receivable accounts (rows 1 and 2) under the Sales account, one can readily determine that \$30,000 of the sales were for cash and \$60,000 were for credit.

Cost-Volume-Profit Model

Costs react on the basis of activity. We can categorise costs into three basic behavior patterns, which are:

1. *Variable cost behavior.* These costs react in direct proportion to changes in activity.
2. *Fixed cost behavior.* These costs remain the same within a specified range of activity.
3. *Semivariable cost behavior.* These costs vary with the level of activity, but not in a strict proportional way. For example, two shifts might be required to produce *X* units. However, to produce *X* + 1 units would require another entire shift.

In knowing cost behavior, we can simulate those profits which might be obtained with changes in volume (activity). This simulated activity can be illustrated in a cost-

	Credits	01	02	03	04	05	06	07	08	09	10	11	12	13	14	15	16	17	18	19
												CO						*BEG*	Σ	*END*
Debits		*CASH*	*AR*	*INV*	*PR*	*PE*	*AD*	*AP*	*CS*	*RE*	*S*	*GS*	*WAGE*	*DEP*	*RENT*	*OTH*	*DIV*	*DR*	*DR*	*DR*
01	Cash		10000						400000		30000								440000	266000
02	Accounts receivable										60000								60000	50000
03	Inventory							150000											150000	150000
04	Prepaid rent	12000																	12000	12000
05	Plant and equipment	75000						25000											100000	100000
06	Accumulated depreciation																			
07	Accounts payable	65000																	65000	0
08	Capital stock																			
09	Retained earnings																			
10	Sales																			
11	Cost of goods sold																			
12	Wages expense	22000																	22000	22000
13	Depreciation expense																			
14	Rent expense																			
15	Other expense							8000											8000	8000
16	Dividends																			
17	Beginning credit balance																			
18	Σ Credit totals this period	174000	10000					183000	400000		90000									
19	Ending credit balances	0	0					118000	400000		90000									

Fig. A.1: An accounting matrix.

volume-profit (CVP) graph, as shown in Figure A.2. In this graph, for simplicity, we delineate only two categories of cost—variable and fixed.

Figure A.2 shows the relationship between cost and profit at various volume levels. The measure of volume is the number of units produced and sold. At lower volumes, a loss is expected; at higher volumes, a profit is expected; somewhere in between a breakeven point exists where total cost equals revenue.

The cost-volume-profit relationship provides a useful way for simulating the profit factors of any organisation. The factors which increase profit are:

1. Increased selling price per unit.
2. Decreased variable cost per unit.
3. Increased volume.
4. For a multiproduct company, a change in its product mix.

A typical question from management may be: What would the profit picture look like if we decreased selling price by 5 per cent, variable cost remained constant, decreased nonvariable cost by 8 per cent, and increased volume of sales by 20 per cent? A variety of questions such as this, proposed by management, could generate information which could effectively enhance planning and decision making.

Budget and Performance Analysis Models

A budget is a plan of action, expressed in quantitative terms, which covers some specific time period. The key concept of a budget is to structure it in terms that equate to the responsibility of those who are charged with its execution. In this way the budget is used not only as a planning device but also as a control device. Budgets are of three types:

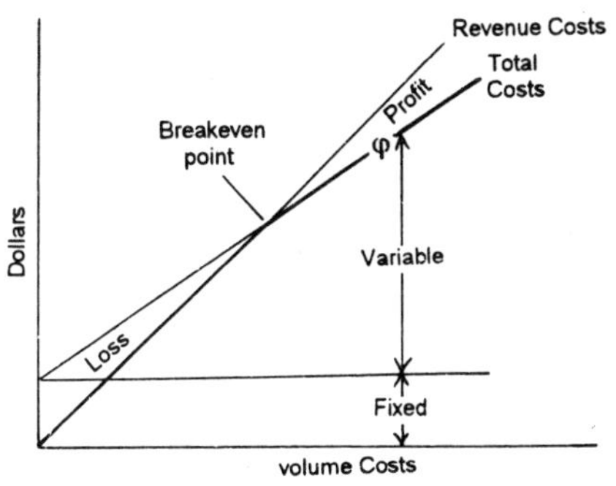

Fig. A.2: The cost-volume-profit relationship.

1. An operating budget showing planned operations for the forthcoming period.
2. A cash budget showing the anticipated sources and uses of cash.
3. A capital budget showing planned changes in a variety of fixed assets.

The budgeting process involves a planning-control-planning life cycle, which is described as follows:

1. Planning which entails selecting objectives and means for their obtainment.
2. Controlling encompasses two activities:
   (a) Translate objectives into units of output and determine specific inputs to.
   (b) Comparison of actual operations with budgeted operations.
3. Planning at this stage uses performance reports for evaluating past operations for planning future operations.

Budgets can also be viewed as being prepared for different levels in an organisation.

Typically, budgets may relate to four levels: (1) entire organisation (master budget), (2) division, (3) department, and (4) subunit. For example, a typical performance report at one level is structured as follows:

	Budgeted	*Actual*	*Variance**
Material	XX	XX	XU
Labor	XX	XX	XF
Other	XX	XX	XU

* U: Unfavorable; F: Favorable.

Budget is a macro concept whereas standards are a micro concept. For example, the standard cost per labor hour may be $5. The budget for 20,000 hours would show a total labor cost of $100,000. The standard itself is a predetermined estimate of what performance should be under stated conditions. In preparing performance information based on standards, we can use three models:

Quantity Variance	=	(Actual Quantity
	-	Standard Quantity)
	x	Standard Cost Per Unit
Cost Variance	=	(Actual Cost - Standard Cost) x Actual Quantity

Total Variance = Quantity Variance + Cost Variance

Payoff Graph Analysis Model

The payoff graph is another tool that can be used effectively by the analyst to enhance the information received by management. Payoff analysis is a simple, straightforward technique which can be used by analysts to compare costs and savings of alternative systems. For example, examine the set of figures given in the table below.

These figures represent the costs of both systems and the resulting savings (or dissavings) when compared to each other. Figure A.3 depicts a payoff analysis graph that, in a meaningful manner, makes this comparison.

The present system's costs are represented by the cross-hatched areas. Savings are calculated by subtracting the proposed system's costs from the present system's costs. The savings are:

YEAR 1:	450,000	-	700,000	=	-250,000
YEAR 2:	500,000	-	510,000	=	-10,000
YEAR 3:	570,000	-	480,000	=	90,000
YEAR 4:	720,000	-	410,000	=	310,000
YEAR 5:	810,000	-	410,000	=	400,000

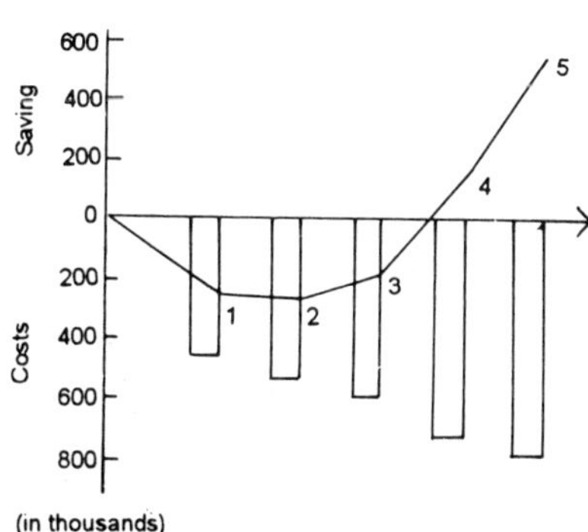

Fig. A.3: Payoff analysis graph comparing the proposed system to the present system.

The plotted points in the graph indicate the accumulated net annual savings. These points are calculated as follows:

Point 1:	0	+	(-250,000)	=	- 250,000
Point 2:	(-250,000)	+	(-10,000)	=	- 260,000
Point 3:	(- 260,000)	+	90,000	=	- 170,000
Point 4:	(-170,000)	+	310,000	=	140,000
Point 5:	140,000	+	400,000	=	540,000

Although this is a useful model in making gross estimates, it ignores the time value of money and a desired rate of return on investments. For these considerations we now turn to the model presented in the next section.

	Year 1	*Year 2*	*Year 3*	*Year 4*	*Year 5*
Costs:					
Semi-automatic (present system)					
Automatic	$450,000	$500,000	$570,000	$720,000	$810,000
(proposed system)	$700,000	$510,000	$480,000	$410,000	$410,000
Savings:	($250,000)	($ 10,000)	$ 90,000	$310,000	$400,000

Net Present Value Model

The net present value model can be used to help management make decisions about investment proposals if such a proposal can be reduced to monetary amounts. Stated simply, neglecting nonmonetary considerations, an investment proposal is accepted if the present value of its earnings or cost savings equals or exceeds the amount of the investment required at some desired rate of return.

		Present Value of $1 Discounted at 30%	Present Value	Cost Savings Streams 0	1	2	3	4	5
Annual Cost Savings:									
$36,000	x	.769	$ 27,684		$ 30,000	$ 100,000	$ 100,000	$ 100,000	$ 80,000
100,000	x	.592	59.200						
100,000	x	.455	45,500						
100,000	x	.350	35,000						
80,000	x	.269	26,900						
Present Value of Future Cost Savings			$ 194,284						
Initial Investment		1.000	-200,000		$200,000				
Net Present Value			$ - 5,716						

For example, suppose that management is thinking of purchasing a computer system for $200,000. The useful life of the computer is five years. The cost savings for the first year is $30,000, for the next three years $100,000, and for the last year $80,000. The minimum desired rate of return is 30%. Neglecting other quantitative or qualitative considerations, should management purchase the computer?

In the example below, the net present value of $ - 5716 means the investment has not earned what it should at a minimum desired rate of return of 30%. Therefore, the investment is undesirable. If the present value were positive or zero, the investment would be desirable because its return either exceeds or meets the desired minimum.

Additional Models

In addition to some of the basic, traditional accounting models presented above other models also help management in planning, controlling, and decision making. In many organisations, these functions are performed on an intuitive basis. That is, minimal effort is made to define and measure variables affecting the organisation. Logico-mathematical models help to systematise and quantify certain variables in a manner where management can make more knowledgeable decisions. In this section, we discuss some of these models.[3]

Probability Concepts

The following concepts of probability and random variables represent the basic knowledge that a systems analyst must have in formulating successful models.

Probability of an Event. The probability that an event E will occur is the ratio between the number, n, of cases in which E occurs and the total number, N, of the elementary cases, all equally likely,

$$P(E) = \frac{n}{N}$$

where the assumption of equally likely outcomes describes such processes as tossing coins, rolling a die, and so on.

Random Variable. A random variable, X, assumes the values

$$X_1, X_2, \ldots, X_n$$

with each of these values having a probability of

$$P((X_1), P(X_2), \ldots. P(X_n)$$

where

$$\sum_{i=1}^{n} P(X_i) = 1$$

and the expected value of *X* is

$$E(X) = X_1P(X_1) + X_2P(X_2) +' \ldots X_nP(X_n)$$

For example, "what will sales revenue be for the next quarter?" is a typical question an analyst might ask. The estimator states a range of possibilities together with an estimate of the probability each will occur. The sum of the possibilities $(X_1, X_2, \ldots, X_n)$ multiplied by the applicable probability $(P(X_1), P(X_2), \ldots, P(X_n))$ equals the expected value $(E(X))$. The expected value of sales for the next quarter is computed as follows:

Sales (X_1)	*Probability* $P(X_1)$	*Amount* $X_1 P(X_1)$
\$100,000	.1	\$ 10,000
120,000	.4	48,000
160,000	.3	48,000
200,000	.2	40,000
	Expected value	\$146,000

Compound Probability. This is the probability that both *A* and *B* will occur and is written: *P(A, B)*. Compound events are shown in a tree diagram model below.

The probability of a compound event is determined by multiplying branch probabilities. The probability of compound event A_1C_2 is:

$$P(A_1C_2) = P(A_1) \times P(C_2) = (.3) \times (.2) = .06$$

Conditional Probability. The probability that an event *A* will occur, if it is known that event *B* has occurred is written *P(A/B)*. For our tree diagram, $P(A_2/B_1) = .1$.

Total Probability. This is the probability of mutually exclusive (nonoverlapping) events occurring. In our example the probability of A_1 or C_1 occurring, written as $P(A_1 + C_1)$ is .6.

Cumulative Probability. This is the process of accumulating the values of *P(X)* which results in the cumulative probability function,

$$P(X) = P(X \leq X) = \Sigma P(X_1)$$

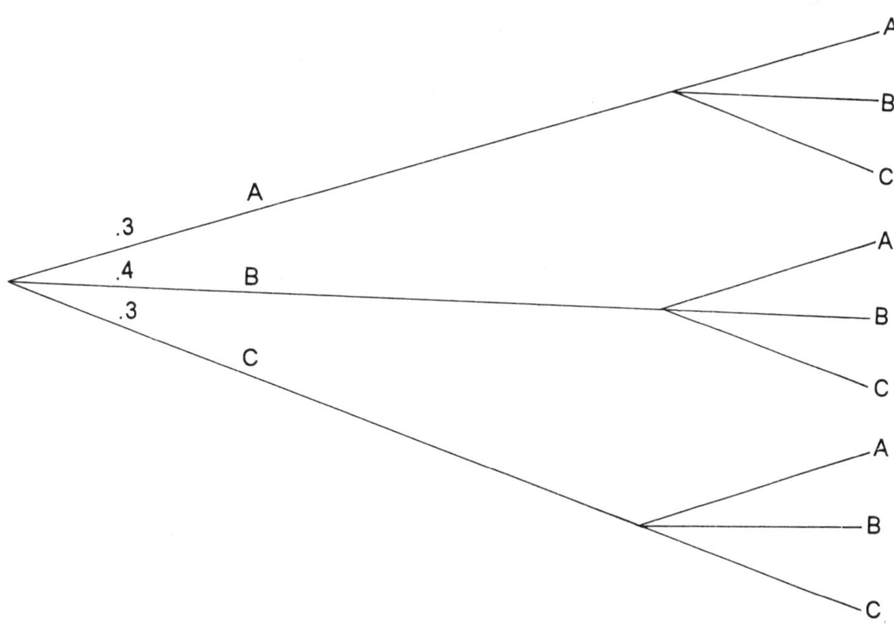

Trial 1 **Tiral 2**

Customer Demand X	*Probability of X*
3	.1
4	.2
5	.3
6	.2
7	2
	1.0

P (number of units *sold* $\leq$ 5) = P (number of units sold = 5) + P (number of units sold = 4) + P (number of units sold = 3) = .3 + .2 + .1 = .6

Statistical Concepts

Statistical concepts represent additional methods of manipulating data to provide information. Some of these basic concepts are indicated here.

Histogram. This is a table showing the number of individual observations falling within each interval or class; this number is called the frequency. Before constructing a histogram, the following must be defined:

1. The limits of the group studied.
2. The data or characteristics measured for each individual.
3. The conditions under which the measurements were made.

Mean. Given a population consisting of *N* individuals, if f_1 is the frequency of the variate X_1, then the mean, $\bar{x}$, is given by the formula:

$$\bar{X} = \frac{1}{N}\sum_{i=1}^{k} f_1 X_1$$

where k is the number of classes and

$$N = \sum_{i=1}^{k} f_1$$

Mean of the Means. If *m* measurements are taken in populations of the same nature:

$$\bar{\chi} = \frac{n_1\bar{\chi}_1 + n_2\bar{\chi}_2 + \ldots + n_m\bar{\chi}_m}{N}$$

Mode. The mode is the value of χi for which fi is greatest (i.e., the most frequently occurring value).

Median. The median is the value of χi (or lying between two consecutive χi) for which

$$cum\, f = \frac{1}{2} N$$

Two Measures of Dispersion. The standard deviation, or mean square deviation:

$$\alpha\chi = \sqrt{\frac{1}{N}\sum_{i=1}^{k} f_1(\chi_1 - \bar{\chi})^2}$$

σ = standard deviation

χ = observations

$\bar{\chi}$ = mean

and the variance is $(\sigma\chi)^2$.

Random Sample. A sample is considered to be random if it consists of observations that are independently drawn from an identically distributed population.

Network Model

PERT (Program Evaluation and Review Technique) is an example of a network model used for planning and controlling projects with well-defined activities and events. PERT is based on a network composed of activities that take time to accomplish. Between the activities are instantaneous events, which designate the completion of each activity. Probably a better interpretation indicates that events represent a start or finish of the Activities.

The activities are placed on a network and are represented by arrows. Generally, the arrows or activities flow from left to right. Four rules to follow when placing an activity on the network are:

1. A determination must be made to see if any activities logically precede the activity that is under consideration.
2. A determination must be made to see if any activities are logically concurrent with the activity under consideration.
3. A determination must be made to spot activities which are logically subsequent to the activity under consideration.
4. Events must be clearly defined relative to their beginning and end.

Expected Time

The activity time should be estimated by someone knowledgeable about particular processes. The three time estimates furnished are:

1. *Most likely time.* How long do you expect it would take to complete this particular activity?
2. *Optimistic time.* What is the minimum possible time in which this particular task or activity can be completed?
3. *Pesimistic time.* What is the longest tine this particular activity or task has ever taken?

The goal in getting three subjective estimate is to use then to calculate a single weighted average or mean time and variance. This average of mean time is called the expected time of the activity. Briefly, the three time estimate are related to the expected time and standard deviation by the following formulas:

$$t_e = \frac{O + 4M + P}{6}$$

$$\sigma_{te} = (P - O)/6$$

where $O =$ optimistic time estimate
$M =$ Most likely time estimate
$P =$ pessimistic time estimate
$t_e =$ expected time (weighted average)
$\sigma_{te} =$ standard deviation of t_e.

The above formulas are based on the assumption that the time estimates approximate a beta distribution.

Critical events on the network are those which, have zero slack time. Slack time equals the latest event time (T_L) less the earliest event time (T_E). The latest event time is the latest time that an event can occur without disrupting the project. Earliest event time is the earliest time that an event can occur. A heavy line connecting the critical events represents the critical path for a network. An increase in time along this path will extend the completion date by the same amount. A decrease in time along this path will shorten the time to completion by the same amount or change the critical path.

The network for a batch-project of okra/tomatoes/corn is shown in Figure A.4. The activities and time estimates are listed in Table A.1.

Frequently, estimates are required concerning the probability of completing an activity on the critical path by a certain date. Based on the assumption that possible completion times for an activity are approximately normally distributed, PERT has the capability to provide such estimates. The probability of completing an activity is determined by the number of standard normal units between the completion deadline and the earliest time the activity can be completed. The formula is as follows:

$$Z = \frac{T_D - T_E}{\sqrt{\Sigma\sigma_{t_e}^2}}$$

where $Z =$ number of standard normal units between T_D and T_E
$T_D =$ completion deadline
$T_E =$ earliest completion time
$\sqrt{\Sigma\sigma_{t_e}^2} =$ the square root of the sum of the variances of the pertinent activities on the critical path.

Once Z has been calculated, reference is then made to a standard normal table.

The probability that time to completion will exceed the deadline date is equal to the area under the normal curve to the right of the Z value.

For example, we may ask the question, "Can activity 3,7 (cutting okra) be completed by day 13?" The variances associated with the pertinent critical path activities are as follows:

Activity	σ_{te}	σ^2_{te}
1,2	.83.	69
2,3	.67	.44
3,7	.50	.25
	Total	1.38

Substituting into our formula for Z,

$$Z = \frac{13 - 11.4}{\sqrt{1.38}}$$

$$= 1.36$$

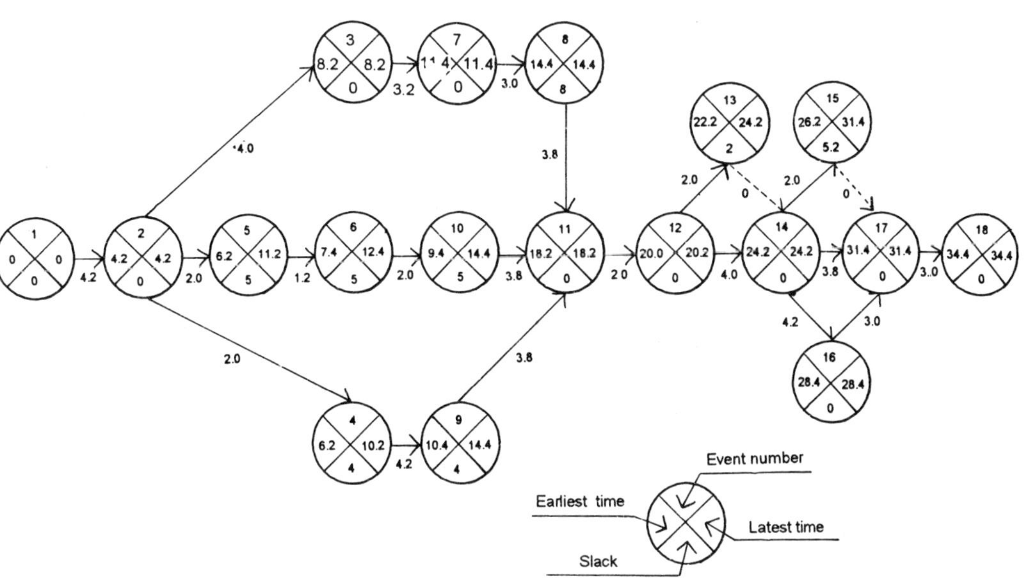

Fig. A.4: Network showing earliest and latest time and slack. The heavy line represents the critical path.

The area under the normal curve to the right of 1.36 is .0869. Therefore, we can say that the probability of completing activity 3,7 later than day 13 is less than 8.69 per cent. Stated another way, the probability that activity 3,7 will be finished by day 13 is 91.31 per cent.

Decision Model

The elements of a simple decision model consist of actions, outcomes, probabilities of outcomes, and utilities. Let us define the following:

TABLE A.1

Activities and Time Estimates for the Okra/Tomatoes/Corn Project

		Time in Days			
Activity	*Description*	*Optimistic*	*Most Likely*	*Pessimistic*	t_e
1,2	Unloading/testing raw produce	2	4	7	4.2
2,3	Washing okra	2	4	6	4.0
2,4	Washing/stemming tomatoes	1	2	3	2.0
2,5	Loading can racks	1	2	3	2.0
3,7	Cutting okra	2	3	5	3.2
4,9	Blanching tomatoes	3	4	6	4.2
5,6	Mixing device changeover	1	1	2	1.2
6,10	Preparation of corn for mixing	1	2	3	2.0
7,8	Preparation of okra for mixing	2	3	4	3.0
8,11	Loading of okra	2	4	5	3.8
9,11	Loading of tomatoes	2	4	5	3.8
10,11	Loading of corn	2	4	5	3.8
11,12	Canning process	1	2	3	2.0
12,13	Quality control-testing	1	2	3	2.0
12,14	Pressure cooker process	2	4	6	4.0
13,14	Dummy	0	0	0	0
14,15	Quality control-testing	1	2	3	2.0
14,16	Cool bath process	3	4	6	4.2
14,17	Warehouse preparation	2	4	5	3.8
15,17	Dummy	0	0	0	0
16,17	Stacking in warehouse	2	3	4	3.0
17,18	Cleanup and retooling	2	3	4	3.0

A = set of alternative resource commitments, or actions ($a \in A$),

O = set of future states or outcomes ($o \in O$),

p(o) = set of probabilities that describe the outcome occurrence,

U(o, a) = utility of an outcome occurring given the selection of an action. If an expected utility approach is taken, then the alternative with the highest expected utility would be selected.

$E(U/a^*) = MAX\ \Sigma.\ (U(o, a) \cdot p(o))\ a \in A\ o \in O$

An example may make this clearer. Suppose you are a raw material inspector for the Swill Wine Co. Your job is to either accept (a_1) or reject (a_2) incoming shipments of grapes. The shipments can either meet standards (o_1) or be substandard (o_2). From past experience you know that the probability of a substandard shipment is .2. Conversely, you know that the probability a shipment will meet standards is .8. Now suppose further that the following utility matrix, in terms of dollars, is applicable:

	Outcomes	
Actions	0_1	0_2
a_1	2	-4
a_2	0	1

Then the expected dollar utility for the alternative resource commitments is as follows:

$$E(U/a_1) = U(o_1,a_1) \cdot p(o_1) + U(o_2,a_1) \cdot p(o_2)$$
$$= \$2 \cdot .8 + (\$ - 4) \cdot .2$$
$$= \$1.60 - .80$$
$$= \$.80$$
$$E(U/a_2) = U(o_1, a_2) \cdot p(o_1) + U(o_2, a_2) \cdot p(o_2)$$
$$= \$0 \cdot .8 + \$1 \cdot .2$$
$$= \$.20$$

Maximising over alternatives leads us to choose action $a_{1,}$ accept the shipment.

Many different types of questions can be answered within this decision framework. One of the most interesting is, "What would be the most you would pay for correct information about the contents of a shipment?" Let us answer this question by again referring to our example.

Suppose your "perfect" information source was a trained German Shepherd dog, who by sniffing the crate could tell with certainty whether or not the grapes were substandard. Your expected utility function would now be,

$$
\begin{aligned}
E(U) &= U(O_1.a_1) \cdot p(o_1) + U(O_2.a_2) \cdot p(o_2) \\
&= \$2 \cdot .8 + \$1 \cdot .2 \\
&= \$1.60 + .20 \\
&= \$\,1.80
\end{aligned}
$$

Notice that the probabilities of the outcomes have not changed. What has changed is that you are no longer making incorrect decisions. You should be willing to pay up to $1.00 ($1.80 – .80) per crate sniffed for this canine's services.

Contribution-by-Value Analysis Model

A very simple, but quite effective, logical model that can be used in almost any kind of performance analysis is termed contribution-by-value analysis (also called ABC analysis). This analysis is based on Pareto's Law, which states that in most situations a relatively small percentage of certain objects contributes a relatively high percentage of output.[5] For instance, it can be shown that in most areas approximately 15-30 per cent of the population contributes 70-90 per cent of the tax revenue. Or, for example, that 20 per cent of the employees in an office do 80 per cent of the work. Many systems analysts find that when inventory items are plotted on a cumulative percentage graph, in order of descending value, Pareto's relationship usually exists. Relative to such a phenomenon, one frequently hears a rule of thumb quoted as: 20 per cent of the items in inventory account for 80 per cent of the sales. Such an analysis is quite effective in that it reveals very clearly the performance of any situation analyzed. For inventory analysis, the contribution-by-value analysis can be applied to sales by customer, by salesperson, by product item, by territory, by warehouse, and so on.

An example of contribution-by-value analysis relative to sales by warehouses is discussed and illustrated in Figure A.5.

To prepare the analysis, the following steps are taken.

1. Dollar annual sales are calculated for each warehouse by multiplying sales price times quantity sold for each product and computing a grand total for all products in each warehouse.
2. All warehouses are arranged by dollar annual sales in descending sequence.

Warehouse Number	*Warehouse Count*	*Number of Warehouse Percentage of Total*	*Annual Sales*	*Cumulative Sales*	*Cumulative Percentage of Total Contribution*
1	2	3	4	5	6
1	1	2.00	4,331,927.34	4,331,927.34	56.00
2	2	4.00	1,331,521.32	5,663,448.66	73.20
41	3	6.00	271,765.00	5,935,213.66	76.70
3	4	8.00	189,880.05	6,125,093.71	79.10
50	5	10.00	157,450.05	6,282,543.76	81.20
94	6	12.00	145,175.00	6,427,718.76	83.10
45	7	14.00	123,044.65	6,550,762.41	84.60
14	8	16.00	98,355.30	6,649,117.71	85.90
48	9	18.00	94,579.75	6,743,697.46	87.10
43	10	20.00	86,769.56	6,830,467.02	88.30
42	11	22.00	75,180.12	6,905,647.14	89.20
25	12	24.00	68,287.65	6,973,934.79	90.10
67	13	26.00	66,245.20	7.040,179.99	91.00
26	14	28.00	60,040.40	7,100,220.39	91.80
64	15	30.00	58,352.45	7,158,572.84	92.50
38	16	32.00	42,587.50	7,201,160.34	93.10
39	17	34.00	36,915.80	7,238,076.14	93.50
15	18	36.00	35,601.80	7,273,677.94	94.00
29	19	38.00	32,322.60	7,306,000.54	94.40
36	20	40.00	29,919.65	7,335,920.19	94.80
4	21	42.00	29,322.25	7,365,242.44	95.20
24	22	44.00	29,184.10	7,394,426.54	95.60
19	23	46.00	28,548.05	7,422,974.59	95.90
57	24	48.00	27,129.90	7,450,104.49	96.30
95	25	50.00	24,260.13	7,474,364.62	96.60
62	26	52.00	23,379.75	7,497,744.37	96.90
47	27	54.00	23,088.10	7,520,832.47	97.20
16	28	56.00	22,110.39	7,542,942.86	97.50
17	29	58.00	19,293.90	7,662,236.76	97.70
66	30	60.00	18,705.50	7,580,942.26	98.00
71	31	62.00	17,925.20	7,598,867.46	98.20
46	32	64.00	15,764.25	7,614,631.71	98.40
68	33	66.00	14,306.00	7,628,937.71	98.60
18	34	68.00	13,304.20	7,642,241.91	98.80

cont...

1	2	3	4	5	6
35	35	70.00	12,741.70	7,654,983.61	98.90
28	36	72.00	11,347.80	7,666,331.41	99 10
65	37	74.00	10,164.25	7,676,495.66	99.20
34	38	76.00	10,087.15	7,686,582.81	99.30
61	39	78.00	9,422.20	7,696,005.01	99.50
27	40	80.00	6,463.10	7,702,468.11	99.50
91	41	82.00	6,196.60	7,708,664.61	99.60
54	42	84.00	5.592.55	7,714,257.16	99.70
55	43	86.00	4,507.80	7,718,764.96	99.70
5	44	88.00	4,049.70	7,722,814.66	99.80
70	45	90.00	3,356.00	7,726,170.96	99.80
37	46	92.00	3,262.10	7,729,433.06	99.90
60	47	94.00	2,402.35	7,731,835.41	99.90
49	48	96.00	1,694.50	7,733,529.91	99.90
23	49	98.00	558.35	7,734,088.26	99.90
68	50	100.00	252.50	7,734,340.76	100.00

Fig. A.5: Contribution-by-warehouse sales report.

3. A list is printed from these ranked warehouses. Included in this report is such information as warehouse number, warehouse count, percentage of total, annual sales of each warehouse, cumulative sales, and percentage of total contribution. The relevant points of this report are:
   a. The top 10 per cent of the warehouses account for 81.20 per cent of the dollar sales. In other words, a mere 5 out of 50 warehouses account for over four-fifths of the sales of the entire business or close to $6.28 million annually.
   b. The upper 20 per cent of the warehouses account for 88.30 per cent of the sales. An additional 10 per cent increase in the number of warehouse's increased sales by 5.20 per cent.
   c. The upper 50 per cent of the warehouses account for 96.60 per cent of the sales.
   d. The upper 74 per cent of the warehouses account for 99.20 per cent of the sales. Conversely, the lower 26 per cent of the warehouses account for only .80 per cent of the sales.

The information from the report is plotted to assist management in visualising the relationships between number of warehouses and their relative contribution to sales volume. A plot of the results of this analysis, with the percentage of cumulative annual sales on the vertical axis, and the percentage of warehouses on the horizontal axis, appears in Figure A.6.

The contribution-by-value analysis shows that the company is operating several warehouses which are probably not necessary for efficient and streamlined operations. As surprising as the above relationships are on first exposure, however, they will probably be found in many organisations. It should also be noted that the discernment of such relationships provides management with valuable information even though the contribution-by-value analysis model is, itself, simplistic.

Forecast Models

Good forecasts are vital to the success of every organisation. The sales forecast, for example, is a basic source of information for production, inventory, procurement, and employment plans. Even though inherent errors exist in any forecasting model, an organisation that bases its operations on intuitive decision making is ignoring the possibilities for a more efficient operation.

The Least-Squares Model

As an extrapolative forecast model, the least-squares technique uses historical data exclusively. When a model of this type is used, two basic assumptions must be made: that the recent level of activity will continue and that the recent rate of change will remain about the same. The least-squares line approximating the set of points $(X_1, Y_1), (X_2, Y_2), \ldots, (X_n, Y_n)$ has the equation

$$Y = a_o + a_1 X$$

where the constants a_o and a_1 can be found from the formulas

$$a_0 = \frac{(\Sigma X^2)(\Sigma Y) - (\Sigma XY)(\Sigma X)}{N\Sigma X^2 - (\Sigma X)^2}$$

$$a_1 = \frac{N\Sigma XY - (\Sigma Y)(\Sigma X)}{N\Sigma X^2 - (\Sigma X)^2}$$

Here, X is the independent variable and Y is the dependent variable. The least-squares line passes through the point $(\overline{X}, \overline{Y})$, called the centroid or center of gravity of the data.

Suppose the value of X represents time, such as months, and the value of Y represents quantities of products sold each month. The value of Y can be extrapolated according to some value of X. In other words, if the independent variable X is time, then the data show the values of Y at various times in the future.

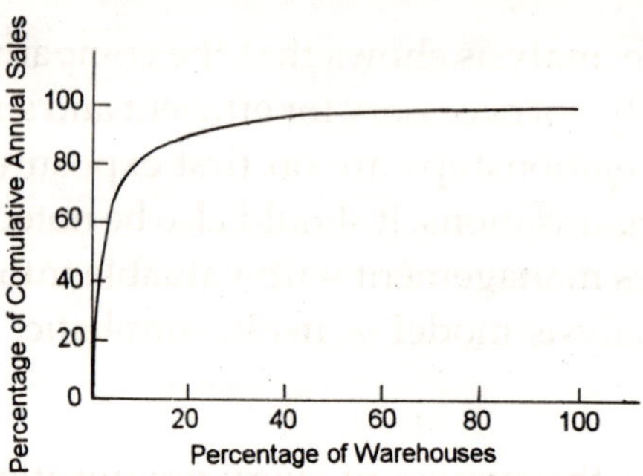

Fig. A.6: Graphic representation of the contribution-by-warehouse sales report.

Since Y is estimated from X, *Y* represents the value of Y for given values of X as estimated from the least-squares regression line of

$$\hat{Y} = a_0 + a_1 X$$

From this, a measure of the scatter about the regression line of X on Y is. supplied by the quantity

$$X_{Y,X} = \sqrt{\frac{(Y - \hat{Y})^2}{N}}$$

which is called the standard error of the estimate of *Y* on *X*.[6]

The Exponential Smoothing Model

Exponential smoothing is similar to a moving average; however, where applicable, exponential smoothing is normally chosen as a forecasting method for the following two reasons:

1. With the moving average all data in the series are weighted equally. In other words, recent data are given the same weight as older data.
2. Forecasting by the moving average method requires that a great deal of data be maintained.

Exponential smoothing is a form of weighted moving average. All that is needed to use the exponential smoothing model is a smoothing constant, the current forecast, and a new observation.

The computational procedure of exponential smoothing is shown by the following formula:

$$\text{New Average} = \text{Old Average} + \alpha\,(\text{New Demand} - \text{Old Average})$$

where α designates a smoothing constant between 0 and 1.

The new average represents the forecast of demand for the subsequent forecast interval. The old average is the new average of the preceding forecast interval, and the new demand is the actual demand for the present period. Said another way, the forecast is part old forecast and part forecast error. If the forecast had been completely accurate, then the new average would equal the old average.

By controlling the weight of the most recent data, α simultaneously determines the average age of the data included in the estimate of the average. The value chosen for the smoothing constant can be such that the estimate is very stable, or reacts very quickly. For example, $\alpha = 0.5$ would give a greater weight to the new data than $\alpha = 0.1$. Regardless of the value of α, the weighting of data follows what is called an exponential curve; therefore, the name exponential smoothing.

One of the crucial questions that arise when one uses exponential smoothing is the size of the smoothing constant that should be used. Conceptually, the answer is simple. Enough weight should be given to provide system stability, but it should be small enough so that real (not random) changes in the level of demand will be recognised.

Inventory Control Model

The problem of planning, scheduling, and controlling production in the face of uncertain market conditions, and of maintaining reasonable levels of inventories, is almost universal. In many organisations with a wide product line, the inventory clerks as well as management may not know with reasonable accuracy what the levels are, and an investigation into the inventory will often indicate a wide variation between the actual conditions, and what is thought to be the inventory. When an inventory item is overstocked, the error may not become evident for a long time, if at all. When an item is understocked and a stockout occurs, customer goodwill is reduced. Any organisation with inventory problems, therefore, needs an inventory management system that accomplishes two things: (1) it makes certain that items are available when they are needed, and (2) it prevents an increase of inventory beyond proper limits. Inventory management assures that an adequate supply of inventory is maintained and requires an optimum balance between shortage and overstock. Too many shortages decrease the customer service level. Conversely, an overstock of items ties up working capital that can be used more profitably elsewhere.

Replenishment, Lead Time, and Safety Stock

The first of two approaches to replenishing inventory is shown in Figure A.7 and is termed a periodic system wherein an order is placed on a specific date. The disadvantage of this method is that stockouts are risked. The second approach, illustrated in Figure A.8, is termed reorder point system in that an order is placed when the inventory level of an item reaches a predetermined level L_{RE}.

The time *T* in the periodic method is always the same, whereas T in the reorder point method is unequal. Of the two methods, the second one is used more often. It consists of placing a constant order quantity when the inventory level reaches the reorder level. The reorder level is computed as follows:

Reorder Level = Lead Time x Forecast of Demand — Safety Stock

The lead time t_1 to t_2 is that time interval between placement of an order and receipt of that order. In Figure A.8, it was assumed that lead time was zero. Such an assumption is normally not realistic. Lead time would probably be similar to that shown in Figure A.9. The safety stock allows for a margin of error in estimating lead time or demand.

The Problem of How Much to Order

The best known model of how much to order is the classic EOQ (economic order quantity) model. This model reveals to the inventory clerk how much to buy (or order) when a reorder point is reached.

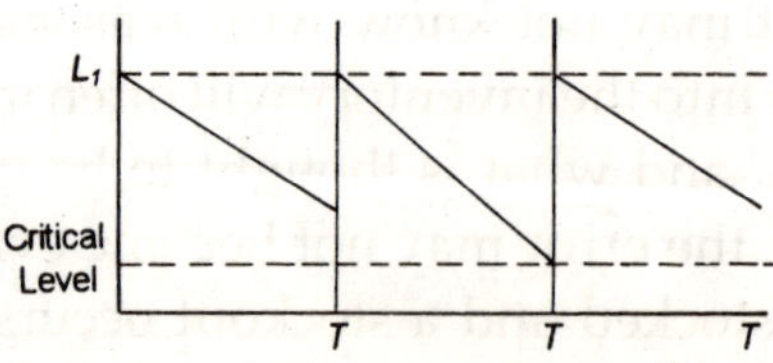

Fig. A.7: Period resplenishment system.

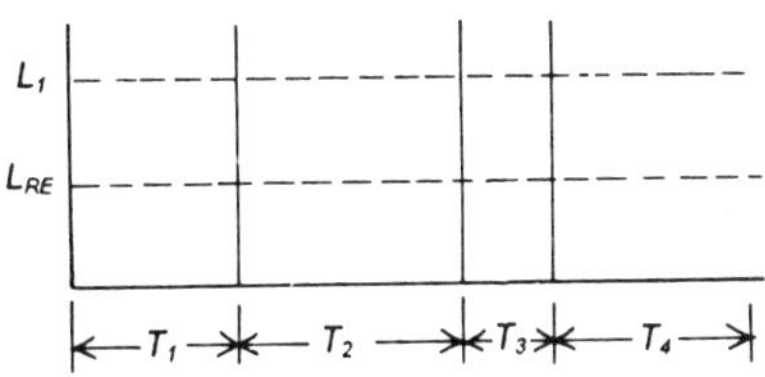

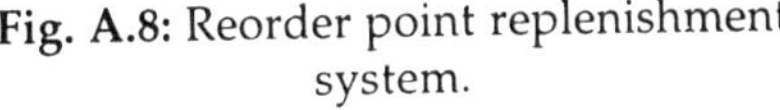

Fig. A.8: Reorder point replenishment system.

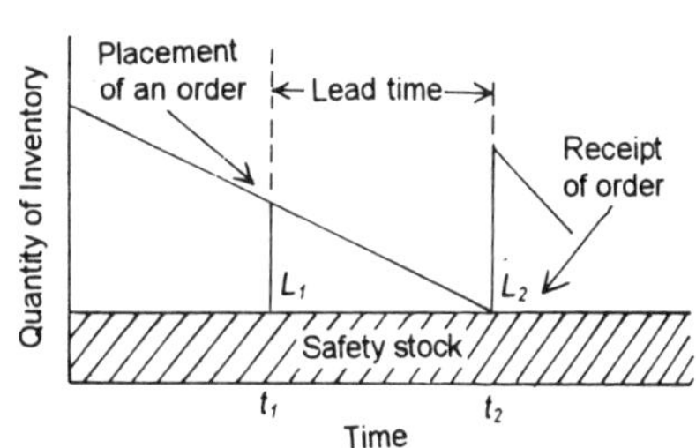

Fig. A.9: Illustration of lead time and safety stock.

The order quantity chosen will incur certain costs. Two different sets of cost factors are considered. If a greater or lesser quantity is ordered, then some costs will increase, while others decrease. Among those costs that increase are interest, obsolescence, risk, and storage, while the set of decreasing costs includes such items as freight and procurement costs. These costs can be lumped into the categories of cost to carry and cost to purchase inventory. The goal is to balance the opposing costs, and thus, obtain a minimum total cost. For an illustration of annual costs versus number of orders, see Figure A: 10. Two facts are illustrated:

1. As orders are placed more frequently, carrying costs decrease because the cycle stock (cycle stock is one-half the order quantity) is less.
2. As orders are placed more frequently, purchasing costs increase.

The total operating cost is the sum of purchasing and carrying coots, and Figure A. 10 shows that it is lowest when thesc two are equal. Notice a relevant range of choices between A and B where the resultant total cost is not greatly affected by slight deviations from the best ordering frequency.

The literature normally handles the cost of purchasing as a constant amount for each order placed, and the cost of carrying is lumped into one percentage figure represented by *P*. Let *Y* designate the expected yearly demand in physical units (determined from the forecast model), let *Q* be the economic lot size in physical units, C be the unit cost, and S be the cost of making one purchase order. Then total annual variable costs *(TVC)* are expressed as follows[7]:

$$TVC = \frac{QC}{2} P + \frac{Y}{Q} S$$

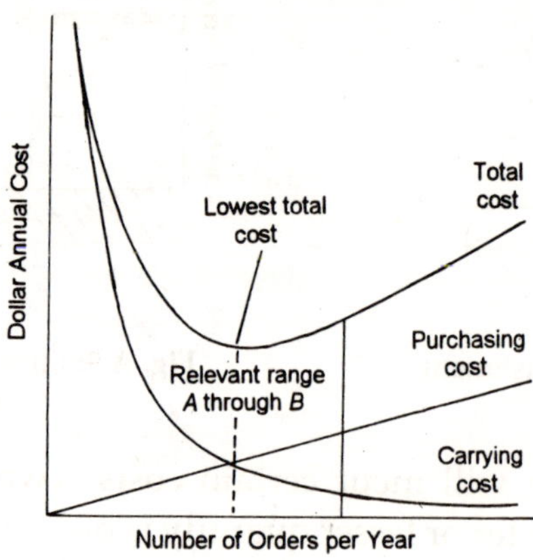

Fig. A.10: Total inventory costs versus number of orders.

In the absence of safety allowances, inventories vary from Q to zero. The average value of inventory is therefore QC/2 if the new order quantity replenishes stock at the time the inventory is depleted. The quantity *QC/2* times *P* represents the annual carrying cost. *Y/Q* represents the number of times a year that orders are placed. Therefore, *(Y/Q)S* represents the total annual purchasing costs.

To determine the amount of *Q* which minimises total cost, the above equation is differentiated with respect to *Q* and set equal to zero. The following equation is obtained:

$$\frac{PC}{2} - \frac{YS}{Q^2} = O$$

which, when solved for *Q*, equals:

$$Q = \sqrt{\frac{2YS}{PC}}$$

This formula states that *Q*, the economic order quantity, varies directly with the square root of the forecasted demand and the square root of the purchasing costs and varies inversely with the square root of the cost of carrying.

Material Yield Analysis Model

In a number of industries, particularly of the process type, material yield plays a significant role in effecting cost reduction and production improvement. Material yield standards are generally set for various types of raw material. In most cases the yield standards are based on laboratory tests or company records. A substantial cost reduction is achieved through the improvement of the yield of good products based on proper procurement and production efforts. A variance analysis programme pointing out and evaluating causes of low yield aids management in minimising shrinkage and waste in purchasing and production. If, for example, the procurement personnel purchase defective raw material, then an excess of shrinkage will occur during preparation of this material for processing. Consequently, a yield analysis and reporting system should be installed to determine the degree of shrinkage or waste.

Standards for material usage during the production phase are of paramount importance to top management. The plant manager and top management personnel need to have feedback which will enable them to detect and measure losses of raw produce during the production process. Not only do the reports of material yield disseminate information to responsible persons, but they ensure a significant degree of control of the processing function.

The basic question is whether the standard amount of raw material is used to obtain a given output of the finished product. The difficulty here is that computation of variances is delayed until the production process is completed. At the Yummy Company, however, production is set up so that a number of subbatches comprise an overall batch.

An example of yield information reporting is shown in Figure A. 11.

The yield analysis report of Figure A. 11 does not tell why the yield of this particular batch of pimiento is unfavorable. It does, however, give feedback to the plant manager, the manager of procurement, the president, and other responsible persons that particular phases in the processing function may be faulty. A retracing of the overall process must be set into motion to isolate the cause of the unfavorable variances and take necessary corrective action.

Quality Control Analysis and Reporting

Every organisation, large or small, faces the problem of attaining and maintaining satisfactory quality of their output. First, the quality attributes must be identified. Next, accurate standard measurements must be set. Finally, the allowable departures from such standard measurements must be determined. Moreover, satisfactory quality must be obtained at a reasonable and competitive cost level.

Product quality variation arises out of the variables which constitute a given process. The following are basic:

1. The raw materials which enter a process themselves vary in form and composition.
2. The production process itself varies and the resulting output may be below satisfactory quality.

The obvious objectives, therefore, are to reduce the amount of defective raw materials going into production and to eliminate defective finished products. These objectives are never fully possible, but a reduction in the number of defectives in the total operation must be sought.

Statistical sampling and control tables can be used effectively in implementing quality control in organisations. A simple table for this purpose is shown in Figure A.12.

Material Yield Report—Sliced Pimiento

Product Number	Description	Weight of Input (Raw Product)	Standard Yield Rate
002	KP SL PIM GL 24/ 4	32,000#	.510

Standard Output	Actual Yield Rate[a]	Actual Output	Variance from Per cent	Variance from Standard Weight
16,360 #	.419	13,400#	9.1% UF	2,960# UF

[a]Actual Yield Rate = $\dfrac{\text{Weight of Actual Output}}{\text{Weight of Input (Raw Produce)}}$

$= \dfrac{13{,}400}{32{,}000}$

$= .419$

Fig. A.11: Yield analysis report.

The table indicates that if 5 or more defectives are in the first sample of 25 from some population (batch or lot), then that population being tested is rejected. If more than 0 and less than 5 defectives are found, then another sample of 25 is taken. If in this next sample the cumulative total of defectives is 3 or less, then the population is accepted. If the number of defectives is greater than 3 but less than 8, then another sample is taken. If the cumulative total of defectives at the second sample is 8 or more, then the population is rejected, and so on.

Basic Queuing Models

Many types of problems are described by the buildup of queues of some input to a service facility. The queues result from stochastic or probabilistic phenomena. In all cases inputs arrive at a facility for processing, and the time of arrival of individual inputs at the service facility is random as is the time of processing. The randomness of one or more parameters in a queue system is responsible for the uncertainties associated with it. In all organisations the queuing phenomena is ever present. In production, machines are idle or overburdened. Patients wait for hours in hospitals. Trucks wait in long lines at loading docks. At times inventories are excessive; at other times, too many stock-outs occur. And so it goes. Management must strike a balance between costs of idleness and costs of overburdened service facilities. Consequently, management must know something about the activity and length of a queue, the demand on the service activity, the capacity of the service facility to handle the random demand, and the time spent waiting in the queue plus the time in the service facility.

Sequence of Samples Which Show Sample Size and Acceptance and Reject Numbers

Sample	*Sample Size*	*Combined Sample Size*	*Acceptance Number (Cumulative)*	*Rejection Number (Cumulative)*
First	25	25	0	5
Second	25	50	3	8
Third	25	75	6	11
Fourth	25	100	9	14
Fifth	25	125	12	17
Sixth	25	150	15	20
Seventh	25	175	18	23
Eighth	25	200	21	26
Ninth	25	225	24	29
Tenth	25	250	27	32

Fig. A.12: A table of acceptance and rejection numbers.

Four basic structures of queuing situations describe the general conditions of a service facility. The simplest situation is where arriving units from a single queue are to be serviced by a single service facility; for example, a car in a car wash. This structure is called a single-channel, single-phase condition. A simple assembly line has a number of service facilities in series or tandem and represents the single-channel, multiple-phase condition. If the number of service facilities is increased (two or more car washes) but still draws on one queue, then this is represented by a multiple-channel, single-phase condition. Finally, the last structure is a multiple-channel, multiple-phase condition which might be illustrated by two or more parallel production lines.[8] These structures are illustrated in Figure A.13.

Simulation Models

In a probabilistic model some dimensions are known while the value of others is based on phenomena of a stochastic nature. The randomness of one or more parameters in a system is responsible for the uncertainties that exist. Random machine breakdowns, customer demand, labor strikes, and competitor price changes, all occur.

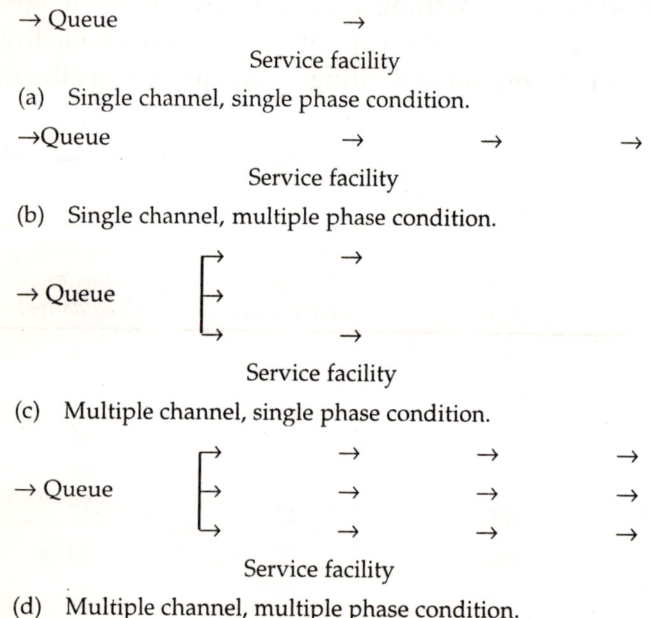

Fig. A.13: Four basic structures of queuing conditions.

Simulation models help to organise disjointed data and activities, and to illustrate interrelationships previously unknown. The perception of combinational aspects of a complex problem and their effect on a system can, in many instances, be handled only by a model. For example, the problem of smog control is amenable to simulation techniques. A complete understanding of the problem involves the interrelationship of climate, the molecular behavior of gases, the chemistry of engine exhaust, the number of vehicles, the geographic layout of the city (including the location of the homes, work places, and highway arteries), the availability of alternate means of transportation, the speed of traffic and the timing of traffic lights, the incomes of the population, the chemistry and biology of the lungs and blood stream, and problems of microbes and virus growth under chemical, light, and temperature conditions produced by smog—among other problems.[9]

The above smog control problem can be attacked through the use of simulation. Decision makers can see more clearly the aspects of the problem and how they interrelate. By so doing, the information produced by the model can aid the decision maker in choosing among a number of alternative courses of action.

Linear Programming Model

The purpose of linear programming is to provide a method of optimising the allocation of scarce resources to competing demands.

Following is a list of kinds of problems which have been solved by linear programming methods. These are the kinds of problems that systems analysts encounter in most organisations; however, this list is not exhaustive and indicates only a few examples.

1. Allocation of energy sources in electrical power generation.
2. Determining optimal mix of food products for beef cattle production.
3. Adapting production to variable and seasonal sales.
4. Allocation of limited raw materials and production facilities to the production of a multiple product line.
5. Optimum multiple plant and warehouse location.

The viewpoint that the analyst should take is to concentrate on the definition of the problem and formulation of the model and leave the technical intricacies and solution of the model to the technical staff of the information system. The technical staff would include, among others, mathematicians, operations research specialists, and application programmers.

Two major assumptions are required in using linear programming techniques: linearity and certainty. Linearity means all the relationships involve variables of the first degree and can be illustrated graphically by straight lines. Certainty requires that the value of all variables must be known and that all variables are non-negative.[10]

An example of the general form which a linear programming problem may take on, follows:

$$\text{maximise} \quad p_1x_1 + p_2x_2 + \cdots + p_nx_n$$
$$\text{subject to} \quad a_{11}x_1 + a_{12}x_2 + \cdots + a_{1n}x_n \leq b_1$$

$$a_{21}x_1 \quad + \quad a_{23}X_2 \quad + \quad \bullet\bullet\bullet \quad + \quad a_{2n}X_n \leq b_2$$

$$\vdots \qquad \vdots \qquad\qquad\qquad \vdots \quad \vdots$$

$$a_{n1}x_1 \quad + \quad a_{n2}X_2 + \bullet\bullet\bullet \quad + \quad a_{nn}X_n \leq b_n$$

The pi's in the objective function may refer to profit contributions of the given products x_1 x_2, . . . , x_n. On the other hand, the a_{ij}'s may refer to the required amounts of manufacturing material for the given products, which are in limited supply according to b_1, b_2, ..., b_n. The linear programming problem would then be to maximise the profit contribution subject to the given limitations on manufacturing material.

Let us consider a simple graphical example of a linear programming problem, as follows:

maximise	$3x_1$	+	$2x_2$		
subject to	$2x_1$	+	$3x_2$	$\leq$	10
	$3x$	-	x_1	$\leq$	6
	x_1			$\geq$	0
			x_2	$\geq$	0

Consider the x_1x_2 coordinate system. Any point (x_1 x_2) can be plotted in this system. For example see Figure A.14. All points lying on or to the right of the x_2, axis satisfy the constraint that $x_1 \geq 0$. Similarly, all points lying on or above the x_1 axis satisfy the constraint $x_2 \geq 0$. Therefore a feasible solution to the problem must be contained in the first section (quadrant) of the coordinate system. Now let us consider the other two constraints. If we allow equality to hold, then we would have equations for straight lines and any point on these lines would satisfy the equations. Refer to Figure A.15. Observe also, that any point (x_1 x_2) in the first quadrant, which lies on or below one of the given lines, satisfies that inequality. For example, the point (1,2) substituted into the equation $2x_1 + 3x_2 = 10$ yields the value 7, which is less than 10. Therefore, the points satisfying all the constraints lie in the region bounded by $2x_1 + 3x_2 = 10$, $3x_1 + x_2 = 6$, and the X_1 and x_2 axes (the shaded areas).

We must now find the point in the region that maximises the objective function, $3x_1 + 2x_2$. Allowing this function to take on different values produces straight lines which are parallel. We must then find the line that gives the objective function its greatest value and at the same time has at least one point in the constrained region. Let us give $3x_1 + 2x_2$ the value 6 and plot this line in the x_1x_2, coordinate system. See Figure A.16. This line has many points within the constrained region, but it should

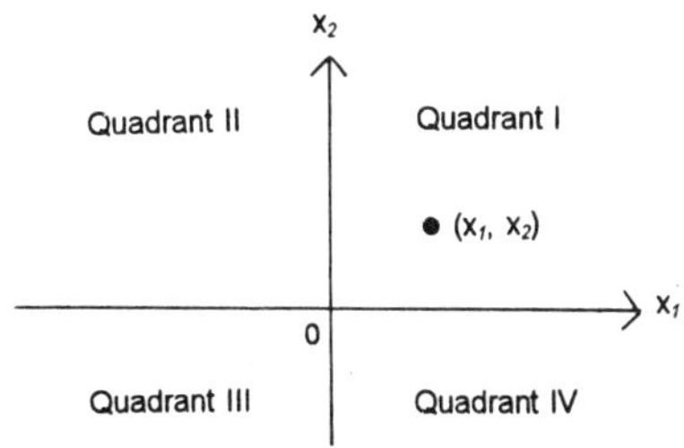

Fig. A.14: The x_1, x_2 coordinate system.

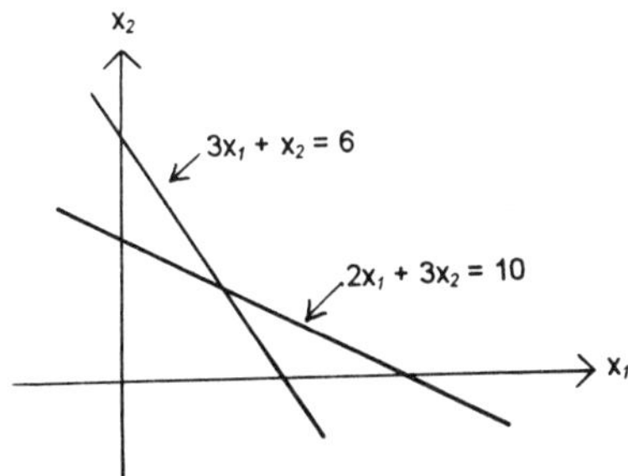

Fig. A.15: Graphical example of constraints in a linear programming problem

be obvious parallel lines exist above this line that give the objective function a greater value and still have at least one point within the constrained region. In fact, the line that gives the objective function its greatest value and still contains at least one point within the given region, passes through the point of intersection of the two lines $2x_1 + 3x_2 = 10$, and $3x_1 + x_2 = 6$. Solving these two equations simultaneously, we find $x_1 = {}^{8}/_{7}$ and $x_2 = {}^{18}/_{7}$. It is these two values that, when substituted into the objective function, give it its maximum value of $= {}^{60}/_{7}$.

For a "real world" application of the linear programming model, assume a company manufactures two products. P_1 and P_2 which are processed by three departments. The products can be processed in any order. Pertinent data are shown in the table above.

The number of minutes each department will be available for operation during the month are as follows:

12,600 minutes for D_1

14,400 minutes for D_2

13,000 minutes for D_3

The questions to answer is, how much of Product *P*1 and Product P_2 should be produced to maximise the total contribution margin? The objective function, therefore is $Z = 8X_1 + 10X_2$, where X_1 is the number of units of product P_1, and X_2 is the number of units of P_2. Then: $Z = 8X1 + 10X_2$ the function to be maximised with the conditions $X_1 \geq 0$, $X_2 \geq 0$.

The constraints are:

$20X_1 + 15X_2 \leq 12{,}600$ for department D_1

$12\ X_1 + 20X_2 \leq 14{,}400$ for department D_2

$26X_1 + 13X_2 \leq 13{,}000$ for department D_3

An infinite number of feasible solutions exist; among them is one or more for which Z is maximum. The graph in Figure A. 17 illustrates a graphical solution of the above problem.

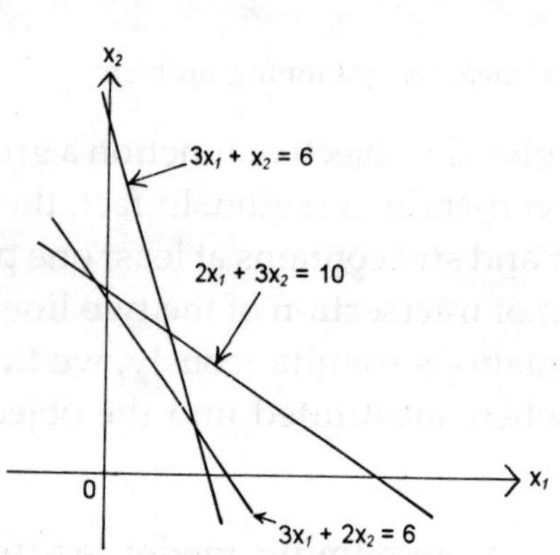

Fig. A.16: Graphical example of the objective function taking on one of many values

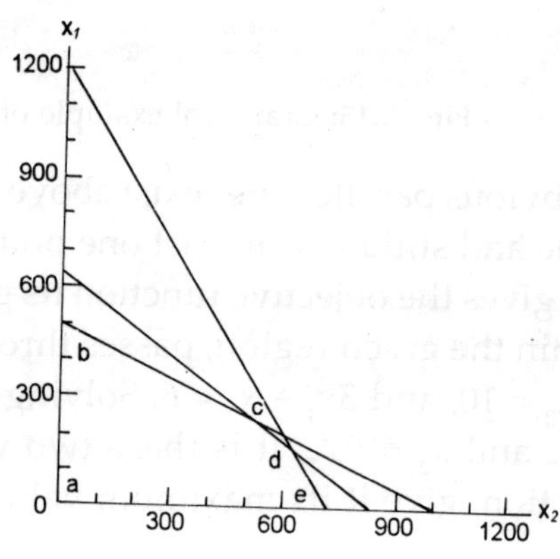

Fig. A.17: Graphical solution.

The area enclosed by abcde includes all feasible solutions to the production problem. The maximum solution can be found by computing the values at each corner of the polygon. These computations are made in the table below.

	D_1	D_2	D_3	*Contribution Margin*[a]
P_1	20 min.	12 min.	26 min.	8.00
P_2	15 min.	20 min.	13 min.	10,00

a. Contribution Margin = Sales Price - Variable Cost.

The maximum Z is represented by a straight line for a particular value of Z equal to \$7600. Since the coefficients \$8 and \$10 are invariant, this line will remain parallel to itself when the value of Z is changed. The maximum will always correspond to one of the extreme points of the constrained region that is furthest from the point of origin. Therefore, the further this line moves from the origin, the greater the value of Z, and vice versa.

Probably the most important single development in the solution of linear programming problems took place in the late 1940s when George Dantzig devised the Simplex Method. Consider for a moment the graphical example of a linear programming problem treated above. Note that a line drawn between any two points in the constrained area lies entirely within that area. This fact holds for any linear programming problem in which a feasible solution exists and this constrained region is said to be convex (bulges outward from the origin). Also note that an optimal point for the objective function will be at one of the corners of the convex region. The Simplex Method gives us a procedure for moving step by step from a given corner (extreme point) to an optimal corner (extreme point).[11]

	Corner	*Product* P_1	*Product* P_2	*(Objective Function) Total Contribution Margin*				
a	0,0	0	0	Z = \$8.00(0)	+	\$10.00(0)	–	\$0.00
b	500,0	500	0	Z \$8.00(120)	+	\$10.00(0)	=	\$4000.00
c.	250,510	250	510	Z = \$8.00(250)	+	\$10.00(510)	=	\$7000.00
d	150,640	150	640	Z = \$ 8.00 (150)	+	\$10.00(640)	=	\$7600.00[a]
e	0,720	0	720	Z = \$8.00(0)	+	\$10.00(720)	=	\$7200.00

a. Optimum solution.

REFERENCES

Anthony and Reece, *Management Accounting*, Fifth Edition, Home-wood, IL.: Richard D. Irwin, Inc., 1975.

Archibald and Villria, *Network-Based Management, Systems (PERT/ CPM)*, New York: John Wiley & Sons, Inc., 1967.

Bierman, Bonini, and Hausman, *Quantitative Analysis for Business Decisions*, Fourth Edition, Homewood, IL.: Richard D. Irwin, Inc., 1973.

Brown, *Smoothing, Forecasting, and Production of Discrete Time Series,* Englewood Cliffs, NJ.: Prentice-Hall, Inc., 1963.

Buffa, *Operations Management,* Third Edition, New York: John Wiley & Sons, Inc., 1972.

Burch, "Computer Application of Contribution Analysis," *Journal of Systems Management,* August 1970.

Demski, *Information Analysis,* Reading, MA.: Addison-Wesley Publishing Co., 1972.

Button and Starbuck, *Computer Simulation of Human Behavior,* New York: John Wiley & Sons, Inc., 1971.

Evarts, *Introduction to PERT,* Boston: Allyn and Bacon, Inc., 1964.

Gass, *Linear Programming,* Second Edition, New York: McGraw-Hill Book Co., 1964.

Hadley, *Linear Algebra,* Reading, MA.: Addison-Wesley Publishing Co., 1961.

Hillier and Lieberman, *Introduction to Operations Research,* Second Edition, San Francisco: Holden-Day, 1974.

Horngren, *Cost Accounting: A Managerial Emphasis,* Fifth Edition, Englewood Cliffs, NJ.: Prentice-Hall, Inc., 1982.

Kuhn, *The Study of Society: A Unified Approach,* Homewood, IL.: Richard D. Irwin, Inc., and The Dorsey Press, 1963.

Maisel and Gnugnoli, *Simulation of Discrete Stochastic Systems,* Chicago: Science Research Associates, Inc., 1972.

Martin, *Computer Modeling and Simulation,* New York: John Wiley & Sons, inc., 1968.

Raiffa, *Decision Analysis,* Reading, MA.: Addison-Wesley Publishing Co., 1968.

Richmond, *Statistical Analysis,* New York: The Ronald Press Company, 1964.

Slaybaugh, "Pareto's Law and Modern Management," *Management Services,* March-April 1967.

Starr and Miller, *Inventory Control: Theory and Practice,* Englewood Cliffs, NJ.: Prentice-Hall, Inc., 1962.

Wagner, *Principles of Operations Research,* Second Edition, Englewood Cliffs, NJ.: Prentice-Hall, Inc., 1975.

Whitin, *The Theory of Inventory Management,* Princeton, NJ.: Princeton University Press, 1957.

NOTES

1. For a turotrial treatment of these methods, we refer you to Robert N. Anthony and James S. Reece, *Management Accounting,* Fifth Edition, Homewood, III.: Richard D. Irwin, Inc., 1975, and Charles T. Horngren, *Cost Accounting: A Managerial Emphasis,* Fifth Edition, Englewood Chiffs, N.J.: Prentice-Hall, Inc., 1982.
2. Anthony and Reece, *op. cit.*, p. 721.
3. For an in-depth treatment of a variety of models, refer to H. Bierman, C.P. Bonini, and W.H. Hausman, *Quantitative Analysis for Business Decisions,* Fourth Edition, Homewood, III.: Richard D. Irwin, Inc., 1973, and Howard Raiffa, *Decision Analysis,* Reading, Ma.: Addison-Wesley, 1968.
4. For full treatment of PERT, refer to Russell D. Archibald and Richard L. Villura, Network-Based Management Systems *(PERT CPM),* New York: John Wiley and Sons, Inc., 1967. Harry F. Evarts, Introduction to PERT, Beston: Allyn and Bacon, Inc., 1964.
5. C. Jay Slaybaugh, "Pareto's Law and Modern Management," *Management Services,* March-April, 1967.

6. The above discussion of the least-squares method represents a summarisation of several comprehensive textbooks. For example, see Samuel B. Richmond, *Statistical Analysis*, New York: The Ronald Press Company, 1964, Chapters 2, 7, 18, and 19.
7. For example, see Thomson M. Whilin, *The Theory of Inventory Management*, Princeton, N.J.: Princeton University Press, 1957, pp. 32-34. Martin K. Starr and David W. Miller, *Inventory Control: Theory and Practice*. Englewood Cliffs, N.J.: Prentice-Hall, Inc., 1962.
8. Elwood S. Buffa, *Operations Management*, Third Edition, New York: John Wiley and Sons, Inc., 1972, p. 465.
9. Alfred Kuhn, *The Study of Society: A Unified Approach*. Homewood, III.: Richard D. Irwin, Inc., and The Dorsey Press, 1963, p. 4.
10. For detailed analyses of linear programming models, refer to S.I. Gass, *Linear Programming*, Second Edition, New York McGraw-Hill Book Company, 1964; G. Hadley, *Linear Algebra*. Reading, Mass.: Addison-Wesley Publishing Company, 1961 FS. Hillier and G.J. Lieberman, *Introduction to Operations Research*, Second Edition, San Francisco: Holden-Day, 1974 and H.M. Wagner, *Principles of Operations Research*, Second Edition, Englewood Cliff's, NJ: Prentice-Hall, Inc., 1975.
11. G. Hadley, *op. cit.*

APPENDIX B

THE COMPUTER AND RELATED TECHNOLOGY

INTRODUCTION

The computer and related technology can be divided into three major sections, which are: (1) the central processor, (2) devices peripheral to the central processor, and (3) data communication devices which connect peripheral devices to the central processor.

THE CENTRAL PROCESSOR

The heart of any computer configuration is the central processing unit, or CPU. First, we will analyze the central processor and then present a few techniques which help to increase its processing power.

Overview of the Central Processor

The central processor is really the "computer" in a computer configuration and all computer configurations perform the following five basic functions:

1. *Input.* The data to be operated upon and the instructions are made available to the central processing unit via input media.
2. *Primary storage.* From the input media, data and instructions are transferred to the main storage section of the central processor. Other storage media (e.g., magnetic tape, magnetic disk) are considered auxiliary to primary storage.
3. *Arithmetic-logic.* The processor manipulates the data in accordance with the set of instructions. These manipulations are performed in the arithmetic-logic section, one operation at a time, with intermediate results being placed back into primary storage. The arithmetic-logic section performs addition, subtraction, multiplication, division, and certain logical operations such as comparing the magnitude of two numbers.
4. *Control.* Control is required inside a computer system to: (1) tell the input media what data to enter into primary storage and when to enter the data; (2) tell the primary storage section where to place these data; (3) tell the arithmetic-logic section what operations to perform, where the data are to be found, and where to place the results; (4) tell what file devices to access and what data to access; and (5) tell what output media on which to write the final results.

5. *Output*. This function refers to the results of the data processed within the central processor. This final result is written on various output media.

A schematic of a computer system, emphasising the central processor, is illustrated in Figure B-1. All digital computers, regardless of size, speed, and details of operation, follow this same basic logical structure.

Size of the Central Processor

When manufacturers state the size of their processor, they are referring to the size of the primary storage. Size of a processor's primary storage helps to determine the maximum size of programmes and the amount of data available for processing at any one time. Each primary storage location has a unique address, analogous to a mailbox in a post office. The address identifies the location of the data for both storing and accessing operations. Although all data are represented as binary digits or bits, the smallest addressable location in main storage differs from one computer to another. Depending on the design of the computer, each addressable location is a character or the beginning of a computer word. These storage locations may be designated as follows:

1. *Byte-addressable combination.* The basic storage unit of some computers is called a byte. The byte is made up of eight bits and an additional parity bit. Although the byte itself is a fixed binary composition, it can be strung together in different ways to provide structures of varying length. The byte-addressable system is flexible in the sense that each byte is addressable and can represent two numbers or one character. This means that a computer with 64K memory where K, or kilo means thousnads has approximately 64,000 bytes of addressable main storage.
2. *Character-addressable.* In a character-addressable system it may require a six-bit set (not including control bits) to encode a character. If the number 47 is in storage, the 4 will take up one storage location having an address; the 7 is in another contiguous storage location with a separate address. An eight-bit byte would provide greater storage than a six-bit character because two decimal digits may be packed in a byte.
3. *Word-addressable.* A computer word consists of an ordered set of bits, which may be of fixed or variable length, depending on the particular computer. Commonly, computers which are designated as word-addressable, have fixed word sizes of 24, 30, 32, 36, 48, 54, and 64 bits.

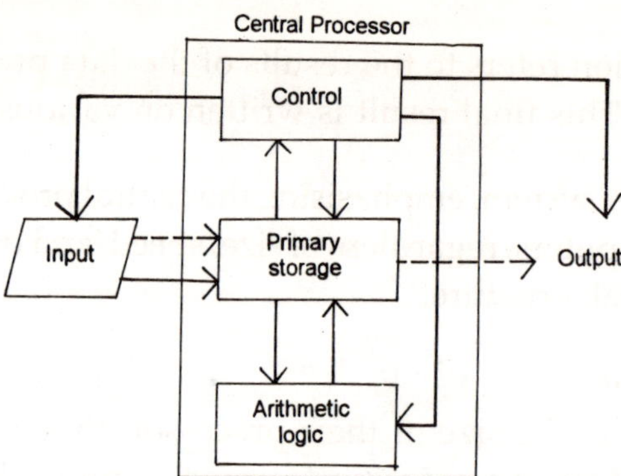

Fig. B-1: General diagram of a central processor. Broken line indicates data flow; solid line indicates instruction flow; and heavy line indicates control flow.

Speed of the Processor

Other aspects to consider when evaluating primary storage are: access and cycle time. These aspects are discussed here.[1]

1. *Access time.* Access time refers to the time it takes for the control section to locate instructions and data for processing. It represents the time interval between initiating a transfer of data to or from storage and the instant when this transfer is completed. This time interval varies from one computer to another. In most primary storage devices, access time is measured in microseconds (one-millionth of a second); however, in some large-scale computers access time is measured in nanoseconds (one-billionth of a second).
2. *Cycle time. A* computer performs its operations on a cycle basis. The computer operates on pulses per length of time like a clock. At any one time, the computer is either in the instruction cycle or the execution cycle. An instruction is obtained from a main memory location and transferred to the arithmetic-logic unit. Here it is decoded according to its operation code, specifying what is to be done, and its operand, specifying the address of the data to be operated upon. The computer then moves into the execution cycle. Here the decoded instruction is executed using the data specified by the instruction. When the execution cycle is complete, the computer automatically goes back into the instruction cycle, and the process begins again.

The amount of data accessed in one cycle depends on the computer design, and is expressed in bytes, characters, or words. For example, Model X may have a slower basic access time than Model Y, but Model X may access four bytes at a time whereas Model Y accesses two bytes. Therefore, two factors combine which result in effective access time: the amount of data accessed during each cycle and the time required to perform each cycle.

Size of storage used is normally based on cost, and cost of storage in turn is based on speed (i.e., as access speed increases, the cost per bit stored also increases). This speed mismatch and cost variation between various storage media have caused a number of processor configuration innovations manifested in different storage hierarchy systems. For example, a hierarchy of storage might consist of very high-speed (nanosecond) semiconductor storage; medium-speed (microsecond) core storage; and large, slow-speed (millisecond) magnetic disk or drum. The hierarchy of storage concept can be illustrated by the virtual storage and buffer storage techniques which are discussed in the following sections.

Virtual Storage Technique

The basic idea behind virtual storage is the dynamic linking of primary storage of the processor to auxiliary storage so that each user (several may be using the system concurrently) appears to have very large primary storage, usually measured in megabytes, at his or her disposal. Parts of a programme, or data associated with the user's programme, may be broken up and scattered both in primary storage and on magnetic disk or drum, thus giving the "virtual" effect of much larger primary storage to the programmer.[2] This technique is illustrated in Figure B-2.

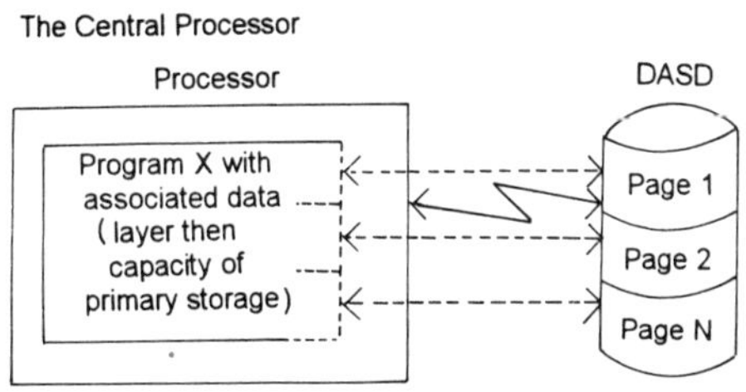

Fig. B-2: Illustration of the virtual storage concept.

Normally only the instructions and data necessary for immediate processing will be located in primary storage, in the form of "pages" which are transferred between primary storage and slower auxiliary (DASD) storage automatically.[3] With this approach, jobs are loaded into partitions or regions of auxiliary storage. During processing, small blocks or pages of instructions and data are transferred between auxiliary storage and processor storage according to the momentary needs of each job.[4]

Buffer Storage Technique

This technique, also called cache memory, uses a limited-capacity but very fast semiconductor storage combined with less expensive, slower, large-capacity core storage to give the overall effect of a faster primary storage. This technique requires careful look-ahead procedures to get the correct data into semiconductor storage when it is required.[5] The buffer storage technique is illustrated in Figure B-3.

It is the function of the buffer to fetch frequently used instructions and data to be used by the arithmetic-logic part of the central processor. In most cases, these instructions and data will be available at the buffer rate, rather than at the slower primary storage rate. This technique is based on the theory that adjacent bytes in primary storage will usually be used at the same time. If the required data are in the buffer, they are transferred to the arithmetic-logic unit at buffer speed. If the required data are not in the buffer then they are obtained from primary storage. On the subject of buffering, studies revealed that the required data are in the buffer 90 per cent of the time. As with, the virtual storage technique, the buffer storage technique provides increased performance without adding new responsibilities to the programmer (i.e., the operation of buffer storage is "transparent" to the programmer).

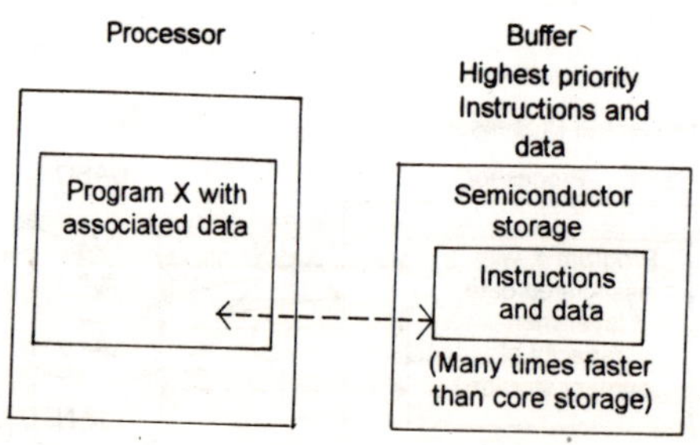

Fig. B-3: Illustration of the buffer storage concept.

Multiprocessors

It should be recognized by the reader that a computer configuration, in many applications, operates with more than one processor unit (multiprocessing). While one can configure a total computer system in endless ways, for one typical illustration of a multiprocessing system, refer to Figure B-4.

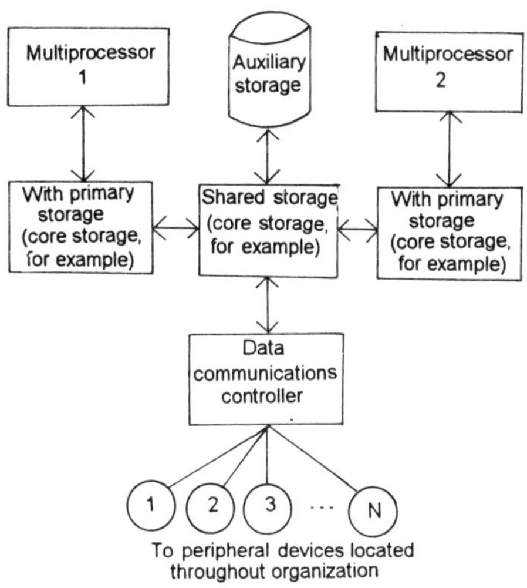

Fig. B-4: Illustration of a multiprocessor configuration.

The system above, for an example, could be used as a fail soft backup system where each processor is equipped with its own dedicated core memory, shares common partitioned storage that is used to access the data base files, and is connected to various peripherals. The partitioned core, storage configuration allows either processor to operate the entire system in the event the other processor fails.

Minicomputers

Minicomputers are distinguished from large computers on the basis of cost, processor speed, memory size, and software. Today, a typical minicomputer fulls within a $15,000 to $75,000 price range. Over three-quarters of all minis support business applications, while about one-half are designed for use in scientific applications.[6]

Features such as virtual memory and small, high-speed cache, memory are becoming increasingly popular in minis. The most common size of main memory is from 128K to 512K bytes. Most minicomputers have 16-bit word sizes. The norm of cycle times for a minicomputer is 700 nanoseconds.

Minicomputers typically support up to four languages, with BASIC being the most popular, followed by FORTRAN, COBOL and RPG.

Microcomputers

The advances in microelectronics that possible the minicomputer in the early

1970s, have led tó the creation of the microcomputer. A system of large-scale integraltion (LSI) chips contains the CPU, internal memory, and input/output interfaces of the microcomputer.

While microcomputers were originally designed for hobbyists, they have become a viable alternative to manual systems for small businesses. This trend will accelerate as hardware prices fall and as the amount of business software for micros grows.

Though the line of distinction between minicomputers and microcomputer is blurred on the dimensions of physical appearance and size we can generally characterize microcomputers as having 4K to 64K bytes of internal memory, data entry via keyboard, and a video screen for output. Beyond a basic configuration, a small business microcomputer system may have additional internal memory, external memory in the form of cassettes or minifloppy disks, and a low-speed printer.

Types of Storage

We will conclude this section by presenting a summary classification of storage media. This classification is presented in Figure B-5.

Name of Storage Media	*Primary Storage*	*Online Auxiliary Storage*	*Offline Auxiliary Storage*
Bubble	X		
LSI	X		
Semiconductor	X		
Magnetic core	X	X	
Thin films	X		
Holographic	X	X	
Plated wire	X		
Magnetic drum	X	X	
Magnetic disks	X	X	X
Mass storage		X	
Magnetic tape			X
Punched paper tape			X
Punched cards			X

Fig. B-5: Types of storage media.

DEVICES AND APPLICATIONS PERIPHERAL TO THE CPU

In Figure B-6 we present a general schematic of devices peripheral to the computer. In this section we will discuss from a systems application viewpoint five basic areas: (1) aspects of auxiliary storage media, specifically magnetic tape, magnetic disk, mass storage, and microfilm; (2) terminal devices; and (3) data entry techniques.

Analysis of Auxiliary Storage Devices

Primary storage is expensive and can only be used economically to hold programmes and data that the computer is presently processing. Auxiliary storage devices are used to store other programmes and data which are made available to the computer when needed. Popular storage devices which transfer data or instructions rapidly between primary storage and an input output drive unit are: magnetic tape, magnetic disk, magnetic drum, and mass storage. Computer output microfilm (COM) can also be considered as auxiliary storage. We will treat, in this section, four of these devices, namely: (1) magnetic tape, (2) magnetic disk, (3) mass storage, and (4) COM.

Magnetic Tape

Magnetic tape is a very popular medium for storage of voluminous amounts of data. It is a sequential medium and is used widely in batch processing environments.

Physical Characteristics of Magnetic Tape

Data are recorded on seven-, eight-, nine-, or ten-channel tape in the form of magnetised spots. Tape widths are normally $^1/_2$ inch, although some tapes are if, $^3/_4$, 1, and 3 inches in width. Some new tapes are being marketed which record data in a fashion similar to videotape, (i.e.. data are recorded across the tape rather than along it. This technique allows bits to be much smaller and closer together. Some manufacturers claim that packing density is 40 times greater than on regular tape. Usually, reels hold 2400 to 3600 feet of magnetic tape; however shorter tapes are sometimes used. Further discussion will be based on nine-channel tape.

Coding Scheme

The recording of data on magnetic tape is similar in concept to a tape recorder. Magnetic tape for data processing, however, records numbers, and alphabetic and special characters. These data are recorded on tape in channels as shown in Figure B-7.

Density

The density of magnetic tape is represented by the number of characters or bits

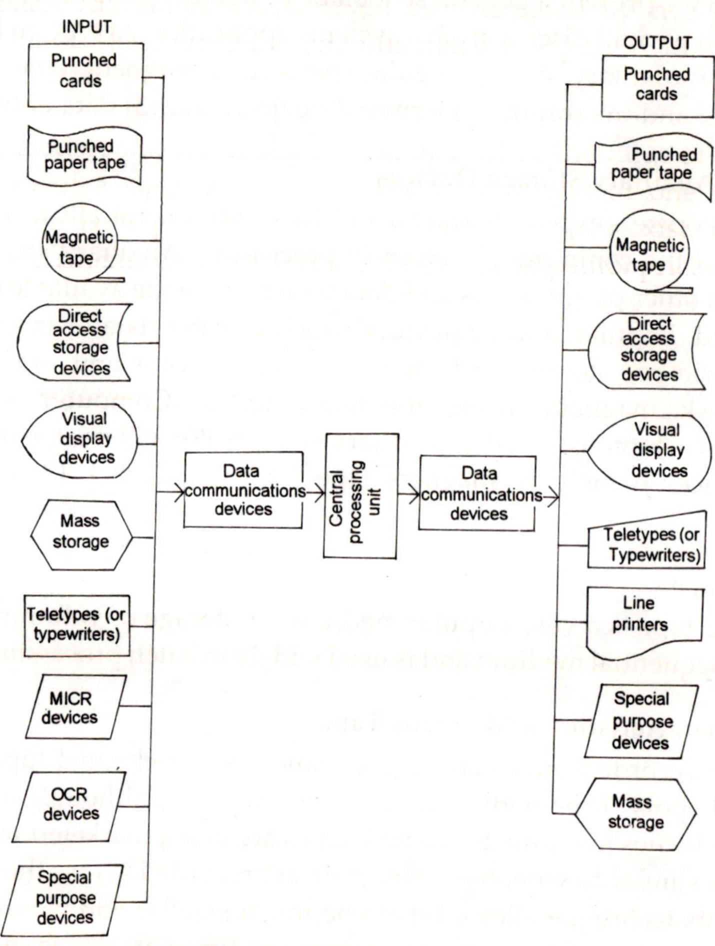

Fig. B-6: The computer and its peripherals.

recorded per inch (CPI or BPI). The most common tape density is 1600 BPL. Higher density tapes can record up to 6250 BPI.

Magnetic Tape Transfer Rate

The transfer rate is determined by the speed of a tape drive unit and the density of characters recorded per inch. The tape drive unit functions in much the same way as a home tape recorder (i.e., the tape is wound from one reel to another, passing through a read/write unit where it can be read repeatedly without destroying the data stored). New data can be written over old data, when desired, and the tape can be rewound and backspaced. If the speed of a tape unit is 112.5 inches per second and the characters per inch are 800 then the data transfer rate is 90,000 characters per second (CPS). The common speeds of tape units are: 18.75, 22.5, 36.0, 37.5, 75.0, 112.5, 125.0, and 200.0 inches per second. Some manufacturers use vacuum systems rather than capstan systems. These vacuum systems literally suck the tape from one reel to another at speeds of 1000 inches per second.

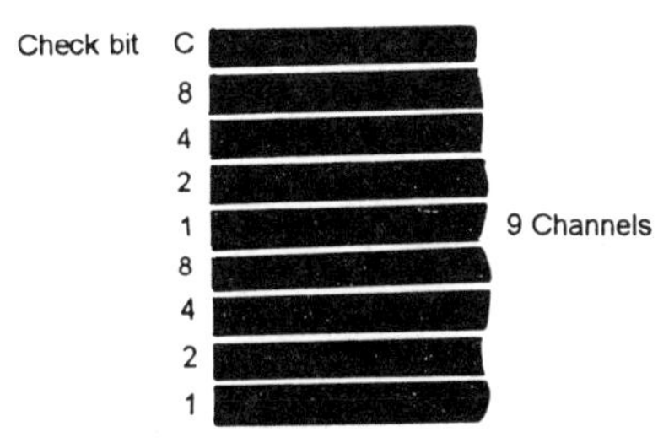

Fig. B-7: Magnetic tape using EBCDIC.

Blocking Records

Each physical record that is written on a tape is separated by a blank ($^1/_2$ inch, $^3/_4$ inch, etc., according to the particular tape system) referred to as an interblock gap (IBG). The IBG has three purposes, which are: (1) it separates a record or block discussed below, (2) it allows space enough for the tape unit to reach its operating speed (i.e., one-half of the IBG is used for starting speed), and (3) it allows space enough for the tape unit to decelerate after a read or write operation. The tape must be moving at its designated speed before it can be read from or written on. Therefore the IBG gives enough space to get the tape moving at full speed. By the same token, when the end of the record (or block) is reached, in reading or writing, the tape cannot be stopped immediately; therefore, space must also be provided to allow the tape to stop.

The IBG contains no data. For example, if a recording density is 1600 BPI this means that a $^1/_2$ inch IBG could hold 800 characters of data. Or looking at it another way, approximately the data found in 20 80-column cards could be stored in two $^1/_2$ inch IBGs. The records in a tape with each record separated by an IBG are shown in Figure B-8. The records contain 800 characters and are unblocked.

Tape economy is realised by combining the records into a block of records by a blocking factor of *N*, where *N* equals the number of records within each block. The block itself becomes a physical group of characters separated by IBGs and the data records within the block become a logical record. A block is therefore said to be a tape-recording concept, whereas a record within the block is a logical record, or a data processing concept. Figure B-9 represents records with a blocking factor of 5.

<—— ½" ——>	<—— ½" ——>	<—— ½" ——>	<—— ½" ——>
1 B G	Record	1 B G	Record

Fig. B-8: Unblocked records.

1 B G	Logical record 1	Logical record 2	Logical record 3	Logical record 4	Logical record 5	1 B G

Fig. B-9: Records with a blocking factor of 5.

The concept of transfer rate is a little misleading because, as a tape unit reads blocks of logical records, it stops each time it comes to an IBG. Consequently, when blocks are being read or written, a certain amount of time is spent at each IBG. The total amount of time required to read or write a given number of blocks is equal to the sum of the time spent reading or writing the data plus the time spent starting and stopping at the IBGs. To realise the effect that start/stop time has on reading and writing speeds, consider the following example:

Tape density	=	1600 BPI
Tape unit speed	=	75.0 inches per second
Therefore, stated transfer rate	=	120,000 CPS
Number of blocks on tape	=	8000
Blocking factor	=	10 where each record contains 30 characters; therefore, each block contains 300 characters or a total of 2,400,000 characters.
Number of IBGs	=	8000
Size of IBG	=	$^{3}/_{4}$ inch
Time to pass over IBG	=	.010 sec.
Therefore,		
Total start/stop time	=	8000 x .010
	=	80 sec.
Total time for reading data	=	2,400,000
	÷	120,000

	=	20 sec.
Therefore,		
Total time to read all records	=	80 + 20
	=	100 sec.
Effective transfer rate	=	1,200,000 ÷ 100
	=	12,000 CS

Consequently, it takes 80 sec. to start and stop the tape, and only 20 sec. to read the data. A waste of tape space and, accordingly, processing time results. To reduce this waste more records should be placed in a block. If the blocking factor is 40, then the number of IBGs would be reduced to 2000 instead of 8000. The total time to read the records is 20 sec. for reading data plus 20 sec. (2000 x .010), or 40 sec. When an installation has thousands of tape reels, reducing wasted space becomes quite significant. The reduction in wasted space results in:

1. *Less cost for tape.* Typical costs for tape reels are between $10 and $100. If a system has 1000 tapes with a cost of $80,000 and the space can be reduced 50 per cent then a cost savings of $40,000 can be effected.
2. *Saves time.* Reduction of wait-time of the processing unit resulting either from tapes being moved from the tape units and/or space in the tape itself. Obviously, an increased blocking factor increases I/O speeds.
3. *Saves storage.* In older systems that have not had proper data management, an increasing number of applications, combined with increasingly stringent requirements for data retention, have resulted in a squeeze on available storage space. In some instances this squeeze has caused an expenditure for a new wing of the tape library. The principle of large blocking factors can be applied to many older systems on two levels: (1) The software system should be investigated to ascertain if the largest possible blocking factor is being used by every programme. This would be particularly applicable in those installations that have upgraded their central processor storage capacity. (2) The reblocking of archival files should be done to contain the highest blocking factor that the hardware can handle. It is often found that multiple-reel tape files can be reduced to a single reel. The re-compilation of source programmes to increase blocking factors, the necessary deblocking and file extraction run, and the reblocking of tapes are methods that use computer time, but the time lost on this fairly infrequent procedure would be more than balanced by the overall cost savings. Incidentally, physical space occupied by tapes can be reduced by writing short files on small reels, which are then stored on special racks to maximise the space savings.

Advantages/Disadvantages of Magnetic Tape

The advantages of Magnetic tape are as follows:

1. It has a much faster transfer rate than punched cards.
2. Tapes play an important role and remain unchallenged for backup storage and for low-cost, high-capacity applications requiring only sequential access.
3. It requires less storage space than other media such as cards.
4. It is erasable and can be used over and over again for many different applications.
5. Tape manufacturers offer a wide range of specifications to meet particular applications.
6. Relatively speaking, tapes are inexpensive where one cent can buy enough tape capacity to store tens of thousands of characters.
7. In card systems, one or more records can be lost from a file. A tape file is continuous, which means that no record of the file can be lost.

The disadvantages of magnetic tape are:

1. Since tape is a sequential medium, the access of a particular record is made only after all records preceding it have been read. It is, therefore, not applicable for jobs which require rapid, direct access to specific records.
2. Since the tape is also continuous in design, a clerk cannot physically remove, insert, or change a record without reading from the original and rewriting it with the change to another tape.
3. The magnetised spots are unreadable by humans. A printed listing of the tape is required to read or verify tape data.
4. The temperature, humidity, and dust content of the tape environment must be tightly controlled. Particles of dust on a tape can cause improper processing. Temperature and humidity conditions that fall outside of prescribed ranges can cause peculiar and mysterious results from processing.

Magnetic Disk

Magnetic disks have now become the medium of choice to serve as auxiliary storage. The price per character or byte stored continues to decrease, and the direct access capability of disks gives the systems analyst far more options and flexibility in designing systems (e.g., capability of online inquiry of large files) than does magnetic tape.

Physical Characteristics of Magnetic Disk

A magnetic disk is made up of a stack of rotating metal platters on which records are stored. Direct access to any record can be made without having to read through a sequence of other, irrelevant records. This direct access capability allows random entry of transaction data and random inquiry into the file from a user. The different disk models range from 5 to 100 disks measuring from 1.5 to 3 feet in diameter. The IBM 3330 Disk Storage Facility is used to illustrate the physical characteristics of magnetic disk. A schematic of it is shown in Figure B-10.

The illustration portrays a disk unit in which 10 of the 12 surfaces are used for recording data. Each surface is divided into 404 tracks, which are analogous to flattened, circular sections of magnetic tape. Each track has a capacity of 13,030 bytes. The read/write mechanism positions the read/write heads over a separate track which forms a vertical cylinder. Since each surface consists of 404 tracks, we can see that, the disk unit is composed of 404 concentric cylinders. In Figure B-10, the read/write heads are positioned over the tracks which make up cylinder 013.

Addressing

In Figure B-11 we have four 3100-byte records stored on cylinder 013, track 02. These records, although not shown, are coded in EBCDIC. Each record on the track is numbered sequentially.

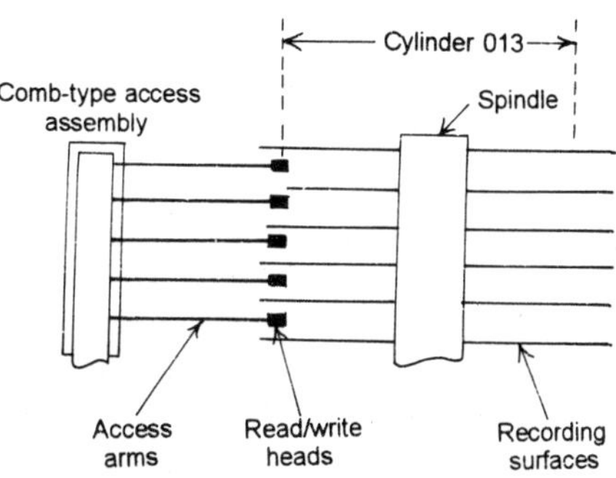

Fig. B-10: Side view of a disk pack.

Therefore, each data record is preceded by a small address record. With these addresses, it is possible to access directly any desired record stored on the disk. Note that records are separated by gaps, similar to an IBG in magnetic tape. Since the addresses and gaps require a portion of the track, it is impossible to store a full 13,030 bytes of data on a track when more than one record per track is stored. As the number of records per track increases, the number of gaps and addresses increases, causing the data per track to decrease. For example, if the record size is 500 bytes, then the track capacity would be 20 records, for a total track capacity of 10,000 bytes of data.

Magnetic Disk Transfer Rate

The disk pack rotates clockwise on a spindle as the access mechanism moves in and out.

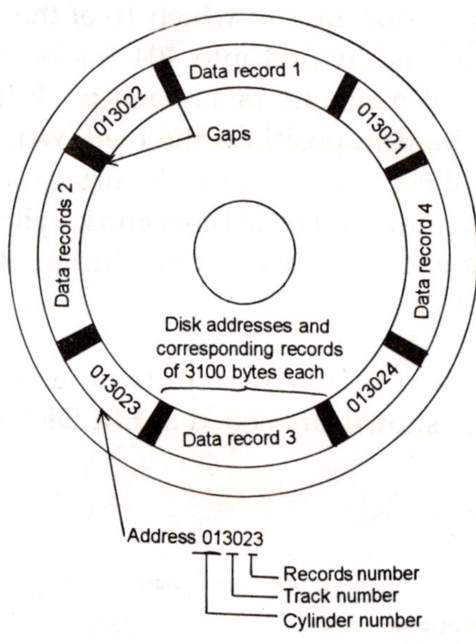

Fig. B-11: Four 3100-byte records stored on disk showing an address for each record.

The speed with which data are read or written is dependent upon these two factors plus read/write head selection and data transfer. These factors are discussed below:

1. *Access mechanism movement time.* This is the time it takes for the access assembly to move the read/write heads to a specified cylinder (called seek time or access time). The access movement time is based on the number of cylinders the read/write heads travel over to reach the one specified, and the speed of the mechanism itself. The movement rate is not uniform because the mechanism is electromechanical and does not move at constant speed (notice the movement of the player arm of a record; the naked eye can detect a somewhat irregular movement). For a movement of one

cylinder, minimum time is 10 milliseconds (msec.); across all 404 cylinders, maximum is 55 msec. The average movement speed over the entire pack is 30 msec. If the read/write heads are already at their proper position during access, they do have to be moved, therefore, the access movement time is zero. On some disk systems the read/write heads are fixed in position over each track (e.g., the IBM 2305 Fixed Head Storage Facility). This eliminates the seek time consideration.

2. *Read/Write Head Selection.* After the access mechanism has been properly positioned on the specified cylinder, the head that is to read or write is switched on. This switching is electronic and the amount of time, therefore, is negligible in all cases.
3. *Rotational Delay.* Before data are read or written the proper location on the track must rotate to the read/write heads. The time spent in rotating to a proper alignment of the read/write heads with the specified location is called *rotational delay.* For the IBM 3330 Disk Storage Facility, a full rotation requires 16.7 msec. If, after positioning the access mechanism over the desired track, the desired record has just passed, then the rotational delay is 16.7 msec. If, on the other hand, the desired record has just reached the read/write head, then the rotational delay is zero. For timing calculations, an average rotational delay of 8.4 msec. is used.
4. *Data transfer.* After the disk pack has been rotated to its proper location, the record can be read or written. The time required to transfer the record between the disk pack and the main storage is the transfer rate and is a function of rotation speed, the density at which the data are recorded, and the length of the record transferred. The transfer rate of a 3330 unit is 806K bytes per second.

In timing a read or write operation, the actual direct accessing consists, therefore, of access mechanism movement time, rotational delay (using average time), and data transfer rate. The total time for a complete processing job requires, in addition, the consideration of additional factors such as programme processing time, access method processing time, and control programme time.

For example, again using the IBM 3330 as the storage medium, Figure B-12 presents an approximate timing summary to read a thousand 5000-byte records randomly distributed over an entire disk pack.

Per record:			
	Average access time	30.0	msec
	Average rotational delay	8.4	msec
	Data transfer time	6.2	msec
	Total	44.6	msec
1000 records—44.6 sec.			

Fig. B-12: A liming summary.

Floppy Disks

Floppy (flexible) disks were introduced by IBM in 1972 as a low-cost, random access storage medium for minicomputers. Floppy disks are punched out of a polyester film that is coated with an iron oxide compound. The flat, 8-inch circular magnetic diskette rotates freely within a jacket that is intended to prevent both data loss and the diskette from being damaged.

The jacket has access and index holes to accommodate the read/write head (which actually touches the disk) and the data timing transducers of the disk drive. Each diskette contains 77 tracks, and has a storage capacity of 512K bytes (double-sided diskettes or "flippies," single density). Track-to-track access time is 3 msec.; average access time over all tracks is approximately 90 msec.

Advantages/Disadvantages of Magnetic Disk

The advantages are as follows:

1. Besides having a direct access capability, a disk file may be organised sequentially and processed like a magnetic tape.
2. All transactions can be processed as they occur, thereby keeping the system current.
3. Multiple files can be stored on a single disk pack.
4. Multiple and interrelated files may be stored in a way which permits a transaction to be processed against all pertinent files simultaneously.

The disadvantages are as follows:

1. Magnetic disk is still more expensive than magnetic tape. Falling prices and improved recording densities, however, have given real economies to users of, magnetic disks (and tapes, too, as far as costs are concerned).

2. For many applications, sequential tape processing is as acceptable and effective as disk.
3. In accounting work, a clearly discernible audit trail is needed. In updating a file on a magnetic disk, the record is read, updated, and written back to the same location, thus destroying the original contents. If no provision for error detection and file reconstruction is made, costly errors may go undetected.

Mass Storage

Although magnetic tape is being replaced by disk units as the medium immediately below processor memory, large data files, backup files, and seldom-used files still need to be stored on a low-cost, medium-to-slow access medium. One such system is Control Data Corporation's 38500 Mass Storage System (another is IBM's 3851).

This system is intended for processing large active files within an environment where performance and equipment costs are the key criteria for evaluation. Storage capacity of the system ranges from 16 billion to over a trillion bytes. A maximum of 5, and an average of 2.5 sec., is required to access data.

The Control Data 38500 system is built around magnetic tape cartridges. Each enclosed cartridge contains a 150-inch-long, 2.7-inch-wide magnetic tape, capable of storing up to 8 million bytes of data. Within a single-file unit, 2052 tape cartridges are clustered in beehive fashion. To retrieve data, an X-Y selector is positioned at the addressable location, the cartridge is picked by the selector, and the cartridge is then moved to a tape transport. At the transport, the cartridge is opened, and the tape is unwound fully and inserted into vacuum columns. It can then be moved past the read/ write station at approximately 129 inches per second, effecting a data transfer rate of over 800,000 bytes per second.

Computer Output Microfilm (COM)

COM provides another medium for storing large amounts of data. This approach is shown in Figure B-13. Data output from the central processor is read into a microfilm recorder which is connected to a film developer. The final microfilm output is in two basic forms: (1) microfiche and (2) roll film. Either one can be viewed directly through special readers.

Advantages of COM are:

1. Although COM is generally considered as a replacement for data on paper, in many situations it can be considered as a replacement for magnetic tape.

2. COM is quite applicable for archival files (five or more years), whereas magnetic tape is not made for long-term storage of data. Tape deteriorates over a long period of nonuse and, in addition, the recorded magnetic signals must be insulated from possible damage caused by environmental conditions such as radiation, heat, humidity, and random signals from electrical fixtures.
3. COM significantly reduces the need for storage space because it reduces the paper explosion.
4. Information is available directly from storage in human readable form with the aid of a microfilm reader.
5. It is relatively inexpensive.

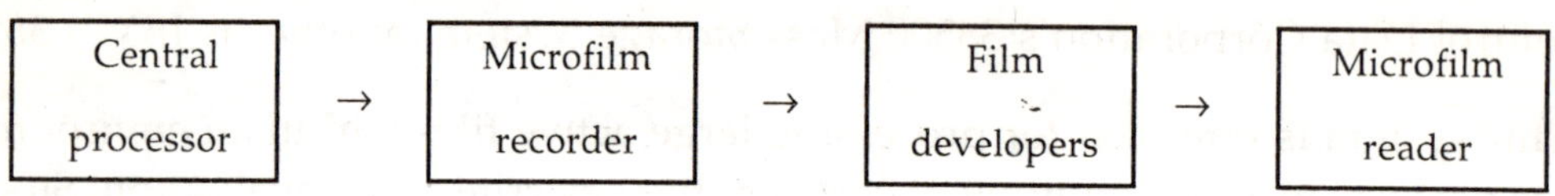

Fig. B-13: An illustration of the processes involved in producing COM.

6. COM, as a replacement for distributed reports, reduces significantly mailing costs.

The major disadvantages of COM are:

1. It is not economical where records within a file require updating continuously.
2. A COM reader is necessary.
3. A COM file cannot be read by a computer.

Summary Characteristics of Auxiliary Storage Devices

We have discussed in detail the four popular auxiliary storage devices—magnetic tape, disk, mass storage, and COM. In seeking the best mix of devices, the high-speed devices such as magnetic drum, magnetic disk, and mass storage are generally the best for quick processing of large quantities of data. In archival files where minimum access speed and high data storage capacity are important, microfilm may be the best choice. Applications that require voluminous amounts of data processed on a periodic basis, requiring little, if any, inquiry capability, are handled best by magnetic tape.

At the slower and lower cost end of the spectrum are punched cards and punched paper tape. It is quite difficult to make a sensible comparison between these two media and other media listed above, because of the great difference in cost, transfer rate, storage capacity, and so on. The decision as to which of the two to select, however, often depends on how the data are to be organised. Paper tape is preferable when files are organised sequentially and there is no need for insertions, modifications, or deletions. On the other hand, punched cards are preferable when the unit-record concept is to be used (i.e., the punched card serves as a record where each card is designed to contain data about a certain transaction).

Terminal Devices

Terminals actually represent devices which are used to get the data into the system and the information from the system. They are fundamental to an online system. Terminal hardware will vary with the needs of the different users throughout the organisation. Terminals vary from simple teletypewriters to card readers, high-speed printers, CRTs, magnetic tape units, and so on. The distance of the terminal from the central processor has no effect on its function. Move a magnetic tape unit to a plant 500 miles from the central processor, add a communication data control unit, connect it to a communication channel, and it becomes a remote job entry (RJE) terminal. Hook up a CRT to the data base and one has an interrogative terminal, and so on.

In this section, we will devote our discussion primarily to two types of terminals: (1) telephone terminals and (2) intelligent terminals.

Telephone Terminals

The Touch-Tone® telephone is an example of a low-speed terminal in the sense that it can handle effectively only low volumes of data. It can be used to update files, retrieve response information by voice answerback, printout, or visual display on other devices. For example, it can be used to provide credit status on credit card customers. Clerks type in to the central processor an access code, the customer's account number, and the amount of the purchase. By voice answerback, heard only by the clerk, the transaction is either approved or the clerk is instructed to call the credit department for further instructions. A similar system to this could be used as an order entry system in conjunction with reporting inventory availability to incoming calls from customers and/or salespersons.

Intelligent Terminals

An intelligent terminal incorporates a processing capability usually in the form of a microcomputer. This microcomputer has the capability to perform operations on the data it handles in addition to transmitting it to a central processor.

Applications of Intelligent Terminals

Intelligent terminals are used to (1) extend the power of the central computer and (2) accept data at its origin and perform some level of processing. Many of the intelligent terminals include microcomputers which can be used for different purposes based on how they are configured and programmed. For instance, by using one set of peripherals and programmes, a remote job entry (RJE) system is developed, and by using a different set of peripherals and programmes a data entry system, such as a remote key-to-disk system, is created.

With the advent of lower costs and greater availability of computers and data communication systems, the use of RJE systems have become cost/effective for small users who cannot economically justify their own data processing systems. Also, this RJE technique is applicable to the distribution information systems structure.

Also, intelligent terminals provide a form of backup for the central computer. With nonintelligent terminals connected to the main processor, if this processor were to fail, the terminals would be disabled, and for all practicable purposes, the entire system would be down. Transactions could not be entered and processed. At most, transactions might be captured on paper tape or magnetic tape for later transmission to the computer. With an intelligent terminal, it is feasible for the terminal to accept transactions and perform some of the processing if the main computer were down or the data communications system were disrupted. This capability is one of the main reasons why banks and retail stores select intelligent terminals. Sales transactions in a store, or savings transactions in a financial institution, can still be recorded at the terminal for processing and later transmission if necessary, even though the central computer is down.

Another reason for using an intelligent terminal is that it can relieve the central processor of some of the processing workload. This situation helps to reduce an overload on the central processor, allowing the system to get along with a smaller central processor than would otherwise be the case.

Data Entry Techniques

More than half the cost of using computers in many organisations is incurred in the capture and conversion of data. Probably no other aspect of computer processing offers more potential for cost savings than does this one area. The preparation of data for computer processing is truly the big bottleneck in the entire system and, as a result, it substantially decreases throughput.

In this section on data entry techniques we will direct our attention to five main areas: (1) keyboard-to-storage, (2) point of sale (POS), (3) optical character recognition

(OCR), (4) magnetic ink character recognition (MICE), and (5) voice recognition (VR).

Keyboard-to-Storage

The keyboard-to-storage technique consists of several keystations (CRT) connected to a minicomputer or programmed controller which collects the data input, verifies it, provides various other functions, and writes it on tape or disk for processing. Some of the functions that this kind of data entry system performs are:

1. Keyed-in data are input to an edit programme to filter out errors.
2. CRT input terminals provide sight verification for the operator; if an error is made, backspacing and deletion allows the operator to correct the error quickly.
3. Operators can work at higher keying rates than is possible with keypunches.
4. Productivity statistics for monitoring and checking operators' efficiency are supplemented by means of a programme in the system.
5. Check digits and batch totals are prepared automatically.
6. Certain reasonableness checks and relevancy checks are made.
7. True modular input of data is allowed because blocks of data are merged together into proper sequence for further processing.

The typical keyboard-to-storage system is referred to as key-to-tape or key-to-disk. It consists of a low-cost minicomputer; direct access intermediate storage; and magnetic disk, tape, floppy disk, or cassette for final output. Most manufacturers of these systems offer 8 to 64 keystations per system. Studies indicate that at the present cost levels, disregarding any other benefits, a system has to replace from 10 to 14 keypunches before a key-to-tape system is cost/effective. With falling prices, in the near future, the same basic system may be cost-effective at a five or six keypunch level. A key-to-tape system is shown in Figure B-14.

An online data entry system works basically the same way except the data flows directly into the central processor. For an example, refer to Figure B-15.

Advantages/Disadvantages of Keyboard-to-Storage Systems

The advantages are as follows:

1. Editing, formatting, combining input data, and dumping data are automatic functions.
2. Supervisors are provided various operational statistics on such things as operators' performance, work in progress, and work completed.

3. Productivity is increased becauses the operations of card feeding, duplication, skipping, and stacking are eliminated.
4. Operators' acceptance is good because it eliminates menial tasks such as card handling and the creation and use of drum cards, and it furnishes a quieter environment.

The disadvantages of keyboard-to-storage systems are:

1. Buffered keypunch/verifiers perform many of the functions that the key-to sterage systems perform.
2. Practically everyone understands the ubiquitous punched card.

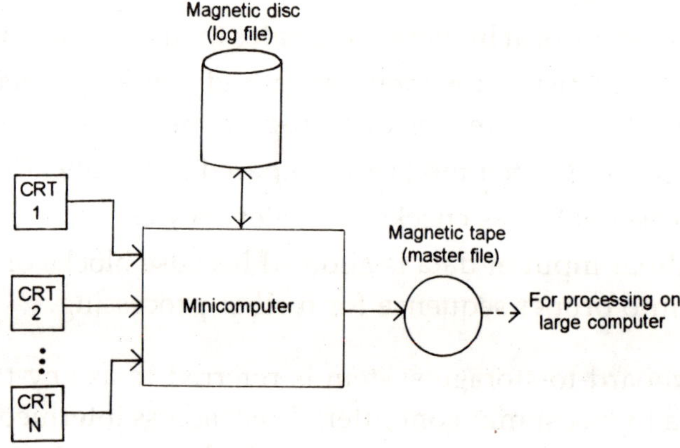

Fig. B-14: Illustration of keyboard-to-tape system.

Point of Sale (POS)

Point of sale systems provide a method by which vital data are captured at the point of transaction in department stores, supermarkets, and large discount stores. The same technique is applicable to other user categories where it is important to capture data at the time of an event or transaction.

This technique uses either hand-held "wand" readers or stationary sensors, which capture data from merchandise tags or tickets containing optical or magnetic characters. All readers are linked either to a central processor or an intelligent terminal. The main advantages of POS are as follows:

1. Provides large-scale data collection and online capabilities.
2. The method of reading optically or magnetically encoded characters on

tickets and product items speeds up the sales transaction to the mutual benefit of the buyer and seller.

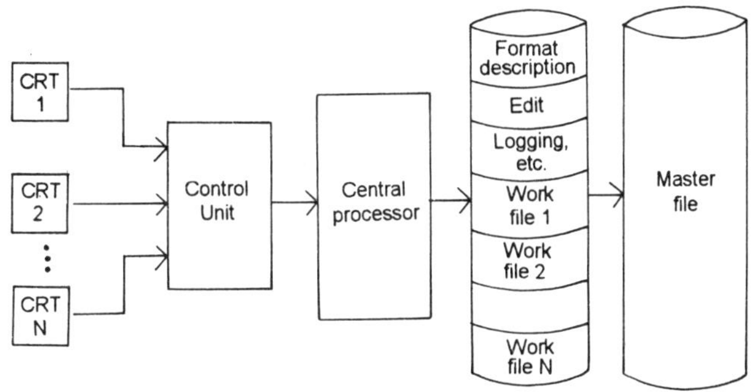

Fig. B-15: Illustration of an online entry system.

3. Input errors are eliminated.

The disadvantages of POS systems are:

1. Currently, many of the systems are too expensive.
2. Requires major revisions to the system in a number of areas (e.g., retagging and recoding).

Optical Character Recognition (OCR)

The purpose of OCR is to decrease the input bottleneck by reducing the number of keying operations and errors in transcription. Ideally, OCR equipment will read any document and transmit the data to a computer, thus eliminating any intermediate data preparation tasks. Most OCR devices being used in organisations are designed to read marks or machine-printed characters. They operate on the basis of sensing a mark in a specific location in the document. Applications for this device are test scoring, surveys, questionnaires, order entry, inventory control, and payroll. Character readers read characters generated by computer printers, accounting machines, cash registers, typewriters, and precisely written handprinted characters. A general flow of data using OCR devices is shown in Figure B-16.

The advantages of OCR are as follows:

1. Since data conversion is handled photographically, data errors are decreased.
2. Increases throughput.

The disadvantages are as follows:

1. Standardisation problems in type fonts and document inputs.
2. Reject rate is sensitive to the condition of the document (i.e., smudges, creased documents, dirt, and poor quality paper).
3. Low-cost OCR devices have limited throughput and a single-font reading capability. Devices with the capability to read several fonts are expensive.
4. The installation of OCR equipment usually requires complete forms redesign.

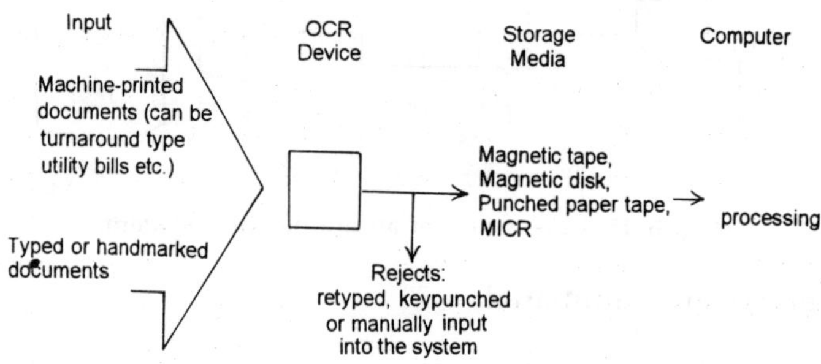

Fig. B-16: Illustration of an OCR application.

Magnetic Ink Character Recognition (MICR)

Magnetic ink character recognition (MICR) is used primarily by financial institutions for sorting and routing financial documents. The MICR characters are preprinted on documents and are composed of the ten decimal digits and four special characters.

Voice Recognition (VR)

On the floor of a commodities exchange, a transaction is completed between two brokers. The reporter speaks into a wireless microphone, "July silver four-four-four." A visual confirmation is given and he says, "Go." Using voice recognition (VR),[7] the data have been captured for further computer processing.

Where a limited amount of data in the form of words and alphanumeric characters are involved, a number of users are finding voice data entry to be cost/effective. By bypassing the writing or keying operations traditionally used to encode data, time may be saved and the cost associated with error correcting minimised. Moreover, VR can serve an important control function, recognising only those commands of authorised personnel.

Operationally, VR systems consist of a microphone or telephone receiver to accept voice input, a spectrum analyzer to filter the audio signal, and an analog-to-digital converter to change the signal to digital code. The digital code is then matched using a minicomputer to specific code patterns stored on disk or cassette.

Most VR systems have a number of characteristics in common. Normally, VR systerns are discrete or isolated. This means that the speaker must pause for a fraction of a second between each sound. Second, each user of the system must train it through repeated utterances to recognise his or her particular enunciation of sounds. Finally, basic voice recognition systems have a limited memory capacity (vocabulary) of 20 to 40 words.

DATA COMMUNICATIONS

Data communications systems transmit data between peripherals and the central processor and, thus, allow people and equipment to be geographically dispersed rather than being at one central location. In computer-based information systems, nearly all of the information produced must be disseminated to a variety of users, some many miles away. This transmission load is increasing each year, making the interdependency of computers and data communications systems even more apparent. Data communications control systems, equipment, and services have, cumulatively, become possibly the fastest growing area of information systems activity.

Typical applications which require design, selection, and implementation of data communications systems are as follows:

1. *Timesharing.* This application allows a number of remote users to gain access to the computational services of a central computer system. Data flow is in both directions (i.e., the terminal is both sending and receiving).
2. *Computer job load sharing.* This application permits the interconnection of two or more computers.
3. *Remote job entry (RJE).* This application entails the linkage of a central large computer with two or more small computers in separate locations, each of which is equipped with high-speed printers, card read-punches, and magnetic disk and tape. The purpose of RJE is to transmit voluminous amounts of data to a central processor for further processing.
4. *Interrogation.* This application requires the implementation of an online inquiry system using such terminal devices as CRTs and teletypewriters to gain access to the data base. Also, similar to RJE, the user may update records within certain integrated files.

The three major areas of data communications systems are:

1. *Communication channels.* These channels provide a path for electrical transmission between two or more points. These channels are also called circuits, lines, or links.
2. *Modems.* The term modem is a contraction of modulator-demodulator. These devices modulate and demodulate signals transmitted over communication channels.
3. *Line management.* Line management encompasses the procedures and equipment necessary to connect several terminals to the same line. Multiplexers, concentrators, and programmable communications processors are devices that enable many different terminals to share a single communications line.

Communication Channels

Communication channels are comprised of one or more of the following: telegraph lines, telephone lines, radio links, coaxial cable, microwave, satellite, laser beam, and helical waveguides. Depending on the terminal equipment and the application required, the channels can be arranged for operation in one or more of the three basic transmission modes:

1. *Simplex.* Transmission is made in one direction only.
2. *Half duplex.* Transmission can be in both directions, but not at the same time.
3. *Full duplex.* Transmission can be made in both directions at the same time.

Data Transmission

Data are transmitted over a wire line (or microwave system) by an electrical signal. It is comprised of three elements: (1) amplitude-strength of the signal, (2) phase-duration of the signal, and (3) frequency-number of times a wave form is repeated during a specified time interval. These elements are illustrated in Figure B-17.

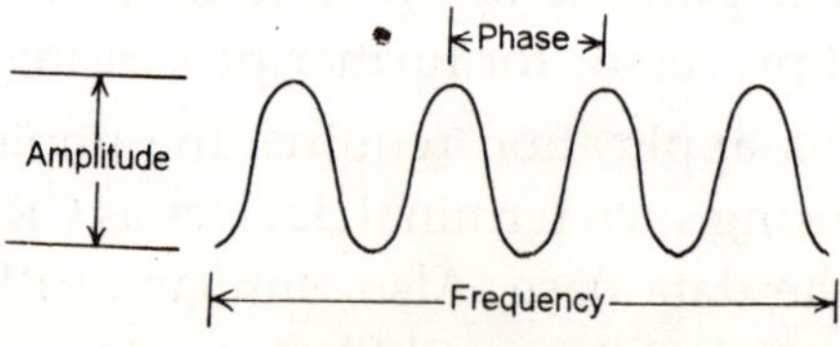

Fig. B-17: Schematic of a wave form.

When the binary numbering system is used to represent characters, a pulse for a defined time interval represents a 1-bit, and no pulse is used to represent a 0-bit. The pulse or no pulse is based on the amplitude, phase, and frequency of the signal, which is termed the "state."

Data transmission is either asynchronous or synchronous. Asynchronous transmission, such as in telegraph communication, is the slower of the two. Signal elements are transmitted to indicate the start and stop of each character. Three common asynchronous codes are:

1. *Baudot.* This is a five-level code with 32 possible combinations. With the use of a shift code (shift from a code for numbers to a code for alphabetics and special characters), it is possible to code 64 combinations. The term, baud, is used for measurement. For example, one baud per second, means one pulse or code element per second. This coding method uses five bits for the character plus a start and stop bit.
2. *Binary Coded Decimal.* The BCD method is similar to the Baudot method. It is, however, a six-level code.
3. *American Standard Code for Information Interchange.* This code, termed ASCII, uses seven- or eight-character bits.

Synchronous transmission is normally used where the transmission rate exceeds 2000 bits per second. The synchronous data transmission requires the receiving terminal to be synchronised bit-for-bit with the sending terminal. This eliminates the need for start and stop bits, thereby improving the efficiency of data transmission. This system requires, however, a clocking mechanism at both the sending and receiving ends.

Grade of Channels

The above discussion considered the directional flow of data and types of transmission and codes used. Another very important consideration is the grade of the channel. Channels are graded on speed of transmission and this attribute is directly proportional to bandwidth. For example, telegraph lines are narrowband, telephone lines are voiceband, and coaxial cable or microwave are broadband. The bandwidth of a channel is measured by a unit called a Hertz (Hz), which means cycles per second. It has been shown that the bandwidth of a channel should be approximately twice the number of bits to be transmitted per second. For example, if one is to transmit data at 1200 bits per second (bps), then a channel with a bandwidth of 2400 Hz is required. Channels may be classified as low-speed, medium-speed, and high-speed.

Low-Speed Channels

This grade was originally developed for use with teletypewriters (TTYs). It transmits data in the range of 55, 75, 110, 150, and 300 bits per second. Data can be transmitted via the teletypewriter online, or paper tape can be prepared offline and transmitted during slack periods. These systems normally use five-channel (Baudot) code, but, at higher speeds, they also have available the eight-channel ASCII Code.

Medium-Speed Channels

This grade is voiceband and is provided by the Bell System and the independent telephone companies. They are used for voice and data communications, interchangeably. Their typical transmission rate is 300 to 9600 bits per second. There are three types of services available: (1) private line, (2) the dial-up network, and (3) WATS.

1. *Private Lines.* The major difference in this system and a dial-up system is that the channel remains connected for the duration of the lease, the routing can be chosen, and the line can be electrically conditioned so that the transmission rate can be increased up to 9600 bits per second. Private lines are leased on a monthly basis with unlimited usage and the rate is a function of airline miles from point to point.

   Conditioning refers to the process by which the quality of a specific, privately leased line is maintained at a certain standard permissible error rate. Such conditioning adjusts the frequency and phase response characteristics of the channel to meet more exact tolerance specifications.
2. *Dial-up or public switched network.* The dial-up or switched network is currently the most commonly used method of transmitting data. The channel is available as long as the connection is made, and payment varies according to mileage, time of day or night, and duration of connect time. The rate approximates the rate for a normal voice telephone call. The average speed of transmission is generally from 2000 to 2400 bits per second.

   Since each dial-up connection may involve a unique combination of channels, the telephone company does not guarantee the characteristics of dial-up channels. Consequently, to achieve high transmission rates on a dial-up network, the required conditioning must be performed within the modem. Such a modem rapidly determines the channel characteristics and compensates for them at the start of the connection and then continuously adapts to any changes during connect time.

3. *Wide area telephone service (WATS).* WATS is a pricing arrangement for users of large volume data (and voice) transmission over long distances. WATS offers two billing plans: (1) a full period service, and (2) a measured time service. Under full period service, the subscriber has unlimited use of the channel at a fixed monthly rate in the geographical area for which he or she subscribes. Under measured time service, the basic monthly rate covers the first ten hours of use per month for calls to Data-Phones (or telephones) within the subscribed service area. An additional charge per hour of actual use is levied beyond the first ten hours; however, the tariff which governs this service is extremely complicated and a full explanation is beyond the scope of this text.

High-Speed Channels

Where data are to be transmitted at high speeds and very high volumes, then a broadband service should be used. Both the Bell System and Western Union offer leased broadband services. These broadband lines comprise a group of channels of voice grade. Each channel, when properly arranged, can carry voice, computer data, or facsimile signals. Two classes of services are offered.

1. *Type 5700 line.* Has a base capacity of 60 voice-grade channels and a maximum equivalent bandwidth of 240 kHz (kilo-hertz).
2. *Type 5800 line.* Has a capacity of 240 voice-grade channels and a maximum equivalent bandwidth of 1000 kHz.

This service is quite flexible because it can be used as a single broadband channel for fast and voluminous data transmission or as several individual lower-speed channels. In certain cases a user group with similar needs may share a line, whereas on an individual basis, they could not afford such a service. A flat monthly rate is charged for this service, regardless of the volume of data transmitted. This rate is based on the number of channels, total capacity, and distance between transmission points.

Some companies have found it more economical and efficient to develop and use their own private-line microwave systems. The First National Bank of Boston, for example, has a microwave link between its head office and its operations center four miles away. The microwave link consists of a 1.544-megabit system that is capable of handling data transmission between the two points at speeds up to 19,200 bits per second.

Massachusetts General Hospital has a microwave link between it and Logan

Airport in Boston. Doctors at the hospital, through audiovisual contact with patients at the airport, direct tests performed by technicians at the airport medical facility. This system is being extended to nursing homes throughout the Boston area so that expert medical care can be brought to patients who are unable to come to the hospital for treatment.

Arthur C. Clarke, an author of several books on space, believes that satellites will have at least the same impact on people as have telephones. Most major telecommunications companies (e.g., AT&T, GTE) have launched or will launch their own satellites. Western Bancorp for instance, uses satellite links to connect three remote data centers to its corporate data center in Los Angeles. The system supports a bankwide teller-transaction processing system consisting of 5000 terminals in 700 banking offices covering 11 western states.

Fiber optics are AT&T's terrestrial answer to satellite communications. Optical fibers are embedded in cables and carry communications by bending and bouncing light waves through tiny strands of glass. Fiber optics the size of a human hair offer 1000 times the carrying capacity of today's copper wire pair. The benefits associated with fiber optics as a transmission medium include high bandwidth, little noise interference because they are nonelectrical, high security since they cannot be tapped, and suitability for digital transmission because light pulses lend themselves well to binary coding.

A data transmission medium of the 1980s and 1990s is infrared. Infrared is an optical transmission system that uses the infrared spectrum of light-emitting diodes. Like microwave, it is a "line-of-sight" system that is most useful for building-to-building data communications up to 1 kilometer apart. A system called Lite-Link operates at a speed of 500 kilobits per second.[8]

Modems

Modems, also known as data sets, are used to handle the data stream from a peripheral device to the central processor, or vice versa, through the common carrier network. The modem can operate in simplex, half duplex, or full duplex mode.

Telephone channels were developed for analog voice transmission. In communication applications involving digital data, the modulator portion of a modem converts digital pulses, representing binary 1's and 0's, generated by the computer or peripheral equipment, into an analog, wavelike signal acceptable for transmission over analog channels. The demodulator reverses this process, converting the analog signal back into a pulse train acceptable to the peripheral or computer at the other end. This is illustrated in Figure B-18. If a modem was not used to convert/

reconvert data signals, and the computer or peripheral was directly connected to the telephone channel, the signal would be degraded and the data would be made unintelligible by the electrical characteristics of the channel.

Line Management

Often a single terminal connected to a dedicated line is not active enough of the time to keep the line busy. A common solution to this problem is to connect several terminals to the same line. Because the terminals are "dropped off" the communications line, the configuration is called a multidrop. A multidrop configuration, while decreasing line costs, can produce a garbled message if two or more terminals use the line simultaneously. To overcome this potential problem a polling or contention method of line management is used.

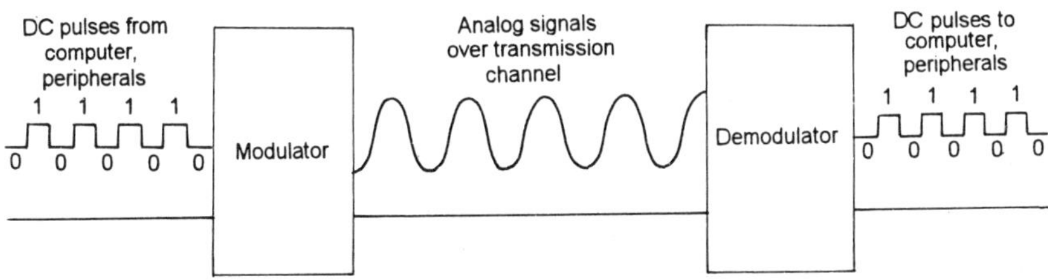

Fig. B-18: Illustration of modulation-demodulation.

With polling, the central computer asks each terminal if it has something; to transmit. If it does, then it is directed to send its message. After transmission of a terminal's message is complete, the computer asks the next terminal if it has something to transmit. This polling continues in turn until all the terminals on the line have the opportunity to transmit. Then, the computer polls the first terminal and the entire polling process is repeated. While polling allows the line to be busier, it can waste processor time if terminals do not have messages to send. An alternative method that overcomes this disadvantage is called contention.

With contention, each terminal listens to the communications line before transmitting its message. If the line is free it sends its message. If the line is busy the terminal wishing to send a message waits awhile before listening again. A serious disadvantage of the contention method of line management is that terminals may experience long delays in sending messages because the communications line is too busy or messages are too long.

Multiplexers, concentrators, and programmable communications processors are devices that permit connection of more peripherals to the central computer using fewer channels.

Multiplexer

Where a number of terminals are in one or more areas outside the toll-free zone of the central processor, the common carrier tariff structure makes it economically attractive to operate a group of such terminals through one voice-grade channel, instead of connecting them separately to the central processor via a number of narrowband channels. In most situations of this type multiplexing will reduce the cost of the communication network by allowing one voiceband grade channel to substitute for many subvoice (slow-speed, telegraph) channels that might otherwise be poorly utilised. Figure B-19 illustrates a communication system before and after multiplexing.

As shown in Figure B-19, the multiplexer accepts input from several terminal sources, combines these inputs, and then transmits the combined input over one channel. At the other end (not shown), a similar unit again separates the discrete data inputs for further processing.

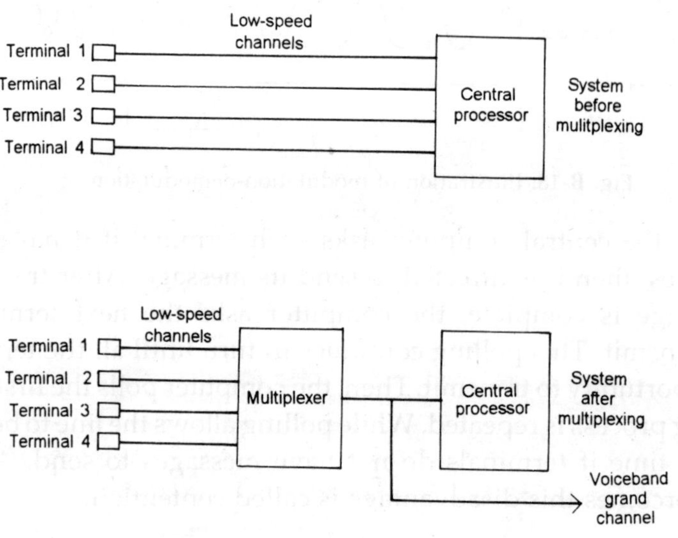

Fig. B-19: Communication system before and after multiplexing.

Two basic techniques are used to multiplex data: (1) frequency division multiplexing (FDM), and (2) time division multiplexing (TDM). In FDM, the digital pulse signal from each terminal is converted by a modem into an analog signal having a frequency unique to the individual terminal. Each separate signal is allocated its own portion of the frequency of the available band. All the signals are electrically combined and then transmitted over the line. The receiving end of a FDM device demultiplexes the individual signals by using a set of filters, each designed to "hear" a particular tone. The tone is then demodulated by a modem back into a digital pulse signal.

The TDM approach uses transmitting capability according to available time elements. Digital inputs from each terminal are continuously sampled, one by one, for a fixed time period. The sampling time per input corresponds to the time expended to designate a bit (bit-interleaved TDM) or a byte/character (byte-interleaved TDM) by the terminal signal. The bit or byte signal so sampled is time compressed and placed into a time slot in the TDM output signal.

FDM is probably better where the system has a number of low-speed terminals, geographically dispersed with less than 16 channels. If the transmission rate is 2400 bits per second or more, or a great many channels are used, then the system should use TDM.

Concentrator

A concentrator differs from a multiplexer in that a concentrator accommodates *X* number of terminals but allows only a portion of them to transmit their data over the available lines. That is, 12 terminals may compete for only six channels. All terminals must contend for the channels and those which do not make connection are busied out. With a multiplexer, all terminals can be accommodated because the basic assumption is that all terminals are used all of the time.

The concentrator works as a normal switching device that polls one terminal at a time. Whenever a channel is idle, the first terminal ready to send or receive gets control of one of the channels and retains it for the duration of its transaction. If several transactions occur simultaneously, then each terminal must wait its turn on a first in, first out basis.

The cost savings in using a multiplexer are based on combining the data while the cost savings using a concentrator are based on the amount of data traffic in the system. In effect, the use of a concentrator is based on the assumption that all of the terminals will not contend for the available facilities , at the same time.

Programmable Communications Processors

As long as the total number of peripherals, local and remote, and the amount of data transmitted are maintained at a certain level, the computer control programme (in residence) can execute the interrupts, move the data into and out of storage, and perform the necessary housekeeping without significant throughput penalty. If the number of terminals and volume of data increase to a point beyond that level, however, then computer throughput is reduced significantly. At this point, it may be more economical to move these functions out of the computer mainframe and into a communications processor.[9] These processors perform some, if not all, of the following functions:

1. Housekeeping—the handling of message queues and priorities, processing of addresses, data requests, message blocks, file management, and updating the executive on peripheral activity.
2. Error checking and retransmission requests to prevent incomplete messages from reaching the host processor.
3. Code translation into the "native" code of the host CPU.
4. Preprocessing and editing.
5. Communications analysis processing— error analysis, the gathering of traffic statistics, and so forth.
6. Establishing and acknowledging the required channel connections including automatic dialing, if this is a feature of the system.
7. Verifying successful completion of the message, or detecting line breaks, and either calling for or executing remedial action.
8. Disconnecting after a completed message, to permit polling to resume.
9. Assembling the serial bit stream into a bit-parallel buffered message.
10. Routing messages to and from required memory locations and notifying the software as required.

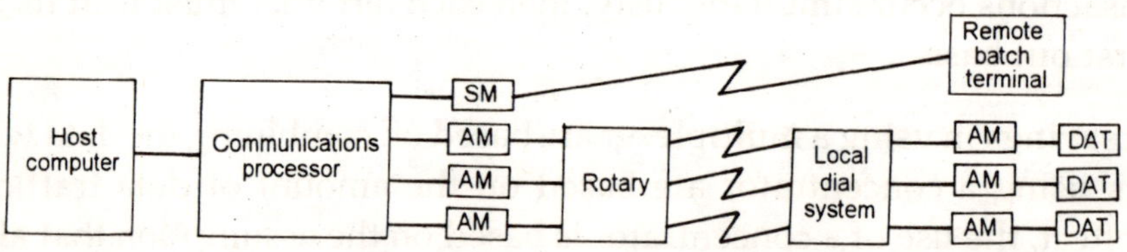

Fig. B-20: Computer system with multiple communication ports served by a communications processor. SM: synchronous modem: AM: asynchronous modem; DAT: dial-up terminal.

The major factor in moving these functions from the central processor (host computer) to a communications processor is economic. With a large number of terminals or communications lines, as much as half the processing time of the host computer (even a large one) can be spent in input/output processing and line control. A separate, specialised computer can perform the same functions with fewer steps and simpler software, reducing direct processor time costs, programming costs, and debugging time. The lease or purchase price of the communications processor is often one or two orders of magnitude lower than that of the main computer; if it can assume work which formerly occupied half the main computer's time, it can obviously be economically justified. In Figure B-20, a typical configuration is illustrated.[10]

The increased use of programmable communications processors can be directly attributed to the current proliferation of low-cost flexible minicomputers and microcomputers, and also to the developments in integrated circuit technology that have enabled digital computers to be manufactured at greatly reduced costs.

RENFERENCES

"All About Minicomputers," *Datapro 70,* Delran, NJ.: Datapro Research Corporation, December 1976.

"Control Data 38500 Mass Storage System, *Datapro 70,* Delran, NJ.: Datapro Research Corporation, September 1975.

Davis, *Computer Data Processing,* New York: McGraw-Hill Book Co., 1969.

Haavind, "A User's Guide to System Evolution," *Computer Decisions,* June 1971.

Howard, "Telecommunications: 1970—1990," *Computerworld/Extra,* March 18, 1981.

"Key to Enhanced Application Development," *Data Processor,* September 1972.

Martin, *Telecommunications and the Computer,* Second Edition, Englewood Cliffs, NJ.: Prentice-Hall, Inc., 1976.

Minicomputer Review, Lexington, MA.: GML Corporation, 1981.

Sardinas, *Computing Today,* Englewood Cliffs, NJ.: Prentice-Hall, Inc., 1981.

"Smart Users 'Deemphasise' Host," *Computerworld,* Supplement, July 27, 1972.

Synnott and Gruber, *Information Resource Management,* New York: John Wiley & Sons, Inc., 1981.

Yasaki, "Voice Recognition Comes of Age" *Datamation,* August 1976.

NOTES

1. Gordon B. Davis, *Computer Data Processing,* New York: McGraw-Hill Book Company, 1969, p. 150. Used with permission of the McGraw-Hill Book Company.
2. Robert Haavind, "A User's Guide to System Evolution," *Computer Decisions,* June 1971, pp. 26-30.
3. *Ibid.*
4. Key to Enhanced Application Development," *Data Processor,* September 1972, pp. 2-9. Used with permission.

5. Haavind, *op. cit.*, p. 26.
6. *Minicomputer Review:* Lexington, Mass.: GML Corporation, 1981.
7. Edward K. Yasaki, "Voice Recognition Comes of Age." *Datamation.* August 1976, pp. 65-68.
8. Summarised from William R. Synnott and William R. Gruber, *Information Resource Management*, New York: John Wiley & Sons, Inc., 1981, pp. 237-240.
9. "Smart Users 'Deemphasise Host'," *Computerworld*, Supplement, July 27, 1972, p. 10. Used with permission. Copyright by *Computerworld*, Newton, Massachusetts 02160.
10. R. L. Aronson, "Data Links and Networks Devices and Techniques," *Control Engineering*, February 1970, pp. 105-116.

APPENDIX C

ONLINE INFORMATION RETRIEVAL

Information is a commercially exploitable commodity. It has to be produced/generated, communicated and used properly. It is "unscare" resource and continues to grow at an explosive rate. The tasks of locating and communicating information presents the following problems:

(i) Large volume of information causes overload at the processing end.

(ii) Increasing time lag between generating and publishing information.

(iii) Interdisciplinary nature of growth in science possesses problems in locating the desired information.

(iv) Proliferation in the growth of primary and secondary journals presents problems in bibliographic control.

(v) Language and other communication barriers.

A vast array of electronic gadgets have been produced to store, organize and communicate the information world wide at a very fast speed. The rapid advancement in computers, storage media and software packages for processing information have eased the situation considerably. It has been possible to convert large volumes of information and data available in abstracting and indexing services in science and technology into machine readable from called databases. At present there are over 7000 such products available for commercial exploitation through over 600 vendors world wide.

History

The concept of using machines for storage and processing of information can be traced as far back as 1960's. In late 1960's online bibliographic databases were made available as a by-product of primary printed publications. The world's first computer produced periodical - Chemical Titles - was introduced by Chemical Abstracts Service (CAS) in 1961. It has covered 750 chemically oriented journals. Each article was indexed by author and keywords with a reference to the journal in which it has appeared. The computers were used for typesetting. Use of computers for typesetting made it possible to accommodate more material in a machine readable form. The creation of machine readable databases helped in providing alerting services. This was beginning of a significant change in information retrieval. The machine readable databases were manipulated further to produce a variety of products such as indexes in printed forms for manual searching. The 1970's witnessed the extensive use of computers in information handling.

The creation of machine readable databases like Chemical Abstracts, Biological Abstracts, Index Medicus by secondary information services coincided with the development of long distance telecommunication networks like Tymnet and Telenet in USA. The online search concept as an industry started when two organisations viz. M/s. Lockheed under M/s. Dialog Information Services in 1972 and M/s System Development Corporation (SDC) in 1973 provided softwares and necessary computing facilities to enable the databases to be sorted and searched interactively in batch mode through telecommunication networks.

COMPUTERISED DATABASES

Extensive use of computers for information storage and processing resulted in creation of computerised databases covering all area of science and technology. These databases are of two major varieties viz. (1) Reference Databases and (2) Source Databases. Reference databases are of two categories such as *(a)* Bibliographic and *(b)* Referral. Records in bibliographic databases contain clues to the intellectual content and physical characteristics of pieces of the graphic or printed record of humanity such as journal article, research report, conference proceedings, book or patent etc. The referral databases contain directory type information such as list of persons, organisations, research projects etc.

Source databases are primary sources of information or data composed of the full texts of the information in question and including materials prepared specifically for distribution by electronic means. These databases could be further subdivided into (a) Full Text, (b) Numeric and (c) A combination of the two—textual numeric.

Full text database contain original textual material belonging to primary sources such as encyclopedia, newspaper, court decisions, journals etc.

Numeric database contains original numeric or statistical data such as financial, census, production trade data.

Textual numeric databases contains fields of mixed textual and numeric data and includes dictionary or handbooks.

Some important databases in science and technology are enumerated in the following paras.

Reference Databases

Bibliographic Databases

(1) *Biosis Previews:* Producer: Biosciences Information Service, USA. Contains Over seven million records.1969 to present.

(2) *CA Search:* Producer: Chemical Abstracts Service, USA. Contain over nine million records. 1967 to present.

(3) *Compendex Plus:* Producer: Institute for Scientific Information (ISI), USA. Contain over two million records. 1970 to present.

Referral Databases

(1) *American Library Directory:* Producer: R.R. Bowker, USA. Contain over thirty six thousand records. Current.

(2) *American men and Women of Science:* Producer: R.R. Bowker, USA Contains over one lakh records. Current.

(3) *Books In Print:* Producer: Thomas Publishing Company Inc., USA. Contains over one lakh fifty thousand records. Current.

Source Databases

Fulltext Databases

(1) *Harvard Business Review:* Producer: John Wiley & Sons Inc., USA. Contains over two thousand five hundred records. 1971 to present.

(2) *Kirk Othmer Online:* Producer: Wiley Electronic Publishing, USA. Contains over thirty three thousand records. 3rd Edition.

(3) *Martindale Online:* Producer: The Pharmaceutical Society of Great Britain, UK. Over forty three thousand records. Current edition.

(4) *PTS Newsletter Database:* Producer: Predicast, USA. Contains over four lakh records. January 1988 to present.

Numeric Databases

(1) *Cendata:* Prodúcer: US Bureau of the Census, USA. Contains over fifty two thousand records current.

(2) *Mediai General Plus:* Producer: Media General Financial Services Inc., USA Contains over seven thousand records. Current.

(3) *D&B Donneley Demographies:* Producer: Donnelley Marketing Services, USA Contains over sixty two thousand records. Current.

(4) *D&B Duns Financial Records Plus:* Producer: Duns and Bradstreet Credit Services, USA Contains over Twenty lakh records. Current.

Textual/Numeric Databases

(1) *ICC International Annual Reports:* Producer: ICC Online Ltd. UK, contains over ninety seven thousand records. Current.

(2) *Extel International News Cards:* Producer: Extel Financial Ltd. UK. Contains over twenty one thousand records. October 1989 to present.

(3) *Investext:* Producer: Technical Data International Inc., USA. Contains over fourteen lakh records. July 1982 to present.

(4) *Moody's Corporate News:* Producer: Moody's Investor Services Inc., USA. Contains over three lakh seventy thousand records, 1988 to present.

TELESEARCHING

Telecommunication Modes

Since 1970 there have been considerable growth in the production of computer readable databases. As on today there are over seven thousand publically available machine readable databases as compared to few hundreds at the beginning. These are marketed through over eight hundred search services providers popularly known as vendors. Improvements in telecommunication system, satellite links and modems transmitting at 2400 baud or higher speeds are commonly used for online searching. The advancements in computer technology and telecommunication systems have also brought down the searching costs considerably.

Following are the three modes of telecommunication available for accessing computerised databases in India.

(i) Telex Mode
(ii) Dialup Data Service (PSTN)
(iii) GPSS/PAD Mode

Telex Mode

Most of the institutes/organisations possess a telex terminal as a means of communication. This system can be used for conducting online searches too. Advancements in telex machines from electrical telex to computerized Message Communication Terminals (MCT) to PC Telex cards have made the transmission more easy. The transmission speed of this system is 50 bauds per seconds. This slow speed makes online searching more costlier as compared to other modes.

Dialup Data Service (PSTN)

Under this mode two computers are connected through telephone lines to transmit data. It is called Dialup Data Service (PSTN). Here modems to inter phase the computer and telephones lines are used at both the ends. The speed of transmission are 300 or 1200 bauds.

GPSS/PAD Mode

With the introduction of Gateway Packet Switching Service (GPSS)and Packet Assembler Disassembler (PAD), data can be transmitted at a rate of 1200 bauds, 2400 bauds and 4800 bauds. This mode is still cheaper for online searching. Average telecommunication cost for a search duration of five minutes will be around Rs. 60 whereas with Dialup data services it will be around Rs. 1200 and telex mode is still costlier.

Vendors

Databases are produced by various organisations, in very few cases the producer of the database provide access to database. It is very common for the database producer to load the database with an online host. The online host provides the computer for storage of database, software to search the database with back-up services to maintain, market and provide documentation for searching the database. They also update the databases periodically. They have developed a powerful computer system to store large volume of information. These online hosts are known as system suppliers of online service or vendors. As on today there are over eight hundred vendors in the world.

Interactive Searching

Search Strategy

The term strategy has been used in different ways in the information retrieval literature. It is commonly referred to as a command put to a search system. Some have referred to as search formulation. Sometimes it is used in the literature to refer to one's action at a particular point in search execution, a decision about what might be the best way to proceed, a methodology to serve an immediate objective. In a broader sense the strategy can be defined as an overall plan for getting the desired results formulated considering the facilities available with the database searched, structure of database and the topic to be searched. The result of the online search depends on the formulation of strategy best suited. It is a skill and can be developed by experience and detailed study of databases.

Preparation of search strategy comprises the following points:

(i) To identify concepts.
(ii) To ascertain index terms, synonyms etc. of these concepts.
(iii) To identify proper databases.
(iv) To study indexing features of the database.
(v) To formulate the query.

(i) *To identify concepts:* To explain this methodology an example is given below: *Search topic:* Dating of fossils using racemization of amino acid studies.

The above topic can be split into the following concepts:

(a) Fossils
(b) Dating
(c) Amino Acid Racemization

Now the concepts in a topic have been identified.

(ii) *Ascertaining index terms, synonyms to these concepts:* With the help of dictionaries, thesaurs index terms, synonyms are identified. These are: *(a)* Fossils, Paleontology, Archeology *(b)* Date, Age, Geochrononlogy.

(iii) *To identify proper database:* After consulting the catalogue of vendor most suitable database is identified which can satisfy the query. In the above example Chemical Abstract database is selected.

(iv) *To study indexing features of the database:* For this purpose one should have a copy of details of database popularly known as database chapter or search tool. The tool describes in detail the various indexes, entry points, facilities and limits available with database with examples.

(v) *Query Formulation:* The query is then formulated keeping in view the synonyms and the database searched.

Conducting Actual Search: The search topic is analysed and a query suitable to database selected is formulated and is executed. It involves logging in with the database vendor, following the protocols of the vendor, then selecting the desired file and finally executing the query. The above query has been executed using GPSS mode. As explained there are three modes viz. Telex, Telephone, PSTN and Telephone (GPSS) mode. GPSS mode is very fast and also cheap.

OUTPUT

The cost structure of database has three cost components viz. (1) connect charges, (2) database use charges or hit charges and *(3)* telecommunication charges. Costs at serial number one and two varies from database to database and also on format of output and option offline or online. For getting the output these cost factors play important role.

(i) Online: Obtaining the output of the search results is the final stage in information retrieval online. Databases offer different formats for outputting the results. The results can be obtained either online or offline. Online results became available to the requestor immediately after the search in other words the results are downloaded to the hard disc, before disconnecting the call.

Costwise, getting results online is expensive as the connect charges and telecommunication cost is added till the typing or displaying is in progress. There is also possibility of loosing the communication link and interrupting the type or display transaction. In this case one has to repeat the type or display command which results increase in search cost. If the number of records are more the time taken for downloading will be more and cost will be also more. In such cases it is advisable to have offline print option.

(ii) Offline: Getting offline output of search results means one has ordered the host computer to print the search results in a desired format and then the call is disconnected. Here the printing is done after the call is disconnected and then the results are mailed to requestor by air. In this option connect charges and telecommunication charges are levied upto the point of disconnecting the call or logoff. Getting the search results offline is economical. Normally the printouts are received with in ten days time.

INDIAN SCENE

India is not behind in adopting new technologies in information handling. Dialog in 1972 and Orbit in 1973 introduced computerised information retrieval on commercial basis. In India INSDOC under NISSAT project arranged a demonstration of online access to the ESA/IRS database from terminals installed in Bombay in November 1976. Encouraged with this successful demonstration, INSDOC submitted a proposal to the Government of India for setting up ESA/IRS terminals in India. However, this proposal could not be implemented. During 1979-80 an experimental project was undertaken by the Information Centre for Aeronautics in NAL Bangalore to access ESA/IRS databases in online mode between Paris-Frascati and offline between Paris-Bangalore: In 1985 NISSAT launched a feasibility study for establishing online information retrieval centres in the country. This was entrusted, to CMC.

Some other institutions also started using ordinary telex machines for information retrieval. Informatics (India) Pvt. Ltd., Bangalore, an Indian party was instrumental in setting up online access centres in several institutions/concerns. Some of them were BHEL, DESIDOC, CFTRI, NCL etc.

NCL established contacts with one of the largest database vendor viz., M/S. DIALOG Information Services, Palo Alto California, USA, for interactive searching of international databases in 1984. The mode of access was telex. One year later similar arrangements were made with M/S. STN International, a subsidiary of Chemical Abstracts Service, Washington, USA. Upto June 1988 this facility was for R&D work of NCL only.

National Centres

National Government under Department of Scientific and Industrial Research (DSIR) has initiated to set up five online access centres to search computerised databases. These centres are called NISSAT Access Centres for International Data Centres (NACID) and are situated at the following places:

(1) INSDOC, New Delhi
(2) NAL, Bangalore
(3) NCL, Pune
(4) CLRI, Madras
(5) IACS, Calcutta

The functions of these centres have been identified as:

(i) To maintain the facility for online access to international data centres.
(ii) To assist the users in formulation of queries and actual conduct of the search.
(iii) To conduct training courses and user orientation programmes in query formulation and search techniques.
(iv) To collect interest profiles from potential users and provide SDI services.
(v) To promote use of online interactive facilities and therefore to promote and communicate relevant publicity materials.
(vi) To recover costs from the users as per the policy laid down for the centre.
(vii) The centre at NCL will cater to the needs of Western Region comprising Gujarat, Madhya Pradesh, Maharashtra, Dadra and Nagar Haveli, Goa, Daman and Diu.

Experiment at NCL: Online search facility was introduced in NCL from 1984 for inhouse user, with access facility to M/S. Dialog Information Services, USA. The mode of access was telex. With the establishment of NACID Centre, this facility was extended to outside users in 1988. The centre has created the following facilities:

Terminals

Telex Mode

Under this mode the databases are accessed through telex line using the under mentioned equipments.

— Message Communication Terminal (MCT)
— Dot Matrix Printer

The data transmission speed is 50 bauds per second.

Dialup Data Service (PSTN) Telephone Mode

Under this mode telephone channels are used to transmit the data. The speed of transmission varies from 300 bauds per second. The following equipment have been procured for this mode.

— PC/AT with 20MB Hard disc, colour monitor, two serial and two parallel ports
— One dot matrix printer
— One modem (300-1200 bps)
— Telephone line with ISTD facility
— Communication Softwares: *(a)* Procomm, *(b)* Dialog link.

Gateway Packet Switched Services (GPSS) / Packet Assembler / Disassember (PAD)

Videsh Sanchar Nigam Ltd. (VSNL) has extended the facility of data transmission from Pune through PAD in 1989. NCL has acquired this facility to conduct online searches of international databases. The equipment procured for PSTN mode are used for this mode also. The only additional facility created was to obtain a nodal point from VSNL for GPSS access. The speed of transmission is 1200 bauds per second.

Database Vendors

NCL has established contacts with (i) Dialog Information Services, USA; (ii) STN International, USA and *(iii)* Easynet. Over six hundred databases are available for online search through these vendors.

Search Tools

Computerised database producers use different technique of indexing and organising the records. Users are to know these techniques for retrieving the desired record effectively. Datacentres has installed mostly mainframe computers to manage the files using their own softwares. Users have to know the searching facilities provided in these softwares. A number of search aids for online accessing are circulated by the database vendors and database producers. These are known as searching manuals and database chapters. The centre has procured 20 database chapters, 30 searching manuals and 10 thesaurii.

Manpower

Sufficient manpower with proper training and expertise has also been created at the centre.

Services

From the very inception the centre has conducted online searches regularly. Over 789 topic have been searched by December, 1991.

COST EFFECTIVENESS

The cost in inter active searching of computerised databases consists of the following components.

(i) *Computer connect charge:* This is the charge database vendor levy on the use of their system. It is dependent on the database to be searched and is measured on connect time basis. To economize this cost the search strategy must be well defined, short and properly structured.

(ii) *Hit charges:* This is the charge levied on the references selected for a given topic. This varies according to details copied or printed minimum for the record number and maximum for the full details. The cost can be controlled by selecting the proper details/format of output and also the relevant records.

(iii) *Terms used:* Some database vendors levy charges on the number of index terms used in searching. This can be economized through judicious selection of index terms and structuring of search strategy.

(iv) *Telecommunication Charges:* This is the charge levied by the agencies providing telecommunication facilities and is dependent on volume of data transferred or duration of connection. Thus if the system is slow, the searching cost will be higher. Even the computer connect charge will also go up, hence effort should be made to use faster transmission media. First preference should be given to GPSS, there after PSTN and lastly Telex mode.

ECONOMY MEASURES

The under mentioned points may be adopted to economize the search cost.

(i) To define the search topic precisely.

(ii) To select proper index terms by consulting database chapters and thesaurus.

(iii) To prepare search strategy before logging in and store it in the computer in advance.

(iv) To use special features of databases e.g. use registry number while searching Chemical Abstracts database, which is faster and precise as compared to index terms.

(v) To use faster mode of communication preferably GPSS if available.

MANUAL Vs COMPUTERISED SEARCHING

From the aforesaid discussion it is evident that the computerised search is much faster than the manual search. Cost wise also the manual search appears to be costlier. But the major point of doubt will be in respect of recall ratio many information science experts have opined that the recall is not very high. This may be true in case of generalist approach. But in precise searching e.g.searching through registry numbers for chemicals must be cent per cent or nearer to it.

It can be safely concluded that computerised searching is quicker and chapter under the present conditions in the country.

Time

It has been observed that average time taken for a search is highest for medicine (10.3 minutes) and the lowest for Engineering Science (4.71 minutes). Topics in economics has taken longer time (8.7 minutes) nearer to medicine while chemical sciences has taken less time very close to engineering (4.9 minutes). This shows that databases on engineering chemicals sciences are faster in searching as compared to medicine and economics.

Hits

Average number of hits are the highest in Medical Sciences (84.4) and the lowest in economics (15.5). Chemicals sciences ranks next to medical sciences (636).

Cost

Average cost of a topic is Rs. 795 in Chemical Sciences (highest) and Rs. 365 (lowest) in engineering. The average costs in other subjects are also on higher side.

REFERENCES

1. Harter, Stephen P. Online Information Retrieval Concepts Principles and Techniques. Academic Press, 1986.
2. Torpie, Geraldine. Going online 1988. *Aslib* 1987.
3. Computer Readable Databases: A Directory and Data Source Book 6th ed. 1990 Gale Research Inc. Detroit.
4. Kirk-Othmer Encylopedia of Chemical Technology 3rd Ed. Vol. 13, Information Retrieval, pp. 278-336.
5. Ullmann's Encyclopedia of Industrial Chemistry 5th ed. 1990 Vol.BI pp. 12-119.
6. NISSAT Access Centre for International Data Centres (NACID) Progress Report (unpublished).
7. Garudadwajan, B. and Subramanya, H.S. Dedicated line-European Space Agency Database NAL's experience. Paper presented at National Seminar on modes of Access to online databases and application of CD-ROM and other optical discs - NAL and AGLIS, Bangalore 27-29 June 1988.
8. Government of India, Ministry of Science and Technology, Department of Scientific and Industrial Research - National Information System for Science and Technology (NISSAT) Detailed Project Report (1985-90) pp. 7-8,47-49.

APPENDIX - D

DECENTRALISED PLANNING (DISNIC)

Introduction

Information is a vital resource and is for use like the other conventional factors such as land, labour, capital and organisation. "Informatisation of economy" is changing the role of economy as an "information movement and management (IM&M)" economy. Information systems (IS) are assuming an ever increasing importance in the developmental process of a nation and becoming an integral part of every sector: economic, cultural, educational, social or political. Developmental process in a country needs a sophisticated information flow from the lowest level of administration to the highest national decision making level and also information access to various agencies (both governmental and non-governmental) who are involved in developmental activities for upliftment of the society with or without financial assistance from government sources.

Information technology (IT) facilitates the development process by applying various IT tools in planning, administration, monitoring and evaluation, coordination and policy making not only in government but also in non-governmental organisations. Even though information collection and process have been identified as a concurrent activity in India, and also through various statistical legislations in the country, the development of informatics in government took a forward jump with the formation of National Informatics Centre (NIC) in 1977 and the establishment of NICNET in the country during 1980-90.

Rural development, community development, and social development have been given due importance and the development planning process in the country is carried out through successive Five-Year Plans, and also through decentralisation by establishing local government bodies (panchayats and nagarpalikas). Socio-economic planning and plan management requires the availability of an extensive information system based on reliable data to facilitate the development and to analyse policy options by employing modelling and forecasting techniques. Informatics network plays an important role in the information flow from the implementation level to the planners at macro (national), meso (state), and micro (district, block, and village) levels.

Distributed Data Bases (DDB) are today the most promising area and a much needed tool for informatics professionals, IS experts and administrators. DDBs are the converging point of networking and data base technologies, respectively representative of distribution and integration. This is due to fast and often explosive evolution of these two domains over the decade. The concept of Distributed Processing (DP) has emerged as a result of technological, economical and organisational factors. The evolutionary watch-word of the distributed processing movement is "power to the people". DDB establishment approach can be viewed as follows:

(i) Top-down where local databases do not pre-exist but result from partitioning and the Global Database Administrator is free to select any partitioning strategy even if the final allocation is more or less dependent on the distributed DBMS (e.g., GISTNIC) and

(ii) Bottom-up where local databases are already implemented on local DBMS and then are integrated in order to constitute a global database, meeting the application requirements (e.g., DISNIC).

Distributed Sectoral Databases for Decentralised Planning

Since India has different types of terrain, resources, climate, socio-economic levels and distinct problems, preparation of a comprehensive micro-level plan either for a village or cluster of village, requires a strong spatially areas/region oriented geo-integrated socio-economic cum-natural resources database for planning, management and decision-making at grassroot level. Over the years, increasing emphasis has been placed on multi-level planning, from the national level to the state and to the district level and to the small area (development block) which was considered as a "suitable and manageable geographical unit area" for planned development within the frame of district planning and other levels in the multi-level planning structure. Rural development represents the major component of decentralised planning.

Decentralised planning calls for an immense amount of data and information specially to meet the new orientations in planning that have emerged in the recent years. Decentralised planning presupposes availability of relevant information at different levels in a desegregated form at as many of these levels as possible. Hence development of distributed information systems and databases at national, State, district and block level (grassroot level) is essential for the effective socio-economic planning for social transformation in the country and also to bridge the information gap for planning at these levels, and has got its evolutionary approach depending upon the data usage and comprehensive understanding of information requirement for planning purposes.

The micro-level planning approach is essentially to meet the objectives of: (i) optimum utilisation of human as well as natural resources available in the area, (ii) improvement in income and employment opportunities for rural masses, and

(iii) integration of area development with the development of people residing therein, and also to address itself to the problems of the rural poor and formulate realistic targets for reducing: (i) poverty, (ii) unemployment, and (iii) inequality.

Data requirements for micro-level planning at block level may be grouped as follows:

A. Plan Formulation: (i) Assessment of the available resources and additional resources required for the development, (ii) To consider the need of the people with particular reference to the weaker section of the society, (iii) Formulation of schemes/programmes with specific objectives on the basis of the above details; here national priorities should be given utmost importance and wherever it is necessary linkage between local programmes and special programmes should be established, and (iv) Setting physical and financial targets to be achieved within the specific time-frame under each scheme/programme.
B. Plan implementation which is a sensitive aspect of the planning process, involves the issues such as: (i) to find out suitable agencies for assigning the responsibility for implementation of the scheme/programmes; (ii) to provide suitable infrastructure to ensure a timely and healthy progress; and (iii) monitoring the progress and timely solution of the problem arisen.
C. Evaluation is a systematic and proper assessment of a programme with reference to the objectives of the schemes/ programmes; the data generated at the implementation and evaluation stages should be input data for future plan formulation.

Infrastructure for Government Informatics Development

Government organisations use and produce information. Information is the essence of their existence. It is a fact that many government ministries/departments and organisations are not so careful about the collection, storage and retrieval of information as the are about money. The realities are: (i) Information collected by government organisations imposes a heavy cost on business; (ii) Information that is not available may cost a great deal of money; (iii) Information that is not used may lose a great deal of money; (iv) Information systems are today and for the foreseeable future a pre-requisite for effective national development; and (v) development within the government administration can be used as a lever for technical development in society as a whole [UN090].

National Informatics Centre (NIC) is the nodal S&T organisation of Government of India, under the Planning Commission, to introduce information technology (IT) tools for management support (MS), development of databases (DB), model-bases (MB) and knowledge-bases (KB), decision support systems (DSS), Geographic Information System (GISNIC), fileless-office concept, electronic mail services (NICMAIL), and tele-informatics services in the Government at the Central, State and district level in the country. NICNET which is a satellite based computer communication network, established during the Seventh Five-Year Plan period (1985-90) provides information network facilities to the government administrations for IT implementation. NICNET is expected to be enhanced during the Eighth Five-Year Plan period (1990-85) to cover about 5300 Blocks/Tehsils through out the country to facilitate grassroot level development planning and administration which has been emphasised during this plan period. NICNET comprises the following:

(a) Very large Computers (NEC-S1000) at the NIC Regional Centres (Delhi, Pune, Bhubaneshwar and Hyderabad);

(b) ND-550 or equivalent super mini-computers at State capitals. for providing informatics service to the States;

(c) Super PC-AT computer systems at each district, to provide services to the district administration;

(d) PC-AT computer systems at each block development office to provide informatics services, to the block level administration (to be implemented during eighth Five-Year Plan period);

(e) Master earth station at NIC headquarters, Delhi and a Micro earth station at each of NIC State units and district informatics centres, for exchange of information via INSAT-1D satellite.

While NICNET makes use of the satellite communication (INSAT-1D) for long distance links, terrestrial communication is used for short distance intra-city network through leased telephone lines or dial-up lines using Public-Switched Telephone Network (PSTN) for integration to NICNET.

In general, NICNET facilitates the Central Government as well as the State Governments for: (i) Monitoring of vital socio-economic products, (ii) On-line retrieval of data, (iii) Optimum utilisation of expensive computer resources, (iv) Emergency communication systems, (v) Sharing latest software tools, (vi) Dissemination of information, and (vii) Exchange of messages and information between Central Government, State Governments and districts.

Application of IT for rural development was given the top priority by the government by launching various government informatics development programmes of NIC such as DISNIC, GRID (grassroot level informatics development programme during the Eight Five-Year-Plan period), CRISP (Sponsored project of the Central Rural Development Department for implementation by NIC at DRDA level), sectoral informatics programme (AGRIS, ARISE, ENVIS, education, industry, etc.), public informatics programme (GISTNIC, NNRMS of DOS and NRDMS of DST, etc.). Multi - functional use of IT facilities for rural upliftment at village level is expected to pave the way for the use of IT for community use and rural development in a broader perspective. Informatics development programme at district and sub - district level are explained in brief in the following sections.

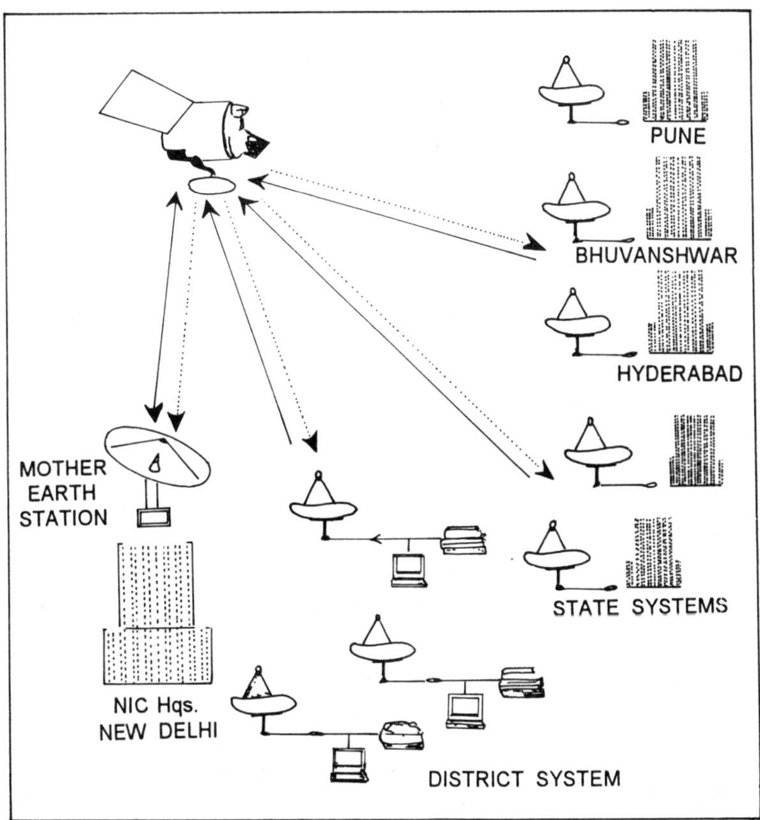

Fig. D1: NICNET: A Nationwide Satellite-Based Computer-Communication Network

(A) DISNIC Informatics Development Programme at District Level

DISNIC programme was launched in 1987 with the specific objective of bringing in IT standards for the government district administration and hence envisaged to: (i) develop the necessary information/data - bases (both spatial and non - spatial) in various sectors of the economy for planning and decision - making at the district level, (ii) promote informatics culture at the district level through appropriate training programmes, (iii) facilitate information standardisation and discipline, wherever required, (iv) improve the analysis capacity and the presentation of the statistics utilised for national, regional and district planning, (v) develop modelling and forecasting techniques that are required for decision - making for socio - economic development, and (vi) promote GIS techniques for planning and also remote sensing data applications for natural resources management at grassroot level.

With the establishment of NICNET, the implementation of the DISNIC Programme has facilitated the development of DDB on NICNET as a bottom - up approach where local DISNIC sectoral databases are already implemented on local DBMS at the district level and then to integrate them in order to constitute a Global Database meeting the End - Users' application requirements at state/national levels, using the distributed database management system (UDMS) of NICNET.

B. DISNIC - PLAN Programme for Facilitating Micro - Level Planning

As per the recommendations of the committee of "Study Group on Information Gap" of the Planning Commission, proformae for information collection for micro - level planning at district, block, and village level were designed and distributed to the State governments, under the DISNIC - PLAN programme. The DISNIC - PLAN programme aims at: (i) creation and maintenance of district, block and village level databases in respect of socio - economic, agro - economic and natural resources, etc., (ii) expert systems development, and (iii) also integration of GIS Techniques for micro - level planning, using NICNET facilities at the district level. Voluntary agencies can look in to the data for its utility with respect to their requirements. Many State governments are in the process of information collection to create to database. Agencies like NABARD would like to use the village data for their credit plans.

(C) GRID Programme of Block Level

With the implementation of DISNIC programme, NIC has initiated information revolution at district level through its various databases to provide demographic, socio-economic and development indicators. With the quick availability of information, the administrators can now devote more time to the actual planning and decision-making. As the block is the smallest developmental unit, especially in implementing development programmes and the block generates basic information, the development of block level information system is expected to go a long way in increasing the availability of information for decision-making, monitoring, evaluation and planning. The GRID programme is expected to facilitate the grass-root level development planning and administration which has been emphasised during this Plan period

Implementation of GRID programme will take place during the enhancement of NTCNET facilities.

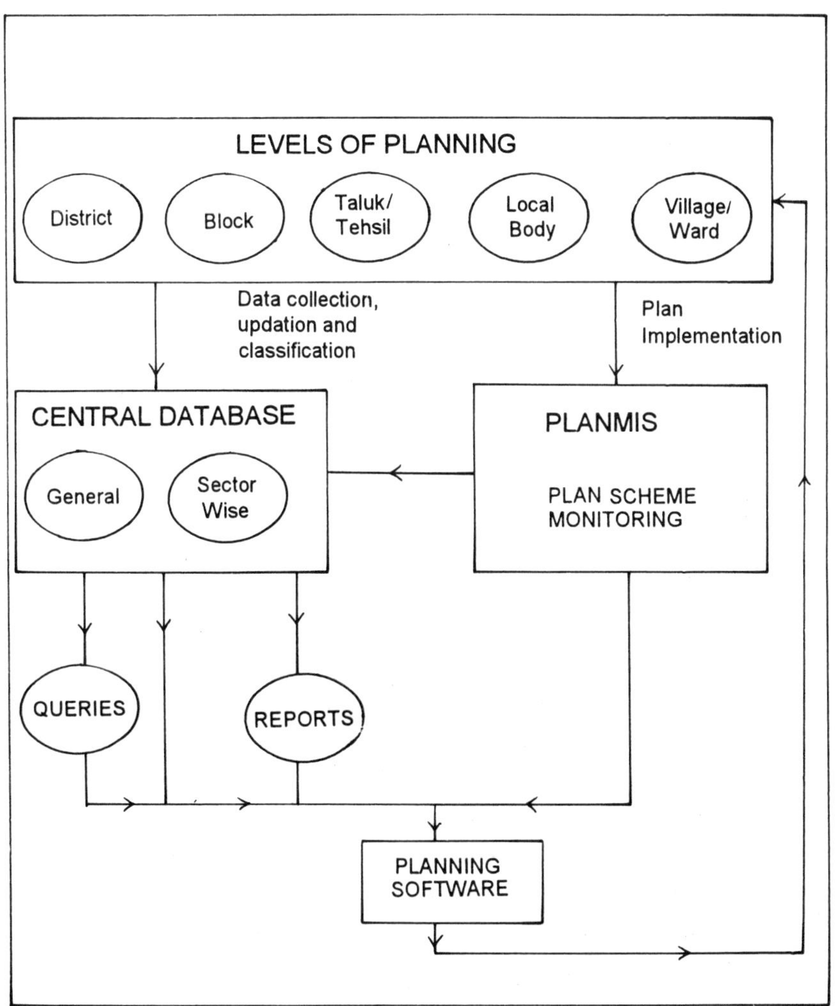

Fig. D2: District Planning Information System

The Working Group on block level planning under the Chairmanship of Prof. M.L. Dantwala has also recommended the desirability of maintenance of data at village level in various areas mentioned below for block level planning. GRID programme is expected to cater to the following areas:

(a) Tehsil/Block level Database Project on Development sectors, e.g., (Rural Labour, Agriculture Development, Animal Husbandry Development, Dairy Development, Minor Irrigation, Soil Conservation, Industry (SSI, Rural,

Agro-based), Social Forestry, Wasteland Development, Wetland Development, Fisheries Development, Community Development, Rural Development), Social Services (Health and Nutrition Education, Drinking Water Supply, Housing, Sanitation, Welfare Programmes, Local Transport), Cooperation, Banking and Financial Institutions for credit facilities, etc.;

(b) Land Records Informatics;

(c) Panchayati Raj Institutions Informatics;

(d) Nagarpalika Informatics;

(e) Employment and Training;

(f) Information system on Women in Agriculture, Women and Rural Development. Women and Environment, Legal Provisions protecting women, Employment opportunities for women, Science and Technology component assisting Women, Women and Education, Women and Health, etc.

(D) Involvement of Voluntary Agencies for Government Informatics Development Programme

Voluntary agencies (VAs) supplement government efforts in the implementation of poverty - alleviation programmes and minimum needs programme, and more and more grass - root level voluntary agencies are getting identified for associating in the implementation of such programmes in the country. VAs play the crucial role of being the "eyes and ears" of the people in the field. Voluntary agencies working for rural development at the village level require access to the information collected by various government agencies at the village level. Information collection at the village level involves: (i) manpower, (ii) money and (iii) time. This can be saved to a great extent, if voluntary agencies have access to the information collected by the government agencies; and also the cooperation among the government agencies, non - governmental agencies and the private agencies, etc. in this regard.

Voluntary agencies assist the district planners in deciding what sorts of assets should be provided to the beneficiary in a particular region depending upon the available infrastructure and resources. VAs are involved in collecting such information by door-to-door canvassing in the rural areas for the identification of IRDP beneficiaries on the basis of annual income. Voluntary agencies have expertise to conduct evaluation studies on programmes run by: (i) grass root level agencies, (ii) social action groups and (iii) activists, and they have systematic orientation and realistic terms of reference of assessing "people and programme".

(E) Information Access to Voluntary Agencies Who are Involved in Rural Upliftment/Advancement

Information is no longer going to be the bottleneck for the social development, as the entire government administration has access to the informatics network (NICNET) and involved in the government informatics development programme at national, State, and district level. The Government Informatics Development Programme by NIC is governed by institutional arrangements, such as, NSCC (NIC - State Coordination Committee) NDCC (NIC District Coordination Committee) and NMCC (NIC - Ministerial Coordination Committee). NIC has signed MOU with all States and UTs for effective implementation of this programme.

Voluntary agencies may like to assess their information needs from NICNET databases, such as, DISNIC, CRISP, GISTNIC and other sectoral databases for utility in rural upliftment, and also for the development of GRID at the block level. VAs can have grants - in - aid from the information technology development programme of NIC for IS - related projects for rural upliftment/ advancement. Problems due to non - availability of proper facilities for information exchange and also information access felt in the planning process by VAs are expected to be eased out by rallying around NICNET.

Conclusion

DISNIC - PLAN project is under implementation in various district nodes of NICNET under the DISNIC programme. State government departments and district level authorities are actively involved in the implementation of the project. Many State Governments have identified pilot districts for the preparation of a comprehensive micro - level plan (decentralised planning) either for a village or cluster of villages using the DISNIC - PLAN project facilities.

APPENDIX - E

WEATHER AND ENVIRONMENT

Introduction

Meteorology is helping man to harness the forces of the atmosphere for social and economic benefits to man kind. The spectrum of its applications in different fields of human activity is growing wider and richer everyday. The meteorological know-how has become essential in almost all fields of economic development, viz., agriculture, water management, industry, transportation, housing, environment control and the utilisation of natural resources. The application of Information Technology (IT) and other modern equipments Including satellites have given a new outlook to the science of weather forecasting.

Application Areas

Meteorology has applications in almost every field which concerns human beings. Computers are being utilised in meteorology starting from observations, preparation of weather forecast and to the point of providing end-product to the user. Various steps involved in this process are given below.

(A) Observing System

Observations form the basis of meteorological studies. A precise weather forecast for any area demands precise facts collected in millions from all over the world at fixed synoptic hours. On fixed hours, large number of land stations, merchant ships and aircrafts record meteorological observations, such as, pressure, temperature, wind, clouds, humidity, rainfall, fog, haze, visibility, etc. Upper air observations are also recorded by releasing balloons with attached Radio-Sonde equipment which are followed by RADARS from the ground. Personal computers are used to make the computations within short time. But still the gap remains over oceans, forests and mountainous regions for understanding and prediction of weather. Satellites have provided a new observing system to cover this gap.

(B) Satellites-The New Tools

The artificial earth-orbitting satellite is a new means of observing the weather; it presents two important advantages over all other known techniques as indicated below:

(i) It provides a means of observing the weather from outside the atmosphere; and

(ii) It provides a means of prompt weather information on a truly global scale.

Meteorological satellites are of two types: (i) polar orbitting satellites and (ii) geostationary satellites. Polar orbitting satellites provide instantaneous pictures of an area around their path while geostationary satellites provide pictures of the same area continuously. Satellites are equipped to take pictures and measure radiations. These observations are used to estimate temperatures, cloud cover, snow cover, areas of dust haze, fog and winds in the various layers of the atmosphere. Pictures help in the detection of cyclonic storms while they are deep into the sea area and also other significant weather systems. Thus satellites help the meteorologist to collect useful meteorological information from otherwise data sparse regions. India was continuously using American and Russian meteorological satellites from 1960 onwards for meteorological information. On 30th August, 1983, INSAT-1B was launched. It became operational on, 15th October, 1983. INSAT-1B was placed into the geostationary orbit over the equator at 74°E at an altitude of approximately 36,000 km. The meteorological Instrument on board were: (i) every high resolution radiometer (VHRR) and (ii) the data collection transponder. INSAT-1D was launched on 12th June, 1990 and is located at 83.0°E at an altitude of 36,000 km. It is being presently used. Its resolution is 2.75 km. in the visible and 11 km. in the infra-red channel.

All data from satellite is received first at Delhi earth station of Department of Telecommunication from where it is transmitted over microwave link to the meteorological data utilisation centre (MDUC) at Lodi Road, New Delhi. Here data is processed round the clock with the help of fast computers. INSAT-II with improved resolution will be launched in the late 1991*. For this purpose new computers to process the data are being installed. A sample picture of a cyclonic storm in the Bay of Bengal at 0430 UTC on 7th May, 1990 is shown in Fig. 11.1. Meteorological satellites thus have really helped in the modernisation of meteorology. Credit for this goes to the development of fast computers and computerised communication system.

(C) Radars

Electronics are having more and more applications in modern Meteorology. Second World War saw the development of RADAR in which ultra-short wireless waves were used to detect high flying enemy aircrafts. These ultra-short waves are reflected not only by metallic bodies, but also by the water droplets in the clouds and the areas of rain in the sky. The reflected intensity increases with the size of the droplets. Areas where large drops are numerous show themselves as bright patches on the Radar screen. Severe cyclonic storms also reveals itself as a bright converging

---

* Since launched in July, 1992.

spiral on the Radar screen when it is within the range of the Radar set. X-band radars have been provided at almost all important aerodromes and S-band at important coastal stations to detect cyclones. Range of cyclone detecting radars is 400 Km. Radars have really helped meteorologists to improve their service to aviation and in storm warning of the coastal areas. Computers are being used to process radars data and incorporate the same in computerised weather forecasting.

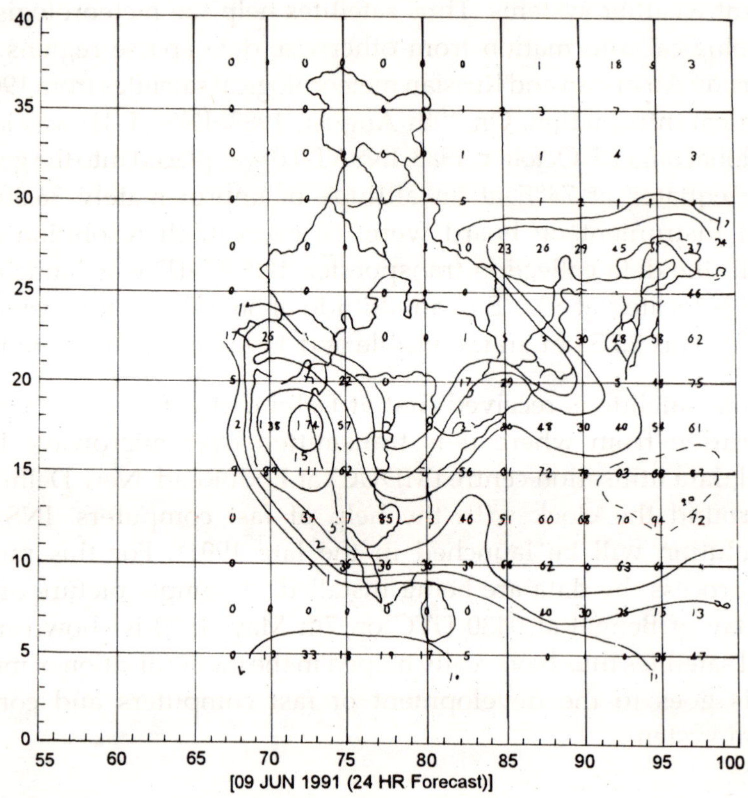

Fig. E1: Rainfall (mm) over India with NCMRWF Improved Model Physics

(D) Computerised Telecommunication

An efficient communication system is a backbone of an efficient meteorological service. All meteorological data collected by various means is required to be exchanged among the user countries. Global exchange of such voluminous data (estimated at 5 million five figures groups per day) on real time basis has become possible only with computerisation of telecommunication facilities. World Meteorological Organisation (WMO) has provided a scheme of Global Telecommunication System (GTS) for quick exchange of data between different countries. India is connected to Moscow,

Melbourne, Tokyo, Cairo and various other international circuits for global reception and transmission of data. In Delhi, VAX-11/750 telecommunication computers are being used for this purpose. Thus Delhi is an important centre for the exchange of international meteorological data. India has also an efficient national telecommunication system. All major airports have been equipped with telecommunication computers. This communication system is also used for exchange of processed meteorological forecast data among different countries. Thus communication also helps in avoiding duplication of work by various countries and, at the same time, ensures the required processed data to all the countries for their work. It may be mentioned that India Meteorological Department was the first to use a telecommunication computer in India.

Corporate Objectives

The main objectives of introduction of IT in the Meteorological Department are as follows:

(i) To provide current and forecast meteorological, information for optimum operation of weather-sensitive activities like agriculture, irrigation, shipping, aviation, off-shore oil exploration, etc.;

(ii) To warn the public in time against severe weather phenomena like tropical cyclones, duststorms, heavy rains and snow, cold & heat waves, etc., which cause destruction of life and property;

(iii) To provide meteorological statistics for agriculture, irrigation, industries, and other nation-building activities; and

(iv) To help in meteorological research and also to process seismological data.

Computer-Based Methodology

(a) Objective Analysis

The data received from the telecommunication computer is decoded by a scientific computer. It is subjected to various quality control checks. The data so received are at irregularly spaced observational stations. The solution of hydrodynamical equations governing the flow of the atmosphere require the values of the meteorological parameters at regularly-spaced grid points. This is necessary because these equations are non-linear and do not have analytical solutions. Their approximate solutions are obtained by numerical methods using finite difference and other numerical schemes. The technique by which the data are obtained at a large number of equally-spaced grid points from irregularly-distributed observations is known as objective analysis. This is being carried out daily in India Meteorological Department using a scientific computer.

(b) Numerical Weather Prediction

Forecast of the pressure fields by numerical solution of the equations of motion using initially observed state of the atmosphere generally with the aid of an electronic computer using numerical techniques is called Numerical Weather Prediction (NWP). This is being carried out in India using simple 5 level models. In other advanced countries more sophisticated models are being used.

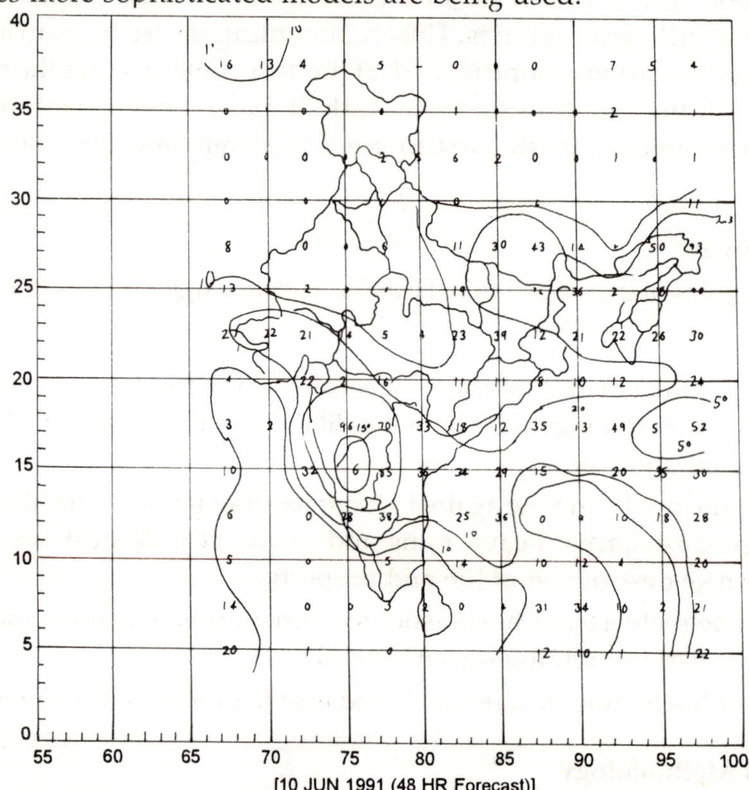

Fig. E2: Rainfal (mm) Over India with NCMRWF Improved Model Physics

(c) Computerised Cyclone Prediction

About 90 years of cyclonic storm data in the Bay of Bengal and Arabian Sea have been analysed with respect to time and location of its formation, direction, and speed of movement, etc. This database is used along with the characteristics of the current storm by an expert system developed for the purpose to predict 24, 48 & 72 hours positions of the cyclonic storm. Mathematical models and computer programmes, have also been developed to predict the storm-surges. The prediction of storm-surges are of immense benefit to the villagers in the coastal areas.

(d) Climatology

Climatology of a place is the average weather of that area. In India, Meteorological Department database for more than 100 years have been created. This data is a valuable asset and is being used to find out future trends of weather and climatic changes. It may be mentioned that in India no definite trends have be found in rainfall.

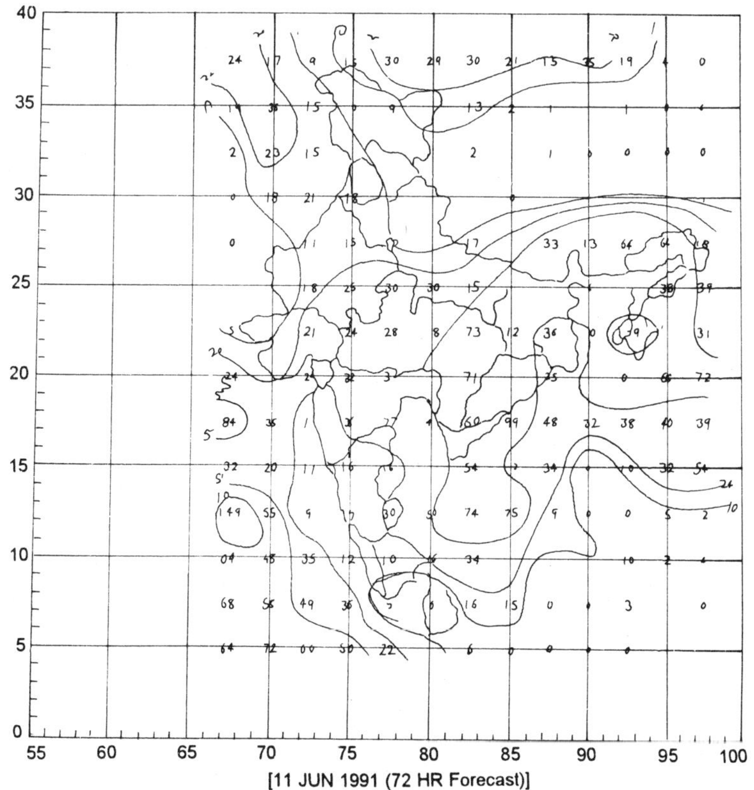

Fig. E3: Rainfal (mm) Over India with NCMRWF Improved Model Physics

(e) Monsoon Forecast

General weather forecasts are issued for 24 hours to 48 hours and in some areas an outlook is issued for a week. But monsoon, which is very important for Indian economy, constitutes about 70 to 80 per cent of the annual rainfall of the country. Special Seasonal Forecast for the period June to September are given. Methods with different parameters have been developed using regression techniques for this purpose. Such forecasts are very useful to the government for planning purpose.

(f) Crop Yield Models

Statistical models have also been developed in India to estimate the principal crops of the country based on long-term weather and technological inputs using computers. The total food production of the country estimated by these models is generally in good agreement with the actual figures.

(g) Air Pollution

Computerised models have also been developed to estimate the pollutions created by the industry and its effect on human beings and agriculture in the area. These models will help in the future town and industrial planning in such a way that the environment pollution will remain under control. For the present state, mankind is responsible by cutting of forests, eliminating some of the animals/birds, construction of large scale concrete jungles in the cities and creating large scale industrial areas. Computerised statistics may help to control this activity by keeping proper records.

Fig. E4: Cyclonic Storm in the Bay of Bengal at 04.30 UTC of 7th May, 1990

Benefits Derived

Computerised information technology has helped the meteorologists to improve the weather forecast for aviation, shipping and agriculture. It has also helped in the improvement of cyclonic storm prediction for coastal areas. It has resulted in enormous saving of human life and property. Environment models developed with the help of computers will also help in keeping the air pollution under control in the existing cities using different preventive measures and also help in the planning of new pollution-tree cities. Thus, use of computers has given a new outlook to the science of weather forecasting and we look forward for further improvement in this respect.

Conclusion

In India, introduction of computerised Information Technology (IT) in meteorology did not pose any problem. In fact, India Meteorological Department introduced Hollerith machines in 1945 and first computer in 1963. A modern scientific computer was acquired in 1973. India Meteorological Department was also first to use a communication computer in 1976. The first super computer CRAY XMP-14 is also being used for medium range weather forecast in meteorology. It is being managed by Department of Science and Technology.

APPENDIX - F

ENVIRONMENT

Introduction

It is universally recognised that information, particularly scientific and technological including environmental information, is one of the basic resources for the socio-economic development of the country. As a resource, information is like electric energy and the impact of reliable, fast and inexpensive information on the national economy will be as great as that of electricity. Some specialists even go as far as to say that information is the resource of resources, i.e., on which depends all other resources because it is information which premits other resources to be identified, evaluated and utilised. Information is an essential ingredient of change and change is nothing but a transformation resulting from a new contribution of data or different treatment of existing data. Information is the only resource which grows as it is sub-divided and spreads. Under development, in the final analysis is a consequence of the lack of capacity to generate information, to handle it properly, to store it, to perform it regularly and to disseminate it equitably.

The flow of fresh and reliable information is the parameter of progress. It is a form of modern currency, an investment for the future. The newly emerging high-tech disciplines such as super computers, telecommunications, micro-electronics, new sources of energy, bio-diversity, environment, etc., are valued more in terms of information generated than anything else. Many advanced countries are said to have entered into a state called "post-industrial society" in which rise of the GNP depends not so much on the production and distribution of goods and commodities but on the generation distribution and application of scientific knowledge and information. In some of these advanced countries, more and more people are working in information-based service sectors than in all other employment sectors put together.

In meeting the information needs of various user groups, it is necessary to distinguish the uses of information and users of information. There are several types of users of information including those engaged in fundamental scientific research, applied scientists working on R&D, technologists, teachers, writers, industrialists, library personnel, business faculty and so on. Each category of these users has different use of information for different purposes.

Corporate Objectives

The information clientele forms a broad spectrum of various sectors. They could be from R&D discipline or entrepreneurs or students or business personnel or others. A scientist may require information for general need to keep himself informed of the latest development over the field of science and technology, an environmentalist may require information to appraise himself the latest environmental development, a business magnet may be in need of information only from business angle. But, whatever may be the need, the user group requires information with a particular objective. Therefore, each information-seeker has a particular path in which his information needs to travel. So according to the diversity of the clientele, the information needs also become diverse. It differs from a researcher, to a policy maker or to an engineer or to an industrialist or even to the general public. Information is required in all parts of public administration system, e.g., in, government departments like Agriculture, Industry or Social Welfare, departmental agencies incharge of commercial operations, Railways, P&T or government corporations like Food Corporation of India or public companies such as, Coal India, Steel Authority of India Ltd. and its subsidiaries. What is most important is to develop a management information system (MIS) to meet the objectives of different clientele.

A comprehensive MIS should have the following characteristics:

(a) It should cover all the salient aspects of the programme with reference to the principles, goals and objectives in view;

(b) It must be selective;

(c) It should he transparent and not opaque, i.e., it should clearly bring out the relationship between the input and output, effort and the result, the money spent and the result derived;

(d) It should bring out outstanding success as well as outstanding failures; and

(e) It should be periodic so that there is a systematic and sustained monitoring over a period of time.

Computer Based Methodology

We are experiencing now what may be termed as the "push of technology" and its impact on every facet of information handling. The advent of digital computer and the advancement in the telecommunication and audio-visual technology have opened up a new possibilities in dealing with problems arising from collecting, organising, disseminating a vast amount of scientific and technical information. Computer and communication technologies are not only merging but are also converging with related technologies such as printing and photography. When all these elements are fully integrated the resultant capability for information transfer and exchange would create a form of material information inter-dependence. Even, one can say that the merger of the computer and the communications with other technologies would result in the development of a total new information infrastructure for the society.

It has been government's endeavour now to provide benefits of computerisation to all nooks and corners in India for accessing all information needs. With the development of various databases, it has become possible to search and sort large quantities of required data rapidly.

In the initial stages, the information networks operated in a batch processing mode which was not a very satisfactory arrangement for information, access and retrieval. However, with the development of the packet switching technology during the 1970s', "on line information network" permitting an attractive man-machine interface has become popular and is being widely used. Improvisation of productivity has resulted in government operations through streamlining of information base, systems analysis of the organisational structure quantitative studies feeding the planning process and, in general, evolving an effective managing information system for each government department with exchange of information among them. This has been catalysed by National informatics Centre (NIC) which was conceived in 1973 and nucleated in 1975 to develop methodologies for implementing a governmental information System and to demonstrate to the government departments the benefits that accrue from computerisation. NIC has also developed, distributed and decentralised informatics and computer network for government management information system. Computer Maintenance Corporation (CMC), has also introduced a commercial computer network INDONET incorporating an integrated information management and distributed data processing facilities spanning the entire country.

Benefits Derived

The NIC has launched its District Information System (DISNIC) under which selected information from the districts can be transmitted to the State computers. Similar information from all the districts will be transferred to the computer at State Capitals under the supervision of the State Governments before passing it on to the regional centre and the national centre. The national centre will be able to query the databases in the States and vice-versa. The relevant decision support information from the districts, thus readily available with the State Governments and with the Central Government DIS-NIC through NICNET, will fill the long-felt, information gap for the planning agencies and will facilitate the decision-making at various levels of Government of India.

National Information System of Science and Technology (NISSAT) set up in the Ministry of Science and Technology, Government of India, has been functioning to meet the scientific and technological information needs through its sectoral information centres.

Environmental Information System

An Environmental Information System (ENVIS) has been set-up by the Ministry of Environment and Forests with a chain of distributed information centres on the priority subject areas of environment and located in the various professional organisations throughout the country to meet the environmental information needs of the users.

Bio-technological Information System (BITS) has been established in the Department of bio-technology for meeting the information requirements in the field of bio-technology of the user community.

Besides, various network of information as given below have been launched/ being launched to make information available to the user community:

1. RAILNET: computer network for the Railways,
2. OILNET: computer network for oil sector,
3. EDUNET: computer network for educational institutions,
4. BANKNET: computer network for banking applications and electronic fund transfer,
5. TRANSNET: a computer network for transport sector,
6. POLICENET: a computer network for the police, and
7. COALNET: a computer network for coal.

Problems Encountered and their Solutions

India, despite its having third largest scientific man power in the world, still is not so well placed in the matter of generating storage, transmission and retrieval of scientific and technical information for the benefit of the scientific community. In spite of the advanced communication systems, a large segment of the science and technology community does not have ready access to current and other information. This is practically impossible for the researchers in the remote location.

There is a serious lack of adequate number of libraries and information centres in the country. There is no adequate bibliographic control of Indian scientific publications and papers, publication of governmental agencies, publications of academies and societies, etc. Even in the area of scientific publications, we lack not only the quantity of the scientific journals but also the quality of production. Still, there is a heavy dependence on foreign information source. It is a common experience that international journals reject publications from developing countries due to their lack of comprehensiveness which, in turn, is due to lack of latest information and incomplete references. By setting up several information systems in the country, the S&T information needs have been partially met.

Conclusion

S&T information can be further improved upon as follow.

— The on-line access to international databases available on many network should be made possible;

— Important databases should be procured and provided to selected information centres for use by our scientists;

— The existing communication facilities should be upgraded to facilitate quick and easy information transfer;

— Training of personnel in information handling should be provided on priority basis;

— A nation-wide campaign should be organised to promote use of the information and its access at various points;

— A National Science Trust should be set-up to increase the facilities for document delivery for the benefit of the scientific community in the common areas; and

— Linkages of the various national information systems should be made immediately to interact the information needs.

Information systems on the other areas should be set-up to meet the information requirements on the S&T community in particular and the people in general.

APPENDIX - G

DESKTOP MAPPING

Introduction

Desktop mapping combines the properties of thematic maps with those of computers: Properties of thematic maps are integrative; wholistic; location-specific; spatial distribution; density; access. Properties of computers are speed; repeatability; precision; neatness; compact storage. Properties of computer storage are portability, copyability; compactness; updateability. Correctly designed thematic mapping software packages can make easy the task of viewing data and finding unusual cases, or locations where norms have not been met. Such identification and selection is the key to effective administrative management as well as ensuring that increasingly scarce state funds are optimally utilised to improve the conditions of the people.

Thematic Maps

Thematic maps are produced by projecting tabular data onto a set of regions for alternatively a set of locations or a set of routes) on a map. Regions can be filled with a choropleth hatching; points can have different markers, or symbols of different sizes, or barcharts or even piecharts. Sometimes piecharts can be projected over a choropleth background, providing an extra dimension information.

The choropleth itself can be many different types — equal interval; user-selected intervals; percentile or even mean/standard deviation. One can also represent the flows between regions (of persons, money, grain, coal etc.) by lines of different thickness, or thick and thin directed arrows. A great variety of thematic techniques are available with desk top mapping.

Desktop thematic maps, can both be viewer on the screen (in black and white or in colour), or examined on paper in user-selected sizes (up to Al). The usual mode of use is to generate, store and view on the screen a number of alternatives making changes in the techniques and symbols used, and editing for aesthetics, before obtaining a high quality printout. In Query Mode, when information about one particular place (or many locations) is required, this can merely be viewed *(in colour?)* without taking a hard copy.

We introduce below and illustrate a few of the possible applications of desktop mapping — first, at Sate headquarters, then at district level and finally at taluk level. This is by no means to be taken as a complete listing of possible applications, for many others too have come up in detailed discussions with various officials. We offer this introduction as a contribution to finding ways to improve the effectiveness and efficiency of State Government with a minimum of additional investment or training.

Applications in the State

Let us look at the applications at the level of departments of government at State headquarters. They are of four main types:

(i) Monitoring performance
(ii) Policy analyses
(iii) Planning and budgeting
(iv) "What if...?" analysis

Desktop mapping can make possible significant easing of the workload at State headquarters in respect of these four activities which concern the officials at that level. This means that more cases can be examined more carefully, that more thought can be given to critical issues, and that more alternatives can be taken up when necessary even within time limitations.

Some of the departments which have some or all of these applications are:

Planning Department
Finance Department
Education Department
Health Department
Agriculture Department
Social Forestry Department
Electricity Department (and State Electricity Board)
Public Works Department (and Area Development Authorities) Buildings
Irrigation (and the Water and Sewerage Boards)
Roads and Bridges
Tribal Development Department.

Taking first applications in the Planning Department, we have:

(a) District-wise and taluka-wise reports sector-wise for printing in annual reports and answers to assembly questions;
(b) Policy analytic support for Annual Plan and Five-Year Plan allocations, sector-wise and district-wise;

(c) Evaluation of the minimum needs status of different talukas and districts and then progress sector-wise, quarterly and annually,
(d) Identification of scarcity-endemic and drought affected talukas;
(e) Evaluation of EGS and similar State-wise programmes on the basis of monthly or seasonal data; and
(f) Evaluation of the 20-point programme results, on a multidimensional basis.

In the Finance Department, we can map sales tax collections by taluka. Cash flows in state treasuries is an important area where net inward and outward flows can be seasonally mapped, grouped and analysed. With suitable base maps accompanying the proposals, it will be possible for the Finance Department to examine the spatial aspects of major schemes coming to it for cost benefit analysis. This will lend strength to the social dimension of such analyses. Spatial analysis of treasury challans will provide valuable policy insights.

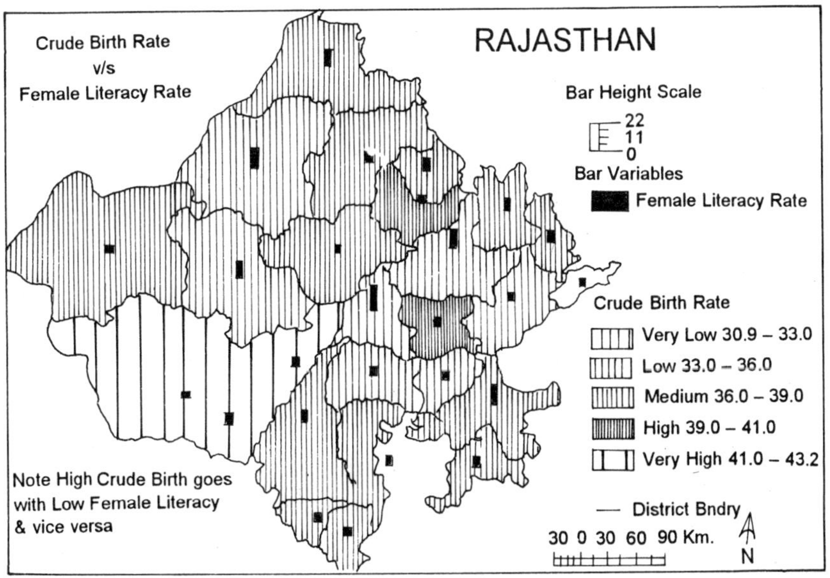

Fig. G1: Policy Analysis: Female Literacy vs Birth Rate

The Education Department has direct responsibility for high schools and above, but receives much useful information on primary and middle schooling. The simplest mapping of boys' and girls' enrolment rates, of the average size of class and of examination results will provide many leads for further detailed study at local level. What is important is that the problem-areas be identified and separated from those that are doing alright. Per-student budgets for teacher salaries, for repairs, for equipment, etc., can be compared spatially to throw up areas needing attention. Because desktop mapping is fast, it can be used to compare school attendance in different months and seasons. Instead of taking two weeks to prepare, a taluka-wise education map can be prepared in 15 minutes and be xeroxed for distribution the same day, thus providing feedback to the concerned regional (district?) officers responsible. Transfers and postings are yet another area where mapping can clarify the situation.

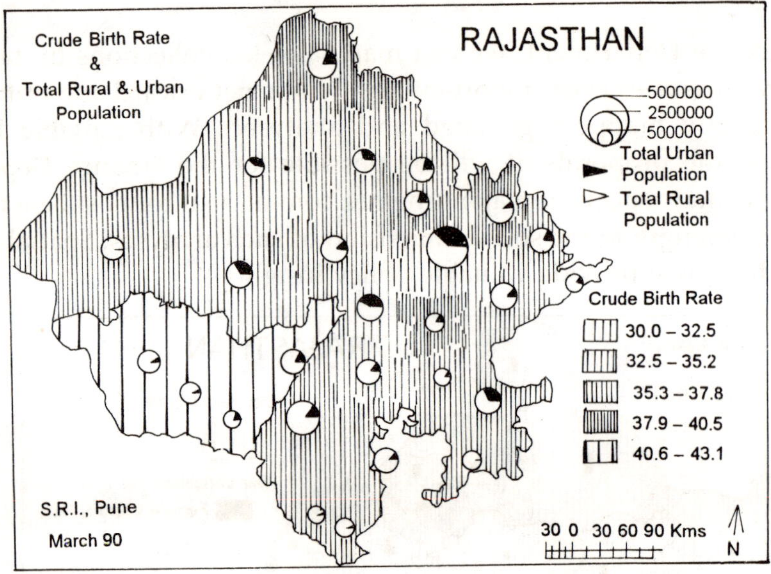

Fig. G2: Urbanisation Inversely Correlated with Birth Rate

Health is a field requiring very rapid response to information because of the short shelf-life of medicines and the speed of epidemics. With child health, maternal care, and preventive medicine assuming greater importance, there is need to monitor performance closely, to map out areas where drinking water is unsafe in future months and to use this as an input to medical programming. Likewise, areas with poor drainage (when and if it rains) become centres of other types of infection. These, too, can be mapped in real time. There is equal need to keep an up-to-date map of all reported infectious cases, so as to help determine the vector and to keep them under control. Desktop mapping can play a big role in medical administration by helping focus attention on needy areas. Mapping will also offer a lot of help in the tasks related to personnel assignments.

Agriculture is a department where at the beginning of the monsoon very rapid decisions must be made about the spatial allocation of seeds, credit, fertiliser, etc. and where it is necessary to monitor the pattern of crop production across the State throughout the year. The ability to plot and to view several variables together will be of special value in relating crop amounts and value to credit, fertiliser usage, etc., spatially. These are all analyses that need to be conducted at aggregate level using taluk or district-wise data. Other related analyses concern irrigation project impacts, the effect of major and minor regulated markets and warehouses on production and prices, and the spatial pattern of prices of agricultural commodities over time. The periodic movement of technical personnel can be rationalised and needy areas identified using maps.

For Social forestry, desktop mapping can be used in project planning ana strategic cost benefit analysis, as well as to compare the display of the programmes in different districts and talukas and the relative unit costs of different components of the programme, which would reveal any problems.

The Electricity Department and the State Electricity Board have a tremendous amount of spatial information on generation, but more importantly on transmission and distribution. In fact, special-purpose modules can be added to THEMAPS to help identify places where the transmission network requires change. Merely monitoring the condition of the State-wide network, which is being continuously upgraded, is a significant step. THEMAPS would also be used to provide a real-time picture of the electricity scene if it were connected on-line to the Electricity Board database. Control and monitoring of extension works on the distribution network across the State can be also effectively done with the help of maps.

The Public Works Department has a unique problem of having to readjust its budget location-wise and responsibility-wise in January, after it is known exactly how much money will be available till March end. Making these decisions can be eased by using a spatial picture of the needs and of the progress of various types of work till then. Forward budgeting for equipment, re-positioning of special equipment and allocation of personnel are other major functions that could be served.

Tribal Development has activities in many more of the talukas than is commonly recognised. Thematic maps will make it possible to monitor the different dimensions of the T.D. Department's work, and also to compare the effectiveness of programmes in different regions. Since it is difficult to travel throughout the State, thematic maps depicting the maning, facilities and the academic and other results, e.g., of Ashram shalas, location-wise, will be useful in evaluating their performance. Such maps can uniquely be used to communicate with tribal leaders and communities about the programme of the T.D. Department.

We have discussed these State Headquarters-level applications at some length partly to indicate how much can be done with — how much value can be obtained from-just ONE digital base map of the state, that includes the taluka boundaries, the districts, the divisions and the 300 to 350 important towns plus rivers and the road (and rail) network. These elements are digitised on different layers, and appear only as needed. It can have a tremendous impact on the rapid recognition of problems, on the clarity of analysis and on the quickness with which solutions are defined.

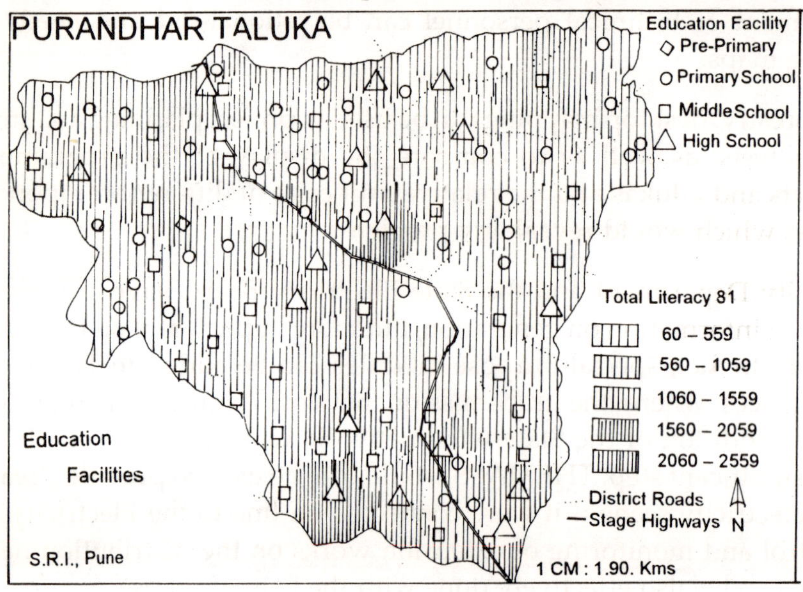

Fig. G3: The Map to Locate New High Schools

Applications of Desktop Mapping at the District Level

For most of the service departments like Health, Education, P.W.D., etc., the district is where the actual planning and later execution is done, and this is where the detailed planning database resides. Nasik district, with the help of NIRD, Hyderabad, has prepared a two-volume Integrated District Plan document which has been much appreciated and commended by the Multi-level Planning Group in the Planning Commission. This is supported by extensive use of maps. Low-cost replication of this methodology through all the districts in the State can be achieved by using a set of district digital base maps with taluka boundaries, locations of villages, with road and rail net-works, rivers canals, with some indication of forest areas (it any) and, in hilly regions, of contours.

One of the most important applications is the ranking of villages and the identification of the Growth Centre hierarchy, so that the location of the next set of services can be logically, economically and most beneficially decided. THEMAPS and its associated relational DBMS, STAT, can be used very efficiently with information about the existing layout of facilities in villages to help plot the Growth Centres and Service Centres, and to indicate the future pattern of growth.

Special attention can be given to the planning and monitoring and analysis of the Minimum Needs Programme — Water Supply, Rural electrification, and so on. Since Zilla Parishads and Collectors are responsible for reporting on achievements under the 20-point programme, this can be effectively planned, monitored, analysed and evaluated by using maps.

Thematic maps of the districts, in the hands of the collectorate planning officer and statistics officer can become a powerful tool for:

(a) Highlighting the problems,
(b) Achieving a consensus on priority areas requiring attention,
(c) Illustrating through "what if' maps the results of various alternative allocation strategies at the ZP among talukas and villages, and
(d) Producing theme-wise pictures of the district for exhibitions and general public education, and for communication to the press about district programmes and progress.

All departments of State Government will find it useful to picture their activity spatially, once this has been adopted by the State Government as the normal means of "viewing" the district. It will also enable the district officials to more easily motivate their village and taluka-level staff, since their areas of responsibility will be clearly seen on the map, they can be classified according to performance, and thematic maps prepared showing the achievement of the areas each person is responsible for. Such maps can also help to identify areas where additional personnel, or training, are required.

In summary, with 1000-1500 village locations depicted on the base map, along with the arteries of communication, supported by the at-tribute data in the database, it will become possible at district level to conduct all kinds of analyses, e.g. of the marketing of agriculture produce, of the movement from village to markets and the seasons therefor (suggesting possible new roads), and so on. Detailed planning, as in the Nasik document, for multi-sectoral development, can also be done. More important, since the information is in the computer, it becomes readily possible first to view various alternatives, and later even to adjust the programme rationally, according to the budget available, without making arbitrary, across-the-board reductions.

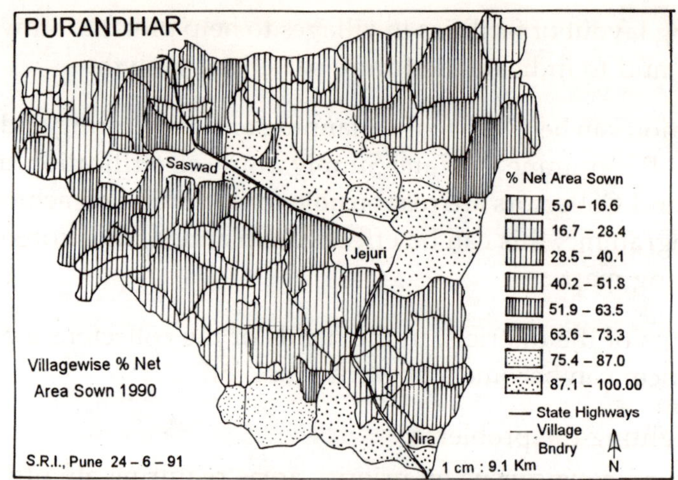

Fig. G4: Taluka Maps used for Detailed Service Plans

Application of Desktop Mapping at Taluka Level

Here it is necessary to distinguish (1) Administrative thematic mapping applications from, (2) Natural-resource-related and remote-sensing-related applications.

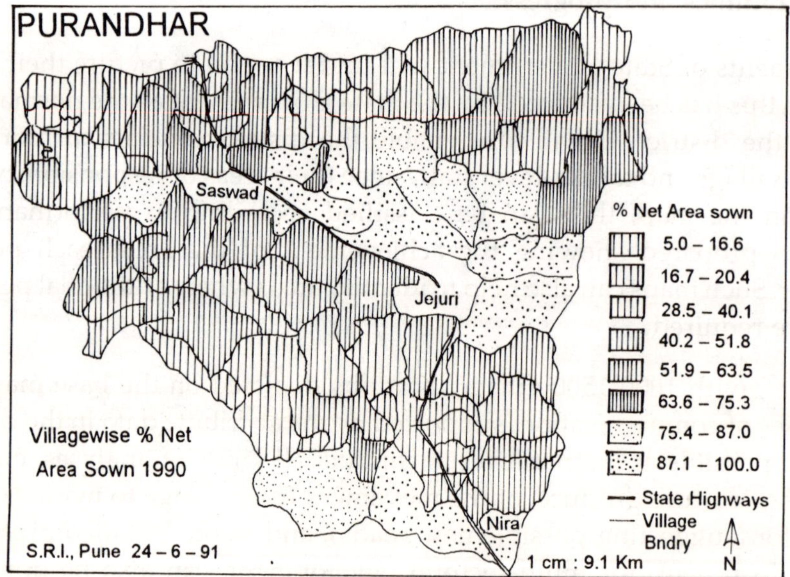

Fig. G5: Village-wise Agriculture Data on a Taluka Map

Desktop mapping by and of itself will fully meet the first set of applications which are concerned with displaying facts about the taluka on what is essentially an administrative/political map of the area. While settlements, village boundaries, forest area boundaries, rivers, roads, railway links, electricity lines, etc., are recorded, only rudimentary geological (soil or contour, information is held in such administrative maps. This makes them easier and quicker to digitise, which is an important consideration when there are 200-400 talukas in the State.

What can be done using these administrative taluka maps, coupled with the attribute data? Detailed planning of education and health facilities, for drinking water and for electrification can only be done at this level. Which village should get a 3-teacher primary school and which should expand into a middle school? Where should the next High School be located? Which road should be upgraded from ODR to MDR? Where should the next health station be located? Which village should get a telephone and which the protected water supply. These decisions can only be made by viewing the situation in full context, which means the demography, patterns of work, the land use in each village should all be available in the database.

Thus while the district is the correct level for controlling and sanctioning programmes, most people-oriented programmes should be initiated using village wise data in a taluka horizon. This can effectively be done with the administrative map. Thus the Minimum needs programme, Social forestry Programme, 20-point programme are all best planned using this map and data.

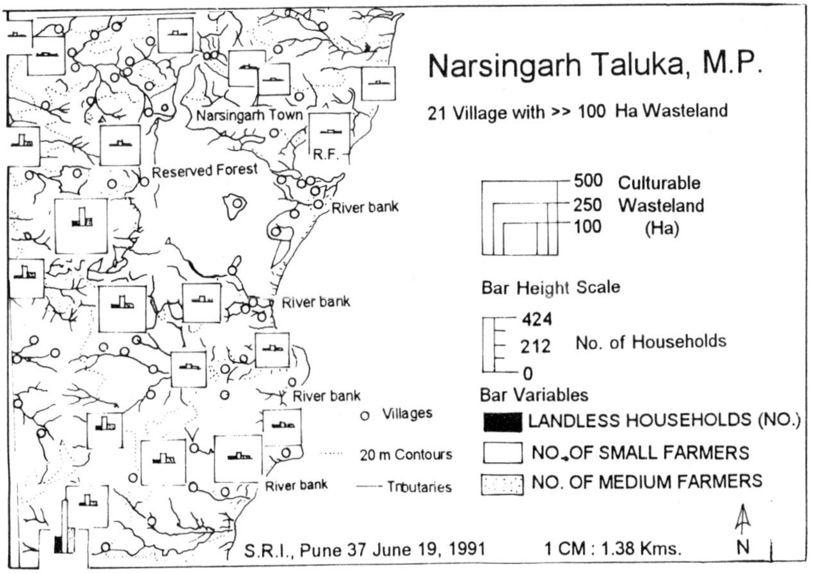

Fig. G6: Social Forestry: Targeting Specific Villages

Let us now look at the second kind of taluka map the natural-resource related 1:50,000 scale Survey of India map carefully digitised so that the remotely sensed imagery can be superimposed. Because of the need for greater accuracy, and the requirement to add layers corresponding to a soil map and a contour map, this map may quite difficult to produce. Once it is available, however, some interesting possibilities do open up.

This high-precision taluka map, which has a soil-type layer, can also be used by the Agriculture Department and Irrigation Department for detailed crop recommendations. If the contours are highly accurate, it is possible that the PWD could use an automated road-routing algorithm for First-cut solutions as well.

Here the increased accuracy of the map enables us to use it for more and more technical purposes which formerly were done by experts or by trial and error. Information about regions which are both digitised, and derived from imagery, can be used to tell about current forest cover, cropping patterns, etc. There is a much higher "initial cost", of course, here both in the digital map and in the additional software modules. The payoff may also be considerable. We do recommend that this type of map be also tried.

Another application of detailed maps, especially useful in agriculture planning, relates to watershed planning and the superposition of survey numbers to watershed maps. Because of the need for contour information, watershed outlines are usually made from 1:25,000 or 1:50,000 sheets. However, the survey number information is generally available only on 1:2000 or 1:4000 sheets. Bringing this information together is easiest done through a digitising process, since the final output maps can be at almost any desired scale. This is an excellent self-sufficient, self-justifying and cost-effective introductory application of desktop mapping for most Agriculture Departments.

Conclusion

In this paper, we have introduced a few State headquarters applications, District-level applications and Taluka-level applications of Desktop Mapping. This has had necessarily to be brief, and we have not been able fully to explain each application.

Implementation of Desktop Mapping in a State Government department will require a close cooperation of design specialists in the subject with decision-makers, and with the officers who have to maintain the databases and keep them up-to-date. The Systems Research Institute, which has over 10 years experience in this field, and a multi-disciplinary team of professional staff, makes its resources available for design, for digital map-making, for custom software development, and also publishes a newsletter and runs regular training courses.

APPENDIX - H

INFORMATION TECHNOLOGY FOR THE VILLAGES AND THE DIGITAL DIVIDE

Although Information Technology has made its mark in rural areas but it has not aimed at the poor and underprivileged but targeted primarily those echelons of the rural area that are part of the market economy or are close to the interfaces of governance. With the Simputer, a low-cost computing gadget, with solar and other localised non-conventional energy-devices, it can be hoped that IT can indeed reach the masses in the rural areas.

Stalwarts in the arena of Information Technology (IT)—and nearly everyone else—are full of enthusiasm over the furious proliferation of inventions, innovations, and equipment that they are witnessing. High-speed wireless networks enable faster connectivity to millions of devices, location sensing will be child's play, devices will recognise speech and even gestures, and computers will hold in their entrails devices possessing artificial intelligence. Such computing will be so pervasive and people and gadgets will get so effectively interconnected that people would routinely be keeping tabs on everything in and around their lives anywhere. An expressive observation says: The tectonic changes in technology have changed the landscape of our existence.... We are now in an era of intelligent devices and ubiquitous computing. Information technology has become all-encompassing due to the convergence of media, telecom, computing technologies and the spread of the Internet.

The earthquake in this statement would in all likelihood roll only the likes of you and me, the globalised lot at the top in this country, and perhaps touch the liberalised middle level lightly. As for the vast bottom level across the Digital Divide one does not know what it would witness.

Some of the enthusiasts however are sure that IT will make a big, pervasive entry into rural India. Says a starry-eyed Fulbright scholar looking at our society: "There seems to be universal consensus that community based access and application of Internet and IT will enable the impoverished rural masses to leapfrog into the Knowledge Era". Even in the highest levels of government extension of ITs benefits to rural people is devoutly desired. Hopes a high dignitary: Innovative designs will help to prove that IT can be used for the uplift of the poor and rural masses. But then, do we take the whole array of technologies in the IT armamentarium to the hinterland? Can we? Should we? Will they cross the Digital Divide and uplift the poor and the deprived— the bottom level? As the respected MIT Professor K. Keniston has put it:

the hopes that "information and communication technologies could enable even the poorest of developing countries to 'leapfrog' traditional problems of development...so as to move them rapidly into the modern Information Age...are largely built on an empirical vacuum". Deplores the Professor: "The wheel is constantly re-invented.... The people in some 'grassroots projects' in India are not usually in touch with each other, rarely publish or write about what they are doing.... There is little accumulation of knowledge, not even the most preliminary kind of on-the-site evaluation, little possibility of learning from successes and failures of other projects".

First, one needs to differentiate hype from reality, and rhetoric from what can be done. *Secondly* there is imperative need to carry out meticulous studies to decide what needs to be done and what strategies are best.

Let us at the outset note that the new technologies, their gadgetry and their connecting networks—optical cables, wireless towers, servers and softwares and so on—do not come cheap. Each of them demands large sums of money and reliable electric power. Their long-term sustainability requires a good match between the services they deliver and the demand for the same. But then new ways of finding money for such purposes have emerged: angel finance, venture capital, corporate investments eyeing a future in the villages, and such. Captive power sources—with similar funding—can take care of grid shortfalls and non-conventional energy can fill up the gaps.

In this scenario the title of a recent article caught one's eye. It read 'e-Villages'. One hoped to see in it some examples of IT facilities catering to a cross-section of village society both rich and poor. That was not to be. The hype of the title got dissipated in the text, which presented a very sobering reality. Notably, IT in these villages turned a blind eye to the Digital Divide.

The picture in the article was of a group of villages, in a prosperous water-rich countryside, whose economy revolved round three sugar mills run by a big industrial house, which had networked its 'watershed' (some 150 villages) with telephones (as the area had sparse telephone density). The industry had an intranet facility, for its own purposes, to get and give market and inventory information. For instance, rates prevailing in nearby markets (eight of them) were gathered from farmers by telephone, put on the intranet; data was updated daily at a fixed hour. The article also spoke of an advanced system based on an access centre (with a 48ft tall tower), which could sustain 1000 Internet connections within a 20-km radius. In portions of the area 38 connections have been given of which eight are taken by the industrial house and two by police stations. The rest are given to entrepreneurs hand-picked (by the industry) for their financial capacity, and trained (at the industry's expense) to run private computer-equipped kiosks. Selected kiosk holders are given access to the industry's intranet.

The chosen kiosk entrepreneurs live up to their choice. Apart from selling Internet services the computers are also used to do typing job, run computer class, and so on. The kiosk premises are also used for other activities—to sell ice-cream, run a phone booth, vend stamps or whatever—to further supplement earnings.

Doubtless this group of villages is not representative of all rural areas and doubtless there are many village groups of diverse character all over the country where IT has manifested itself in different modalities. In this example, IT rides on the back of corporate enterprise, a widely prevalent model for IT's thrust into the rural area. The model envisages funding tie-ups for IT services with corporates operating in the rural area concerned integrating, tightly or lightly, those services with IT facilities of the enterprise itself, delivering economic benefits to the villages. However, in most such instances IT touches, *ad hoc,* only a small part of the life of a small section of the villagers. The under-privileged and the impoverished exist nowhere in its ambit. Also, IT comes in without any prior survey of the felt needs of the populace, not even of the top layer of the villages.

Furthermore, not all of rural India is rich sugarcane countryside. Compared to dry rain-fed areas the water rich areas are likely to be better endowed with financially sound middle class entrepreneurs.

Although no mention is made of the investment made on the IT facilities as a whole, one can surmise that in this example alone, the cost will be, not in thousands but in millions of rupees. This means, does it not, that a vision of IT suffusing all rural areas of the country everywhere would be looking at outlays of many lakh of millions of rupees. Can one contemplate this order of investment with a top down thrust of IT employed to serve a narrow band of end users?

The rural areas are witnessing a major IT thrust from a variety of organs of governance, at the citizen-government interface and at intra-government interfaces, with the former getting maximum attention. The public domain of IT will provide specialised services with sharply focused departmental purposes. For example the district administration, police, excise, sales tax, and road transport, not to speak of the banks have computer-based facilities that, though mainly city-centric, have thin strands stretching into the rural area. The postal department is said to be planning several city-based IT facilities. Under an impetus provided by the Central Government, land records are being computerised at sub-district level — to start with as a service to the land users, eventually as an aid to government's operations and policy-making as well. Likewise, providing rural connectivity is a prime objective of the Central Government's Agriculture Department which has laid out more than Rs 1000 crore for it. It extends to half a dozen states. A four-member team is looking for the ideal technology for it, which can sustain itself without subsidies. The prospect is that in the medium-term, technologies would use more of voice and less of data. CorDECT wireless Loop technology, Webox linked to TV sets, Minnow ISP in a box, PT, and "i2it", it is said, would come up for consideration. The railways have quad copper cables laid between stations and this vast network is going to be used for augmenting rural connectivity.

Technologies yielding low-cost computing gadgets would modify this picture somewhat. One such gadget is the Simputer. Soon the armamentarium of devices of IT will be joined by this sensible and practical innovation. With the Simputer coupled with solar and other localised non-conventional energy-devices, there is some hope that IT could indeed reach the masses in the rural areas. Cautions Prof. Keniston however, that low-cost technological solutions alone are not solutions to the problems of development, but they are prerequisites for IT in India. What is required is a well-articulated vision.

Focused activities of particular agencies of government and *ad hoc* schemes of public utility—these seem to spearhead the penetration of IT into the rural area at present. What we witness seems to be technology (from the top) hunting for applications and users in the villages, without much lateral coordination and with too little thought about the poor. In Prof. Keniston's view the 'IT for the masses'/ 'bridging the digital divide' movement has an inordinate amount of exaggeration and wishful thinking, and we need to define the characteristics of our projects and spread the word about what works and what does not. A doyen among IT professionals has summarised the situation thus: Every time a new technology tends to be sold 'bullishly' in the West we jump on that bandwagon without pausing to assess whether it is a relevant technology for addressing our home-grown problems.... (or taking time) to live with any one technology long enough to invest in it for the long-term and to assess its strengths and weaknesses for solving our indigenous problems. While it could be all right to have projects here and there as pilot experiments to demonstrate technology, fine-tune systems, test their scalability, or establish marketability, extending IT to all corners of the country and both sides of the Divide, is a vastly different matter. One needs to look at all the rural requirements, from the ground up, comprehensively and be clear about the priorities to be assigned to competing demands for investment.

The challenge, as Prof. Keniston says, is to learn if, when and how ITs (of all kinds) can be the most cost effective means to help people, especially poor people, to meet their basic needs and assert their fundamental rights. IT in the rural areas, it must be remembered, has so far not aimed at the poor and the underprivileged but targeted primarily those echelons of the rural area that are part of the market economy or are close to the interfaces of governance. What is the desirable 'architecture' for sustainable future use. That is what rural IT has to fit into. Furthermore, conscious of the enormous investment and effort involved one should pause to consider what activities give the greatest benefits by being computer aided and what should continue to be 'manual'. Not all present-day technology is un-cool retrograde and inefficient just because it is computer independent. Interestingly it was an eminent globalised author writing about e-mail as an *avatar* of progress that has remarked how the telephone did not supplant but only complemented, the postal system, the fax did not replace the telegram, and e-mail sits alongside of all these prior methods of communication. Likewise typewriter and word processor coexist, so too the bullock cart and the 200 kmph motorcar. The IT thrust into the rural area needs to take counsel from these examples of selective absorption of frontier technology before attempting to go across the Digital Divides.

One hopes that the IT visionaries scanning the Digital Divide running across the rural landscape in the far distance, will choose the wise and compassionate ways to go across it, rather than the greedy and the opportunistic.

APPENDIX - I

KRISHINET: THE AGRICULTURAL INFORMATION NETWORK FOR INDIA

Introduction

Some time back a young farmer from Haryana wrapped in a blanket, entered my room. He was searching for more information on growing chrysanthemums. While viewing, Ankur—a Sunday morning programme on kitchen gardening on T.V he was encouraged to grow chrysanthemums. He rushed to the Hortriculture Division of Indian Agricultural Research Institute to get more information. A scientist in the Division of Horticulture guided him to me. I showed him a book on chrysanthemum in Hindi and suggested him to purchase it and to subscribe to 'Phal-Phool'. Then he enquired if he can get a book which informs about growing all kind of flowers. No book was available.

We receive all kinds of enquiries from enthusiastic farmers from all parts of the country and most of their questions remain unanswered because we have not yet developed a system which can provide factual information on latest varieties, place of their availability and new techniques of increasing production etc. Recently a farmer from Mehsana, Gujarat, wanted to know how can he take 4 crops from his land. I have no option except marking it to an agronomist. Most of such letters gathers dust in corridors of Krishi Bhawan in absence of a 'data bank' and agricultural information services.

Information-Hunger and Poverty of Knowledge

One may ask a question here about the role of widespread agricultural extension network in India. Of course we have Directorates of Extension under Ministries of Agriculture in the centre and states having district level and village level extension workers including 'gram-sevake' as the link between Information and Farmer. We have a T&V—Training and Visit System supported by World Bank. ICAR itself has developed a first line extension system of testing emerging technologies in the field, through National Demonstration, Operational Research Project, Lab to Land programme and Krishi Vigyan Kendras (KVK). There are 109 KVKs established so far and it is proposed to have one KVK in each district by the end of English Five Year Plan. All the 28 Agricultural Universities of the country and more than 40 Agro-Research Institutes of ICAR and most of the undertakings, and organisations and companies dealing in Agricultural inputs like fertilizers, pesticides, agricultural implements and rural credit and rural cooperatives also have their own extension system. The All India Radio has its Farm Radio Service and Television beams rural programmes in almost all the Indian languages from different stations.

Even then the percentage of new technologies percolating from laboratories to the farmers' field is very low—only 15 to 20%. Most of them are grabbed by influential rich farmers who regularly visit farmers' fairs, Universities, Institutes and Block Development Office who play host to every government visitor in the village.

It is not only the farmers who are hungry of information, even the policy makers and decision makers, scientists and research workers are not being fed with updated information and the exercise to collect information on any aspect of agriculture is very tiresome, time-consuming and result ultimately in half-baked unreliable and often outdated information. On the eve of new year a round up of the agricultural activities of 1991/were presented on Doordarshan based on my script for which I had to run virtually from pillar to post to get estimates of crop-production, dairy development, fisheries, poultry and agricultural export. When I contacted the Press Information Bureau, they in turn requested me to send a copy of the script so that it can be released to the press. A PTI story released supposed to be a review of the year could not add anything to my information.

Caps in Lab and Land

What we are loosing in absence of a strong agricultural information network can be gauged by the facts of production potential of different crops and livestocks emerged from the years of painstaking research. The production of wheat can be increased by two and a half times, rice by three times, maize by three and a half times, sorghum by five times and pearl-millet by five and a half times. Even the production of pulses and oilseeds can be raised to 3 or 4 times. Same is true of horticulture and plantation crops, dairy fishery and poultry production. All of this potential can be achieved only through the application of existing technologies.

Early pioneering works to help develop rural poor were sporadic attempts like Gandhian experiment in rural Reconstruction (1920), Sriniketan Project (1921), Marthondam Scheme (1921), Gurgaon Project (1927) and Rural Reconstruction Movement (1932). These were followed by Grow More Food Campign (1942), Indian Village Upliftment Scheme (1945), Etawa Pilot Project (1948), Nilokheri Experiment (1948) Sarvodaya Programme (1948) and Community Development Programme (1952). The concept of National Extension Service (NES) was introducted in 1953. The country was covered by over 5000 community development blocks by 1966-67, covering all the 6.3 lakh villages and over 600 million rural people. A new approach called Intensive Agricultural District programme (IADP) was introduced in 1960-61. It envisaged concentration of efforts and resources in potentially productive areas. This concept was extended to longer areas as Intensive Agricultural Areas Programme (IAAP) in 1964., Then came the High Yielding Varieties Programme (1960-67).

The Key Village Scheme was started in 1952 to increase livestock production followed by Intensive Cattle Development Project (ICDP) in 1964-65.

A series of special programmes were also launched—The Drought Prone Area Programme (DPAP) and Small Fanners Development Agencies (SFDA) in 1970-71. SFDA was started to help small farmers (land holing 1 to 2 hectares), marginal farmers (less than 1 hectare) and agricultural labourers. These were followed by Hill Areas Development Programme (1973-74), Tribal Areas Development Programme (1971-72), Whole Village Development Programme (1975-76), Command Area Development (1974-75) and Voluntary Action Scheme (1974-75).

All these programmes have no doubt helped millions of rural people to develop. Wherever it failed the communication gap was the culprit. Even the Training and Visit System introduced in 1970s could bridge the communication gap and its failure has earned a nickname—T&V means Touch and Vanish. The system provides monthly training for the Subject Matter Specialists (SMSs), fornightly training of Village Extension Workers (VEWs) and contacting 750 farmers in a given area by the VEW every month.

The present extension system involves (i) research institutions, (ii) educational institutions, (iii) training institutions/centres, (IV) marketing systems, (v) extension organisations/sub-systems, (vi) input agencies, (vii) Village institutions, and (viii) the farming communities.

There are four major organizational streams to deal with the formidable task of transfer of technology. First the *first-line* extention work organised by ICAR; Second, extension system of the Ministry of Agriculture/State Department of Agriculture; Third, rural development effort of the Department of Rural Development; and fourth, Rural Development work of the Non-Government Organisations (NGOs).

A study of the infrastructure envisaged for Transfer of Technology in Agriculture in India reveals a strange phenomenon that the role of mass media has been over looked from the very beginning, The Print and Audio visual media touched the whole system only at the periphery. The other missing link is the use of modern methods of information and communication.

New Thrust in Eighth Plan

In this context it is heartening to note that while formulating the Eight Plan following proposals have been included by ICAR :

National Institute of Communication of Agricultural Sciences (NICAS)

The existing Publication and Information Division of ICAR is proposed to be strengthened and upgraded to the status of a national institute to foster research and training in agricultural communication in addition to publication and information activities. It will have an agricultural database and facilities to produce audio and video cassetts on agricultural technologies. The G.V.K. Rao Committee (1988) has already recommended that the Publications and Information Division and the Agricultural Research Information Centre (ARIC) should be suitably strengthened to fulfill its role as a premier institution of its kind in the country.

National Agricultural Library of India

Established in 1905, the IARI library is proposed to be upgraded to the National status. Since 1944 this library has created Indian Agricultural Data Base to the extent of 1,40,000 references of Indian Agriculture in card form. It needs to be computerised. With more than 1 lakh books, 3 lakh old periodicals and 75000 research bulletins and totalling 6 lakh publications on agriculture it is the largest Agricultural Library in India. It will have a AGLICNET-INDIA to join all the agricultural libraries through computer network with headquarters in IARI, New Delhi.

KRISHINET

Indian Agricultural Statistical Institute situated in IARI campus in New Delhi has proposed to implement the recommendations of the Working Group on Agricultural Research and Education headed by Dr. M.S. Swaminathan. Dr. Swaminathan wanted KRISHINET to accelerate the pace and increase productivity and efficiency of agricultural research, education and development. According to him, 'It is necessary to take up a systematic and comprehensive study of the information exchange back-up with efficient information processing through an effective computer network'.

He has further suggested that all research institutes and State Agricultural Universities will be equipped with need based minicomputers for creating local capabilities. A national research facility as an apex body with a powerful computer system such as VZX/8200 system will be developed at a central place like IASRI where computerised agricultural information system to be termed KRISHINET will be established. The KRISHINET system will also be linked with space and remote sensing organisations and IMD. Earlier the ICAR Review Committee appointed in 1987 also made the recommendation for establishing an Agricultural Information Network called ICARNET. However, this committee headed by an IAS Mr. G.V.K. Rao wanted ICARNET to aid the decision making process at the various levels in Governmental agencies. The committee says, "We also recommend that the ICAR should develop its computerised satellite-based information network (ICARNET) which should be available to scientists in the Institutes and the Agricultural Universities on online terminals. The network could be engaged to (a) institute online agricultural research information network, (b) develop research project monitoring system, (c) organise scientist profiles in the data bank, (d) build equipment data, (e) develop systems to monitor personnel and equipment usage and (f) feed the information and data to the headquarters as also to the Institutes, the SAUs and other agencies.

The Review Committee has further stressed that The ICAR should take necessary steps to provide adequate documentation, information storage and retrieval services in all its institutes including the council's headquarters so that its scientists are able to keep pace with the scientific development in the rest of the world. Modern day gadgets like computers should invariably be used by the ICAR. It should also make efforts to provide sufficiently qualified manpower in required numbers to operate these services more effectively. These services in the individual institutes should form a part of the national network for establishing inter-institutional scientific linkages which in turn should be linked to the international information networks like the AGRIS, ARIS etc. for international coverage.

GRAMSAT

ISRO-Indian Space Research Organisation, has proposed a rural-channel satellite to telecast rural programmes directly to select villages. The 'GRAMSAT' is proposed mainly to help in rural literacy programmes and to disseminate information about farm-technologies. Rupees 100 crore worth project of 'GRAMSAT' needs full support to achieve the targets of rural development and agricultural research. It will help in networking of agricultural information systems also nationally as well as internationally.

International Agro Network

1. 'CAB International' (CAB I)

Formerly the Commonwealth Agricultural Bureaux is a cooperative not-for-profit organisation owned, administered and financed by member governments. It was established in 1928 and currently has 28 member nations with headquarters at Wallingford, Oxon in UK. Over 100 scientists/linguists and CABI's Bureaux and institutes scan the world literature, select the significant items and prepare an informative abstract of each item which is entered into the CAB ABSTRACTS database. With some 2 million records in the databases since 1973 and 3 million more in printed journals back to 1930, the total archives provide a unique encyclopaedic resource of unsurpassed reliability and quality. Outputs are supplied as magnetic tape, computer printout, microfieshe or floppy disk. The database is also available on optical disk (CD-ROM). CAB has four international institutes on Entomology, Mycology, Parasitology and Biological control.

Food and Agriculture Organisation (FAO)

Started in 1945 the FAO is providing Research, Development and Information support worldwide. With its Headquarters in Rome it is running AGRIS—International Information System for Agricultural Sciences and Technology with its database at Vienna (Austria). In 1974 ARIC-Agricultural Research Information Centre of ICAR was made responsible to function as a National Input Centre on the AGRIS for collection, documentation and indexing of current agricultural research information available in the country. Since 1975 the ARIC has been compiling bibliographic information from 200 Indian Journals. It has adopted AGROVOC multilingual' for providing inputs for greater flexibility in computer retrieval. In return the ARIC is receiving AGRIS magnetic tapes every month from the FAO. The tapes contain the entire bibliographic information of the AGRIS database, contributed by about 120 participating nations and are used for SDI services to the scientists.

International Agricultural Institutes

There are about 16 International Agricultural Research Institutes on different crops, agro-climatic regions and problems such as CIMMYT for wheat and maize in Mexico, IRRI for rice in Philippines, CIP for Patato in Peru, IITA, ICARDA and ICRISAT etc. All these institutes have modernised agricultural communication systems including strong publication and audio visual and computerised information services. The most developed system is still with USDA—United States Department of Agriculture with US National Library and Network. There are rural satellite information network beaming climatic information to rural channels around United States. Even China has developed a unique agricultural system where a technology finalized today is transferred tomorrow to the field with zero gap in agricultural communication. Their agricultural publications are printed in billions.

Urgent Need of Indian Agro-Network

In comparison to the situation of agricultural communication at the international level the condition in our country is very dismal. It is especially week at the farmers level where it should be very strong. There is not one place where you can get all the information. It is as scattered as the different institutions connected with agriculture throughout the country.

Most of the extension workers do not have access to latest technologies. The technology is generated in ICAR and University system while the responsibility to transfer it to the field lies with the extension agencies of state departments. Here the left hand hardly knows what the right hand is doing.

The communication gap is further widened by the ill-planned efforts in mass-media. The time-slot of 'Krishi Darshan' has been reduced by 5 minutes from 30 to

25 minutes. The facilities provided to the TV and Radio stations for rural programmes are extremely poor. The people running the show are mostly technically illiterate. Leaving the lip service, it is in the lowest priority, with entertainment topping the list. The media-moghuls claims that they can only create awareness. Transferring technologies is not their responsibility. It is totally wrong. If somebody takes pains to find out the basic document which was used to start Television in India, he will discover that it was started on the pretext of educating rural masses. A separate Rural channel was also conceived but never delivered.

The printmedia is almost sleeping so far as agricultural communication is concerned. With 5000 publications brought out so far only the P&I Division of ICAR is serving through its publications. Even here the subscription rates of popular farm journals of Hindi and English are increased beyond the purchase capacity of small and marginal farmers.

When the government is spending thousands of crores of rupees on subsidising various agricultural inputs like fertilizers, pesticides and implements, why should not it subsidise agricultural information—the most important input?

We have only eight years left to prepare ourselves to race the challenge of feeding about 1000 million people in the year 2000. While delivering his Honda Prize speech at Tokyo on November 15, 1991, Dr. M.S. Swaminathan has mentioned the following targets of food production for India agreed to by the International Commission of Peace and Food:

1. Raise foodgrain production from 177 million tonnes to 220 million tonnes.
2. Triple the area under irrigated cotton to maize total production from 13.3 million bales to 26 million bales. It will generate employment for 11 million persons and earn Rs. 250,000 million worth of foreign exchange through textile export.
3. Extend the area under sugarcane by additional 1.6 million hectares to increase sugar production from 11 million tonnes to 26 million tonnes.
4. Raise fruit production by 50% and vegetable production by 100% to meet the full nutritional requirement of the people.
5. Raise inland fish providing full-time employment for one million women and men.
6. Expand the area under irrigated oilseeds and improve yields to produce an additional 7.5 million tonnes of oilseeds.
7. Raise milk production from the present 51.4 million tonnes to 70 million tonnes.

Achieving the above targets will require a strong agricultural communication backup. An agricultural database and network is a must to modernise agricultural communication systems in the country. The world has recently witnessed fall of a great nation like Soviet Union. Among the various reasons of its downfall the failure in agriculture has been mentioned as one of the final causes. We shall not repeat the mistake of ignoring the agriculture sector in the name of economy or otherwise.

In the words of Dr. Swaminathan, the great agricultural visionary of our times "The present information age has provided a unique opportunity to mobilise the mass media for stimulating awareness, analysis and action on matters of national importance. Software development for media use needs more support to spread the knowledge-intensive and ecologically substainable agriculture".

REFERENCES

1. Bhatt, V.S., Information Resources in Agricultural Research, 40 *Years of Agric. Res. in India,* 1989, pp. 272-232.
2. Lal, C., *Making IARI Library as the National Agricultural Library (NAL) of India—A proposal,* 1991.
3. Prasad, C, *Linkages between Agricultural Research, Education and Extension in India* (A country paper for FAO of the U.N.), August, 1985.
4. Rao, C.V.K, *Report of the ICAR Review Committee,* 1988.
5. Swaminathan, M.S. Challenges Ahead: Time for new orientation. *Survey of Indian Agriculture, (The Hindu),* 1988.
6. Swaminathan, M.S., *Honda Prize Speech,* November, 1991.
7. Swaminathan, M.S., *Report of the Working Group on Agricultural Research and Education for the Formulation of Eighth Plan,* Planning Commission, August, 1989.

BIBLIOGRAPHY

Anthony and Reece, *Management Accounting*, Fifth Edition, Home-wood, IL.: Richard D. Irwin, Inc., 1975.

Archibald and Villria, *Network-Based Management, Systems (PERT/ CPM)*, New York: John Wiley & Sons, Inc., 1967.

Bhatt, V.S., Information Resources in Agricultural Research, 40 *Years of Agric. Res. in India*, 1989, pp. 272-232.

Bierman, Bonini, and Hausman, *Quantitative Analysis for Business Decisions*, Fourth Edition, Homewood, IL.: Richard D. Irwin, Inc., 1973.

Brown, *Smoothing, Forecasting, and Production of Discrete Time Series*, Englewood Cliffs, NJ.: Prentice-Hall, Inc., 1963.

Buffa, *Operations Management*, Third Edition, New York: John Wiley & Sons, Inc., 1972.

Burch, "Computer Application of Contribution Analysis," *Journal of Systems Management*, August 1970.

Button and Starbuck, *Computer Simulation of Human Behavior*, New York: John Wiley & Sons, Inc., 1971.

Canning, "COBOL Aid Packages," *EDP Analyzer*, January 1972.

Canning, "Computer Security: Backup and Recovery Methods," *EDP Analyzer*, January 1972.

Canning, "Project Management Systems," *EDP Analyzer*, September 1976.

Canning, "That Maintenance 'Iceberg'," *EDP Analyzer*, October 1972.

Davis, *Computer Data Processing*, Second Edition, New York: McGraw-Hill Book Company, 1973.

Davis, *Human Behavior at Work*, New York: McGraw-Hill Book Co., 1972.

Davis, *Management Information Systems: Conceptual Foundations, Structure, and Development*, New York: McGraw-Hill Book Company, 1974.

Dean, "A Comparison of Decision Tables Against Conventional COBOL as a Programming Tool for Commercial Applications," *Software World*, Spring 1971.

Demski, *Information Analysis*, Reading, MA.: Addison-Wesley Publishing Co., 1972.

Dwyer, "Some Observations on Management Information Systems," *Advances in EDP and Information Systems,* New York: American Management Association, 1961.

Evarts, *Introduction to PERT,* Boston: Allyn and Bacon, Inc., 1964.

Forkner and McLeod, Jr., *Computerised Business Systems,* New York: John Wiley & Sons, Inc., 1973.

Gass, *Linear Programming,* Second Edition, New York: McGraw-Hill Book Co., 1964.

Gupta, B.M. and Nathan, S.S. Handbook of Libraries, Archives and Information Centres in India, Vol. 7 Science and Technology Information Systems Centres. Delhi, Aditya Prakashan, 1990.

Hadley, *Linear Algebra,* Reading, MA.: Addison-Wesley Publishing Co., 1961.

Hersey and Blanchard, *Management of Organisation Behavior,* Englewood Cliffs, NJ.: Prentice-Hall, Inc., 1972.

Hillier and Lieberman, *Introduction to Operations Research,* Second Edition, San Francisco: Holden-Day, 1974.

Horngren, *Cost Accounting: A Managerial Emphasis,* Fifth Edition, Englewood Cliffs, NJ.: Prentice-Hall, Inc., 1982.

Hudson, "Determining Organisational Information Requirements," *Journal of Systems Management,* January 1981.

Isaac, K.A., Library and information science education in India: Sinning or sinned against? *In* Sewa Singh (Ed.). *Librarianship and library science education,* New Delhi: Ess Ess Publications, 1988, pp. 79-84.

Kirk, *Total System Development for Information Systems,* New York: John Wiley & Sons, Inc., 1973.

Kubr (ed.), *Management Consulting,* Geneva, Switzerland: International Labour Office, 1976.

Kuhn, *The Study of Society: A Unified Approach,* Homewood, IL.: Richard D. Irwin, Inc., and The Dorsey Press, 1963.

Kuldip Chand Impact of Information Technology on S and T Information Systems and University Libraries in India. Paper presented at the UGC Seminar on Information Technology and Libraries 2-3 February, 1990. Punjabi University, Patiala.

Kumar, P.S.G., *Hundred years of library education and its future: Seminar papers,* Nagpur : Dept. of Library and information Science , Nagpur University, 1987.

Lal, C., *Making IARI Library as the National Agricultural Library (NAL) of India—A proposal,* 1991.

Langefors & Samuelson, *Information and Data in Systems,* New York: Petrocelli Charter, 1976.

Lasden, "Overcoming Obstacles to Project Success," *Computer Decisions,* December 1981.

Lucas, *The Analysis, Design, and Implementation of Information Systems,* New York: McGraw-Hill Book Company, 1976.

Maisel and Gnugnoli, *Simulation of Discrete Stochastic Systems,* Chicago: Science Research Associates, Inc., 1972.

Martin, *Computer Modeling and Simulation,* New York: John Wiley & Sons, inc., 1968.

McClelland and Winter, *Motivating Economic Achievement,* New York: The Free Press, 1969.

McLean, "The Human Side of Systems: The User's Perspective," paper presented to the *1976 Western Systems Conference,* Los Angeles.

Miller, "Problem Avoidance in the User/Analyst Relationship—Part 1," *Journal of Systems Management,* May 1981.

Murdick and Ross, *Information Systems for Modern Management,* Second Edition, Englewood Cliffs, NJ: Prentice-Hall, Inc., 1975.

Murdick and Ross, *Introduction to Management Information Systems,* Englewood Cliffs, NJ: Prentice-Hall, Inc., 1977.

Perry and Adams, "SMF—An Untapped Audit Resource," *EDPACS,* September 1974.

Perry and Fitzgerald, "Designing for Auditability," *Datamation,* August 1977.

Perry, "Using SMF as an Audit Tool-Accounting Information," *EDPACS,* February 1975.

Porter and Perry, *EDP Controls and Auditing,* Third Edition, Belmont, Calif: Wadsworth Publishing Company, Inc., 1980.

Prasad, C, *Linkages between Agricultural Research, Education and Extension in India* (A country paper for FAO of the U.N.), August, 1985.

Raiffa, *Decision Analysis,* Reading, MA.: Addison-Wesley Publishing Co., 1968.

Rajan, T.N., Manpower needs for information work in India, *In* B.M. Gupta (Ed) *Handbook of libraries, archives, and information centres in India,* v 1, New Delhi: Information Industry Publication, 1934. pp. 303-315.

Ramakrishnan, M.N., et al, *eds, Library and information science education in India; New perspectives,* Trivandrum : Dept. of Library and Information Science, Kerala University, 1989.

Richmond, *Statistical Analysis,* New York: The Ronald Press Company, 1964.

Sadek and Tomeski, "Different Approaches to Information Systems," *Journal of Systems Management,* April 1981.

Sewa Singh, Library science as a carrer, *Careers,* Punjab Government Chandigarh, June 1987:1-7

Slaybaugh, "Pareto's Law and Modern Management," *Management Services,* March-April 1967.

Starr and Miller, *Inventory Control: Theory and Practice,* Englewood Cliffs, NJ.: Prentice-Hall, Inc., 1962.

Sutherland, *Systems—Analysis, Administrations and Architecture,* New York: Van Nostrand Reinhold, 1975.

Swaminathan, M.S., *Report of the Working Group on Agricultural Research and Education for the Formulation of Eighth Plan,* Planning Commission, August, 1989.

Thierauf, *Data Processing for Business and Management,* New York: John Wiley & Sons, Inc., 1973.

Wadsworth, *The Human Side of Data Processing Management,* Englewood Cliffs, NJ.: Prentice-Hall, Inc., 1973.

Wagner, *Principles of Operations Research,* Second Edition, Englewood Cliffs, NJ.: Prentice-Hall, Inc., 1975.

Weinberg, *An Introduction to General Systems Thinking,* New York: John Wiley & Sons, Inc., 1975.

Whitin, *The Theory of Inventory Management,* Princeton, NJ.: Princeton University Press, 1957.

Zorkoczy, Peter, *Information technology ; an introduction,* New Delhi Affiliated East-West Press, 1989.

INDEX

W

Y

❑❑❑